HUMAN SACRIFICE

HUMAN SACRIFICE

IN HISTORY AND TODAY

Nigel Davies

DORSET PRESS
New York

To Vera Kaspar

Preface

After writing *The Aztecs*, I decided for my next book, *Voyagers to the New World*, to tackle a more general aspect of ancient American history. This time, in writing of human sacrifice, I have chosen a theme that embraces the globe. Admittedly, ancient Mexico has again served as an excellent point of departure. For I remember vividly that when I first climbed a Mexican pyramid in 1951, I had already read my Bernal Díaz, and was conscious of the grim scenes that had been enacted at the top of those steep steps.

At that time I, like many other people, tended to think of human offering as a kind of Aztec speciality, rarely to be equalled in the New World let alone in the Old. But as I became more absorbed in the study of the Aztecs and began to compare them with other peoples, I soon came to realize that sacrifice was a common heritage of mankind, present in every continent in every era. My researches revealed the lack of modern studies of human sacrifice in different parts of the world that went beyond short papers in scholarly publications. Several books have, of course, been written on cannibalism, but recipes for cooking the victims' remains are only one aspect of the whole question.

When I first felt the urge to write on this strange theme, an old friend who is a noted anthropologist gave me invaluable guidance, but ruefully added that he was not sure if the book could be written at all; how was I to make a distinction between the offering of a man and that of a cow or a cucumber? Undaunted, I wrote back agreeing that the distinction was a fine one but confident that it would not be too hard to explain. I trust that my readers will find the results of my labours have justified my optimism.

Finally, I hope that the reader will bear with a good many gory details, unavoidable in dealing with this subject. Rather than recite a catalogue of horrors, I have tried at least to rationalize and explain why people did these things to each other.

Acknowledgements

I would like to express my gratitude to all who have helped me in the preparation of this book, and in particular to Dr Patricia Anawalt, Dr Christopher Donnan, Madame Sonya de la Rozière, Professor C. von Fuerer-Haimendorf, Mrs Lucy Haksar, Dr Helen A. Kanitkar, Père J. Laval, Dr L. Lauerhaus, Professor Joan Lewis, Dr Sally Moore, Professor Antoinette Nelken, Dr Erwin Palm, Professor Julian Pitt-Rivers, Mr Bruce Rogers, Mrs Thelma Sulivan, Dr Johannes Wilbert, and Mr Ian Johnson of The British Council, Manila.

Contents

I

The Man, the Cow
and the Cucumber

In essence human sacrifice was an act of piety. Both sacrificer and victim knew that the act was required, to save the people from calamity and the cosmos from collapse. Their object was, therefore, more to preserve than to destroy life. This paradox lies at the root of the weird drama of humans who slew other humans in order to sustain their gods. Obviously, in writing of human sacrifice, the author must at once face the difficulty of defining the term and say to which kind of killings it applies and to which it does not. To include the story of every kidnapped child since the Lindbergh baby, and of every massacre in history from Saint Bartholomew to Buchenwald, would make nonsense of our basic concept. Perhaps we can begin by considering what purposes human offering was meant to serve, and what general principles can be applied to sacrifice throughout the world, whether of men or beasts.

Many leading works on the subject date from the early decades of this century when it came to be studied more seriously. Since then the theme has appealed to fewer scholars. The modern social anthropologist does not best endear himself to the élite of the Third World by an obsessive interest in how great-grandfather shrunk the heads he hunted or in the quality of the wood needed to burn great-grandmother alive. The best accounts not of the theory but of actual practices are mostly over a hundred years old, often published in obscure journals, whose back numbers can still be found in a few libraries. Much can be gleaned, for instance, from the reports of British officers in India or of visitors to Africa, such as Sir Richard Burton. His great description of the kingdom of Dahomey is admirable not only for its wealth of personally gathered information but because this expert observer goes out of his way to pour cold water on the more absurd tales then current, such as the popular fable of the "cities of blood", where canoes were paddled in rivers and lakes of human gore. While theories derive from scholars of diverse nations, many of the eye-witness reports of human sacrifice come from Englishmen, simply because they ruled so many of the lands where it thrived and were invited to many a grim ceremony. The Spanish chroniclers in Central America also wrote down what they were told by men who had seen the rites, but they themselves never attended them—except, in a few cases, as victims. For what went on in the Mediterranean world, we depend on rather cryptic texts, but those of China are more informative on the subject.

Several modern books have been written on cannibalism but they throw little light on the central tenets of sacrifice, since cannibalism stands somewhat apart as an effect, rather than a cause; to eat the victim is a convenient means of disposal, a useful alternative to burning or burying him alive. Books on this subject view matters from a rather special angle, since they focus on the more primitive peoples, who went on eating each other until quite recently. They often lapse into mere cookbooks, with every recipe for preparing human flesh, whether freshly slaughtered or completely putrefied, as some gourmets preferred. Such books on cannibalism therefore miss the point, because it is simply one aspect of sacrifice and can only be understood in a broader context. This applies in particular to recent works on the subject that have engendered fierce controversy. Anthropologists Michael Harner and Marvin Harris in their writings ignore rituals and consider that they have "proved" that the Aztecs' primary concern was not to please their gods but to make up for a chronic shortage of animal protein. Their arguments will be discussed in Chapter IX, which deals with Aztec practices. While it will not be denied that the Aztecs at times ate parts of the human body, cogent reasons will be given to show that their motive was not a lack of protein.

In a recent conversation with Michael Harner—and the point was well taken—I made the obvious observation that the Aztecs are only a single case and that the protein shortage theory cannot be sustained unless it can be shown to apply to other parts of the world where human flesh was consumed. In the course of this book it will become

abundantly clear that this is not so and that the incidence of cannibalism, say in Africa or Oceania, is patchy and its presence in one
tribe and absence among its neighbours cannot be explained in terms
of proteins and calories. Moreover, as we shall see, in India, where
proteins were never superabundant, human sacrifice was rife but
there was no cannibalism. Another anthropologist, William Arens, has
gone to the other extreme from Harner and Harris by denying the
existence of cannibalism altogether. The Arens theory will be dealt
with in connection with sacrifice in Africa. He claims that man-eating
never took place and that all accounts derive from mere hearsay but,
whilst I am the first to insist that reports from missionaries and others
should be examined with discrimination, too many eye-witness accounts of cannibalism survive for Arens' opinions to be taken very
seriously.

Many forms of sacrifice do not involve cannibalism and these have
received less attention in recent years, in spite of a certain interest in
the theme—an interest perhaps stimulated by the daily impact of violence in its latest form: terrorism. Some people may look on this as
nothing but a new type of human sacrifice. And indeed, the fate of
an ambassador, kidnapped and even killed as scapegoat for the alleged
sins of others, might at first sight be viewed in terms of those ritual
victims chosen to die for more ancient dogmas; but while I shall seek
some modern instances of human sacrifice, neither the methods nor
the motives of terrorists place their victims in this category. Ancient
gods would have spurned a money ransom. They expected flesh and
blood, obtained through the medium of a ritual, without which the
gift had neither worth nor meaning. Ritual and religion are inseparable
from human sacrifice; indeed, we may define the term as killing with
a spiritual or religious motivation, usually, but not exclusively, accompanied by ritual. Normally it was performed in a sacred place or
one that had been made sacred for the occasion; in the absence of a
temple or in primitive circumstances a magic ring drawn on the
ground would serve.

In terms of this definition, when Stalin murdered millions in his
gulags, or, simpler still, just left them to die of cold, this was not a
sacrifice; their end, though wretched, was neither ritual nor religi-
ously inspired, even if they were victims of an ideology whose dis-
regard for human life rivalled the gods of old. Yet, as supreme head
of the Marxist camp and guardian of its orthodoxy, Stalin was Em-

peror and Pope in one, and certain of his victims—those who died not in gulags but after show trials—were subjected to a peculiar form of ritual in which they were judged for sacrilege as much as for sabotage. By the same token, public hangings at Tyburn and later in front of Newgate prison in London, which went on until the mid-nineteenth century, were not sacrificial, even if a certain ritual was observed and notwithstanding the presence of a huge and turbulent crowd who had assembled to see the fun. The culprits were hanged for offences against a secular state and their deaths fall outside the range of our definition. To decide how far the execution of criminals in older societies was a sacrifice is far more difficult, since in many of these, including Rome, there was no such thing as an offence against the state that was not also a crime against the gods, whose anger was only to be stilled by killing the offender. Among certain African cannibals, murderers and thieves were fattened up in prison before being eaten at a ritual banquet.

 Human sacrifice may reach its highest expression in a voluntary act, undertaken by the man who offers his life as a pledge for the common good, although the term cannot apply exclusively to those who die of their own free will. Moreover, if the nobler forms of sacrifice concerned the individual—the one who died for the many—the more debased rites, claiming scores of victims whose skulls were then impaled on grisly racks, were nonetheless true offerings. Such multiple killings, whether in Aztec Mexico or in African Dahomey, were part of an elaborate ritual and their ends were strictly religious. The principle was the same as for the death of a single man; it had merely been subjected to a process of inflation. Where one victim had been the ransom for the god's bounty, it was now set at a hundred.

Whatever the numbers involved, human sacrifice went hand in hand with a firm belief in an existence beyond the grave that was more or less a replica of life on this planet. People who held such views would have been aghast at the idea that their king, so glorious in life, should be abandoned in death, that he who had been their vital force in this world should be left to fend for himself in the next; those who allowed this to happen would be cursed by the gods. Added to this was the fear, since man had first learned to till the soil, that the crop cycle might cease unless the gods were diverted with the highest gift that man could give, the life of a fellow human being or, in the final resort, that of the king. If the gods were not sated, the sun might simply go down to the nether world and stay there. The change of seasons and the ripening of crops were believed to be gifts of the deities, from whom the earthly rulers descended. Human sacrifice gained a new impetus to ensure that this vital process was not halted.

In the earliest civilizations of the Near and Far East all the principle forms of sacrifice are present: the burial of children to dedicate and protect buildings, the offering of war prisoners, the drowning of virgin brides to honour river gods. But two themes predominate: mass provision of attendants for the dead and annual offerings to the gods on whose bounty plentiful crops depended. These became much more elaborate than the simple burial of human heads and pieces of flesh in the fields. The two themes served a common purpose: in these ancient realms, the king was in effect the kingdom and the fate of his subjects depended on his wellbeing. They could not prosper if he were not properly cared for, both in this world and in the next. Sacrifice of the one for the many—to make the seed sprout—and of the many for the one—to attend the dead king—were thus two means to a single end: the good of the community, if not its very existence. Hence sacrifice was a necessity, the supreme gesture without which humanity would perish.

Whether or not the victim died of his own choice, it was important for him to display at least a show of willingness for the solemn ceremony to be successful. The gods would have been outraged if men chosen for their service had to be dragged kicking and screaming up the side of a pyramid or led to the altar fighting every inch of the way. (An exception might be found in the children sacrificed to the Mexican Rain God, who were encouraged to cry as their tears brought promise of rain.) A degree of compliance was assured once the victim was imbued with the knowledge that he would live again as the result of his act. In Ur the king's servant gained a new life if he followed his master to the tomb; in Mexico the war captives, called collectively the Children of the Sun, knew that they would be privileged to follow the sun on its daily course, after meeting their death with dignity on the top of the pyramid.

Misguided theories have made human sacrifice even more mysterious and incomprehensible to the modern student. The notion dies hard, for instance, though denied by leading scholars, that the noble savage performed no such acts or at best confined himself to animals. According to this premise early man was innocent; only at a later stage did the depraved city dweller embrace the vice of giving his own kind to the gods, a practice that offered the king the twin advantages of terrorizing his subjects into submission and of reducing the number of mouths that he had to feed. While I do not accept the more extreme view of man as an inveterate killer from the very start of his career, enough examples will be cited to make it perfectly plain that a ritual cult of the human head, linked to the notion of sacrifice, can be traced back tens if not hundreds of thousands of years.

A second fallacy arose out of the first: if the noble savage, once innocent of guilt, picked up barbarous habits in the course of becoming civilized and took to killing his fellow men on the altars, this—so the theory runs—was a temporary phase. After such a deplorable lapse on the road to salvation, a reaction would always occur, when man adopted a moral view of life and abjured these bloody rituals. As an invariable rule, he then replaced human offerings with animals and objects and later with gifts of money, or with nothing at all, on the principle that the gods were good and could not be bribed in this way. Such a simplistic view was based on an all-too-literal reading of a single case, the Old Testament, for modern scholarship interprets its sequence of events differently. The story of Abraham, asked to sacrifice his son Isaac, whom God then replaced with the ram caught in the thicket, might suggest at first sight that the Israelites—perhaps led astray in Egypt—originally made human offerings but then, at the very dawn of their history, saw the error of their ways and were prompted by their god to kill animals instead of men. As we shall see later in more detail, the true course of events was the reverse of this. The early Hebrews probably did sacrifice humans on a limited scale when they came out of Egypt and entered the Promised Land, but once they had settled there, ritual killing, far from dying out, reached new heights as they adopted the child burnings of their Canaanite neighbours, an abomination against which the great prophets never ceased to rail.

On the other hand, hundreds of cases are indeed known in which animals or even objects replaced men as sacrificial victims, but such instances do not add up to any hard and fast rule that beasts always took the place of humans if a civilization were given enough time to develop and to become "enlightened". In China, Confucius complained that men were sacrificed in place of wooden dolls; in Rome also, human offerings almost ceased and then increased in number again in the wake of Oriental cults that became popular under the Empire; in Africa, new forms were devised that had not existed when the first Europeans reached that continent. There are cases of ritual killing being reduced and then reviving, while there are others where the level of killing remained fairly constant for a long time, then rose dramatically. The Aztecs are a case in point: they did not invent sacrifice and evidence has come to light of its presence among the first cultures of Mexico; the Aztecs merely increased the tempo until it reached a crescendo at the time of the Spanish Conquest. In many lands the substitution of animals for humans came about at the behest of conquerors from across the sea, Christians or in a few cases Muslims. People were offered no choice; in Mexico they bowed to their conquerors' god, while in India and Africa they were told to kill goats instead of men.

Another major question now arises, if we grant that animals or objects did take the place of humans in the majority of countries. Where formerly a human had been sacrificed, if a cow were made to serve the purpose, or even a cucumber, then did the principle remain the same or was the whole concept of sacrifice altered beyond recognition? Leaving aside those exalted beings who died to save their city or as a ransom for mankind, the distinction seems to be more one of form than of substance. E. Evans Pritchard, in his study of Nuer religion, has made a classic contribution to the problems of sacrifice. He explains that among the Nuer, a cattle-herding people of southern Sudan, since herds were small an animal was simply not available on every occasion and for every form of sacrifice. Fertile cows were only used in major ceremonies such as the funerals of the rich; for a poor man, a castrated he-goat would serve instead. (In Nuer rites male victims first had to be made neuter.) When a lesser favour was sought of the gods or simply when no beast was available, a small knobbly cucumber would be used. It was of minimal value, since it grows wild, and for minor emergencies such as a bad dream or a case of petty incest it was thought quite sufficient. But to maintain the fiction that the value of the gift was not being lowered, not only was the castrated goat referred to in any sacrificial context as "yang", the word for "cow", but even the cucumber would be called "yang".[1] The cucumber was treated in every way as if it were an animal and was even "slain" with a spear. By the same token, Evans Pritchard suggests, if people who sacrificed men for some reason substituted a cow, they would be at equal pains to minimize the difference in order to keep their god happy.

This view finds support among earlier scholars such as the great Biblical authority W. Robertson Smith, who went so far as to say that in oldest times (he was writing of pastoral tribes in Israel and elsewhere) there is no reason to suppose that a man's life was better than that of a sheep or a camel as a vehicle for winning the god's favour. On the contrary, in terms of basic notions that lay at the root of Semitic sacrifice, animals would probably have been deemed purer and more perfect.[2] If we turn to recent writers who tackle the subject, Georges Gusdorf also refuses to make a marked distinction between animal and human victims.[3] Frequently men and animals were offered together on the same altar, to the same god, to obtain the same favours. Romans, Greeks, Vikings and Druids, to name only a few, had rites in which man and beast shared a single ceremony.

There is no disputing that the cow was vastly more precious than the little wild cucumber and in some cases the cow may have also been more valuable than the man. The latter could often be bought as a slave in the same market as the cow; he ate less and was scarcely more productive. In any process of reducing the worth of the victim, the step down from nobleman's son to human slave was probably a more drastic form of sacrificial devaluation than the use of an animal instead of a slave. For to view the life of every human as sacred is a modern notion, hardly shared, for instance, by the eighteenth-century English, who would hang a man for stealing a sheep as well as for a hundred other trifling offences; and in other parts of the world life was held far cheaper still. Supported by an unshakable belief in the blessings in store for him in the hereafter, a man could be led to the sacrificial altar with the same air of indifference as if he were a goat. Europeans who saw humans sacrificed in other regions were always amazed by the bemused calm with which the chosen victim faced his gruesome fate. One difference between human and animal sacrifice is that man was often deliberately made to suffer as a preparation for death. No one thought of scalping a ram, though in Africa animals were sometimes ill-treated, and in certain rites beasts were torn limb from limb when still alive and then eaten raw.

But regardless of whether humans, animals or objects were used, what main purposes was sacrifice meant to serve? The German scholar, Edward Westermarck, in his massive study *The Origin and Development of the Moral Ideas*, published in English in 1906, lists the objects of sacrifice and adds many concrete examples to illustrate each category. Pride of place must surely be given to the universal and ancient practice of burying the living with the dead. Offerings were usually multiple since a great man could hardly be sent off on his journey to the next world accompanied by a single factotum. His prestige often depended on the numbers interred in his tomb. The burning or burying of widows to accompany their husbands in the after-life belongs to the same category, though the act, if voluntary, amounted to suicide. In this, too, prestige was often involved and an Indian Rajah might be burned with a whole cohort of wives and concubines.

Success in war was often sought by means of sacrifice. The Phoenicians and their Carthaginian kinsmen specialized in this form of offering. When Carthage was in desperate straits in its struggle against Rome, noble families gave up two hundred of their sons to be offered to Baal. To stave off epidemics was another, often urgent need since man was defenceless against disease, usually thought of as a punishment from the gods. The Scandinavians, before their conversion to Christianity, would bury children alive to stop a plague. Such sacrifices might serve to preserve a single life as well as the whole community; among the Incas, children from four to six years old were slain to keep the Emperor in good health or cure him if he were ill. Individuals sacrificed to control sickness were often treated as messengers to the gods. In Benin, in West Africa, when the head witch-doctor uttered the prayer in which he asked the god Ogiwo to ward off plague, he said to the slaves who were about to be clubbed and tied to the sacrifice tree: "So you shall tell Ogiwo. Salute him proper." [4] The making of medicine out of the bodies of men or infants especially killed for the purpose was another kind of sacrifice; cases of this in Basutoland (now Lesotho) as late as 1949 led to public trials.

Another very common form of human sacrifice was the rite of interring adults or children in the foundations of new buildings or under city gates and bridges. Foundation sacrifice springs from a primitive fear of anything new or of doing an act for the first time.

A new building is also a form of intrusion on the domain of the local spirit, whose anger may be aroused and who therefore has to be appeased. The buried person is not only a peace offering to this local spirit; his soul becomes a protective demon for the building. When the city of Tavoy in the extreme south of Burma was built, an eye-witness was able to testify that a criminal was put into each post-hole in order to become a guardian spirit.⁵ Foundation sacrifice was as widespread in Europe as in Asia; Westermarck relates that when the Bridge Gate of Bremen had been recently demolished (he was writing in 1906) the skeleton of a child had been found embedded in the groundwork. The Druids also practised this rite. When Dinas Emris was founded in Wales, all the materials for the fortress were carried away in one night; three times they were gathered and three times removed. Finally the leader, Gortigern, was told by his Druid priests that he must find a child whose father was unknown, put him to death, and sprinkle with his blood the ground on which the citadel was to be built.⁶

Last but not least come those offerings connected in one way or another with fertility. Civilized man's prime need was to obtain good harvests or, the reverse of the coin, to ward off famine. In their most basic forms, fertility rites required the sprinkling of human blood or the burial of pieces of human flesh in the fields before sowing; the practice survived into the nineteenth century among certain tribes of India, who reared and fattened victims specially for the purpose. Sacrifices to river gods belong to the same category since the waters that they brought were needed to make plants grow. This class of offering includes rites intended both to make plants fertile and to make women fecund. People were sacrificed not only to preserve existing lives but to help bring new beings into the world. Barrenness was often held to be an act of God, who deliberately kept back children who would otherwise have been born. The best remedy was to send him other infants to take the place of those he had with-held; slave children usually served the purpose. In some places, in India, for example, the practice was carried to such lengths that if a wife had one son and wanted more, the first-born was slain on the supposition that the gods would then provide a series of children to take his place. In certain Australian aboriginal tribes, the mother would kill and eat her first child as a means of obtaining more. The practice of sacrificing the first-born of every species, both animal and human, was not uncommon; it is mentioned in the Old Testament.

It might seem that with a definition of sacrifice, and of the typical ends it may serve, enough has been said in the way of a general background to the study of the special rites of different peoples. But such definitions leave untouched the mechanism that lay behind the act; they fail to explain how and why a certain rite is supposed to produce a given result. In the course of many millennia, legions of men have been offered up to the gods, as well as herds of animals, mountains of fruit and vegetables, rivers of wine and milk, together with countless numbers of objects ranging from precious jewels to cheap figurines. In return the gods were expected to ward off famines, stay the course of plagues, guard buildings, care for the departed, enrich harvests and win battles. These were the favours man needed from his gods. The latter usually responded in the end; it was merely a question of waiting or, if necessary, of making bigger offerings; given time, the rains came again, the floods subsided, or the pestilence ran its course. Perhaps the most elusive request was success in war—unattainable by both sides in the same battle.

While these outward objects may be plain, one is bound to ask whether sacrifice, human or animal, is more than just a straight deal, by which divine favour is bought at a set price. This "gift" theory, as the sole aim of sacrifice, prevailed in the latter part of the nineteenth century—even if *gift* is not a very exact term for an offering that amounts more to a purchase. Other ideas were then advanced that helped to explain the mystery more clearly. Among the earlier theorists, W. Robertson Smith in his classic work *The Religion of the Semites*, published in 1894, carried matters a stage further. He saw sacrifice as going back to the time when people worshipped totems, meaning particular animals or plants, with which each tribe came to identify itself. Sacrifice was aimed at cementing the bonds between man and god by killing the totem animal, who was both god and kinsman to the tribe. Totemism gradually died out, surviving longest among the Australian aboriginal tribes. Only when man saw god not as an animal but in his own image did he begin to kill his own kind, as the likeness of his deity. For Robertson Smith, therefore, animal came before human sacrifice.

In *The Golden Bough* Sir James Frazer's central concept of the slain god, whose death marked the cycle of the crops, owes much to the teaching of Robertson Smith. The principle is the same: it is the god himself who dies, and for Frazer the god is no longer the animal symbol of his tribe but possesses human form. Not the beast but the king, as representative of his people, is made tabu and must be ritually slain. Frazer stressed this theme to a point that many anthropologists find exaggerated, though he has found more favour among the general reading public, spellbound by his lucid prose and his vivid imagery.

In 1909 two French scholars, H. Hubert and M. Mauss, published a work, *Mélanges d'Histoire des Religions*, that rather altered the perspective. For Hubert and Mauss, sacrifice was not easily reduced to a single principle or aim. They saw it not as a gift but as an act of communion, in which the victim serves as intermediary between the human and the divine. They paid closer attention to the mechanisms of sacrifice and to the key role played by the actual ritual. The sacrificer and his victim were not themselves sanctified; it was only the rite that changed their state in such a way that the god would enter into the victim—hence the importance of the priest, who alone knew how to arrange this, and of priestly acts such as the laying on -of hands, whereby the victim became part of the divinity and the sacrificer himself was brought into a state of union with his god.

Edward Westermarck made a valuable contribution to the subject since he dealt more specifically with the sacrifice of humans than of animals. Although he concluded that human sacrifice was a gift to ward off evil, he also refused, like Hubert and Mauss, to accept that in its higher forms it amounted to mere celestial bribery. The rite in which the one died for the many was more an act of atonement, in which a single victim served to ward off god's general wrath against man, rather than simply to save the community from a single calamity or to secure a single blessing. Westermarck describes as "untenable" Frazer's claim that the central theme of sacrifice is to nourish the gods, that they in turn may give good harvests. In support of this assertion the German scholar cites many examples of peoples, from Peru to West Africa, who killed men in order to provide the gods not with food but with attendants or simply sacrificed those who in some way had angered the deity; he stresses the absence of any cruel intent in such rituals:

> I think there is sufficient evidence to prove that, when men offer the lives of their fellow-men in sacrifice to their gods, they do so as a rule in the hopes of thereby saving their own. Human

sacrifice is essentially a method of life-insurance—absurd, no doubt, according to our ideas, but not an act of wanton cruelty. When practised for the benefit of the community or in a case of national distress, it is hardly more cruel than to advocate the infliction of capital punishment on the ground of social expediency, or to compel thousands of men to suffer death on the battle-field on behalf of their country. The custom of human sacrifice admits that the life of one is taken to save the lives of many, or that an inferior individual is put to death for the purpose of preventing the death of somebody who has a higher right to live. Sometimes the king or chief is sacrificed in times of scarcity or pestilence, but then he is probably held personally responsible for the calamity. Very frequently the victims are prisoners of war or other aliens, or slaves, or criminals, that is, persons whose lives are held in little regard. And in many cases these are the only victims allowed by custom.[7]

For Westermarck, in every instance sacrifice is motivated by fear of occult powers, whose workings man cannot fathom, though they hold him at their mercy and with supreme indifference shower curses and blessings upon his head. To stay these powers and to win their favour, some form of down payment or, as he aptly puts it, a life insurance policy is needed. Written into this policy are both protection against immediate disasters brought about by the god's anger, in the form of, say, crop failure, and also clauses offering longer-term benefits, such as the safeguarding of a building during its lifespan. But sacrifice also has a more generalized aim: if men regularly perform certain rituals, they will achieve a state of closer union with their god whose protection they crave.

Modern writers have on the whole accepted such premises but with a difference of emphasis. Many of the more recent contributions have come from French anthropologists. The greatest of these, Claude Lévi-Strauss, writes on sacrifice sparingly but to the point. He roundly rejects the view that among primitive tribes it was centered upon their totem animal; he insists that, far from being taken from a single species, the choice of victim varied widely, in accordance with what was available at the time.[8] Writing in 1948, Georges Gusdorf does not discard the older notion of sacrifice as a kind of salary paid to the gods but insists that this is not the whole story.[9] He concurs with Hubert and Mauss' view that it is an act of communion between man and god and defines sacrifice as "a religious act, tending to reestablish a lost alliance between the sacred and the profane." All offerings, therefore, form a link between these two orders, normally distinct. "To sacrifice is to render sacred." [10] Gusdorf also avoids any clearcut distinction between animal and human sacrifice and explains that man is merely the highest gift that man can offer; to give animals or objects is simply to reduce the price paid. But Gusdorf adds a new perspective by underlining the effect of the rite on the sacrificer as much as on the victim. He stresses its moral impact on those who take part as a kind of "liberation" that brings the individual or the society back into a state of balance. He cites the example of King David, who, in offering his son as a penance for his own sin, thereby regains his moral integrity; so that sacrifice becomes an act of hope rather than of fear: victim and sacrificer join in seeking to bring about a better world.

The most stimulating contemporary study comes from the French scholar René Girard. In 1972 he published *La violence et le sacré*, in which he challenges earlier notions and, along with Gusdorf, insists that to explain sacrifice as a mere gift or even as an act of communion was to miss the point. He concentrated on what he calls the "sacrificial crisis", which ferments in a society and can only be resolved by shedding human blood. The Chinese *Book of Rites* is quoted as affirming that sacrifice "along with music, punishment and law" has as its main aim to bring back social union and to restore the cosmic order.[11] Girard maintains that primitive societies, in the absence of a true judicial system to deal with cases of murder, are forever exposed to an escalation of violence, on the principle of an eye for an eye and a tooth for a tooth; the only end to violence is more violence. The social fabric of such peoples is at best fragile and to strengthen it is an urgent task. Without a proper code of civil law, violence and counter-violence are part of the divine order and for Girard this situation is eternally self-repeating. Tension mounts until flashpoint is reached, the "sacrificial crisis" that demands a victim. He takes as an example ancient Thebes, ruled by King Oedipus. Plague threatened, and everything was falling apart. A victim, a scapegoat, had to be found. In this case it was the king, who was driven into exile, almost equivalent to a death sentence in a Greek city. The tension was then reduced and the crisis resolved. Girard traces this never-ending process of crisis and solution back to a myth, common to all mankind, of an original deed of violence. This single deed has to be re-enacted over and over again. Like Freud, therefore, he looks to a primaeval crime, expurgated by repeated ritual, though he rejects Freud's insistence that the crime is always—as in Thebes—patricide and incest.

Modern thinkers, while not rejecting out of hand the notion of sacrifice as an exchange of gifts with the gods, thus seek a deeper meaning to the practice of taking a man's life in order to save the lives of others. But the two proposed objects of sacrifice, to satisfy the appetites of the gods and to ease the tensions of society, are not diametrically opposed. Rumanian scholar Mircea Eliade helps to bridge the gap between the two. Like Girard, he proposes that among primitive peoples blood sacrifices go back to an original act in which a monster was slain and carved up in order to create the cosmos. In the myths of so many peoples man is what he is today, mortal, sexualized and forced to toil and eat, because of a primordial sin, involving murder, in which a divine being, a man, a maiden or sometimes a child, suffered the pangs of death. To meet man's need to eat, the body of this divine being was then changed into food. His soul went down to the Realm of the Dead, to emerge reborn each year.[12] The act of sacrifice both restores the general equilibrium of society, by re-enacting the original deed of violence, and at the same time caters for the specific needs created by that deed, in particular the granting of good harvests by the gods. Both crop failure and social breakdown are dire threats to the cosmic order, which human offering is thus destined to uphold, whether by a single act of devotion or by filling stone vessels to the brim with palpitating hearts. In all instances the ritual itself is vital as a means to those ends. The gods continued to exact the highest gift, that of a fellow-being, as the price of meeting man's pressing needs. They were only forced to settle for less when human beings ceased—in a handful of societies—to be regarded as mere chattels or a means of exchange like any other.

2

The Gaily Dressed Crowd

Great libraries of Cuneiform texts, written on stone slabs, were unearthed in Mesopotamia in the nineteenth century. Many were deciphered by scholars and gave an ample account of the ritual of the Sumerian civilization and its successors. But in 1927 Sir Leonard Woolley started to dig in the Royal Cemetery of Ur and startled the world by bringing to light funeral practices that were strange and sumptuous and about which the texts of Sumer had been oddly silent.

In his *Excavations at Ur* Woolley recreates the wonder and horror of the stately funeral procession of musicians with their harps, of soldiers fully armed, and of court ladies in all their finery, as they followed their royal master into the burial pit and drank the death potion before being engulfed by earth. "It must have been a very gaily dressed crowd that assembled in the mat-lined pit for the royal obsequies, a blaze of colour with the crimson coats, the silver and the gold; clearly these people were not the wretched slaves killed as oxen might be killed, but persons held in honour, wearing their robes of office, and coming, one hopes, voluntarily to a rite which would be in their belief but a passing from one world to another, from the service of a god on earth to that of the same god in another sphere." [1] From Ur, therefore, comes evidence concerning the first great kings who ruled on earth, whose servants and perhaps their wives had the sacred duty to follow them to the next world, as part of a sumptuous ritual. The sixteen royal graves found in the cemetery date from about 2800 B.C. and the number of victims varies from a mere half-dozen to between seventy and eighty. Though the burials were never exactly alike, in no case had it been a simple matter of throwing back the earth onto a heap of bodies; a prolonged ceremony had clearly taken place, forming part of an elaborate ritual.

Of all the graves, the most revealing was that of King A-bar-gi and Queen Shub-ad. Woolley's team first came upon five bodies lying side by side in a sloping trench and, beyond these, another group, consisting of ten women carefully arranged in two rows, with no tomb furnishings of their own. This was because they themselves were part of the tomb furnishing of their king, just as Egyptian and Mesopotamian monarchs were later buried with substitute retainers in the form of statuettes or figures painted in low relief on the walls of their tombs. At the end of these rows lay the remains of a wonderful harp, the wood decayed but the decoration intact. [This and the other treasures of the Royal Cemetery can now be seen in the British Museum, meticulously restored to their former state.] A little further inside the entrance shaft stood a wooden sledge-chariot decorated with red, white and blue mosaic along the edge of the framework and surmounted by golden lions' heads with manes of lapiz lazuli. In front of the chariot lay the crushed skeletons of two asses with the bodies of their grooms by their heads. Further digging uncovered a confused medley of golden chisels and saws, drinking cups and other vessels in silver, copper and stone, together with yet more bodies.

The royal place of burial lay in another pit about six feet deeper in the earth. The ramp which led to it was guarded by six soldiers, their bodies stretched out in two ranks, complete with copper spears and helmets crushed flat on the broken skulls. Against the end of the royal tomb lay the remains of nine more "court ladies" wearing gala headdresses of lapiz lazuli beads. In the king's chamber, which had been thoroughly pillaged, several other skeletons were found besides that of King A-bar-gi. A second stone chamber contained the body of the Queen, the upper part hidden by a mass of beads, made of every kind of precious stone, whilst crouched against her bier were two women attendants, who must have been killed or drugged before the chamber was walled up. Though Woolley does not say so, it is possible that the Queen, in common with the rest of the great retinue, was herself a victim, and had died from the contents of a gold cup that was found near her hand; the custom of wives accompanying their husbands into the next world is ancient and almost universal.

The King's burial had taken place in two stages: after his closest attendants had been entombed with their master and the doors blocked with stone, the first phase was complete. The second, the filling of the open pit at a higher level with its human furniture, was more spectacular:

> Down into the open pit, with its mat-covered floor and mat-lined walls, empty and unfurnished, comes a procession of people, the members of the dead ruler's court, soldiers, men-servants and women, the latter in all their finery of brightly coloured garments and head-dresses of carnelian and lapiz lazuli, silver and gold, officers with the insignia of their rank, musicians bearing harps or lyres, and then, driven or backed down the slope, the chariots drawn by oxen or by asses, the drivers in the cars, the grooms holding the heads of the draught animals, and all take up their allotted places at the bottom of the shaft and finally a guard of soldiers forms up at the entrance. Each man and woman had brought a little cup of clay or stone or metal, the only equipment needed for the rite that was to follow. There would seem to have been some kind of service down there, at least it is certain that the musicians played up to the last; then each of them drank from their cups a potion which they had brought with them or found prepared for them on the spot—in one case we found in the middle of the pit a great copper pot, into which they could have dipped—and they lay down and composed themselves for death.[2]

When the human victims were unconscious or dead, having drunk their fatal draught of opium or hashish, someone had come down and killed the animals and placed the women's lyres on top of their bodies. After this the earth was flung in from above and the shaft filled in. Curious details were revealed in a great grave pit that formed part of another royal tomb. Here bodies of sixty-four court ladies were found; twenty-eight of these wore golden hair-ribbons, while the rest had silver ones. Of these little remained, as silver has low acid-resistance, but in one case the hair-ribbon was found in a tight coil and was well preserved, since it had formed a solid piece of metal. Woolley suggests that the owner had arrived late for the ceremony and, not having had time to dress properly, gave to posterity the only example of this kind of silver hair-ribbon.

Owing to the absence of any mention of these rites in Sumerian texts, some scholars would not believe that they were burials of real kings, insisting that they were carried out for substitute or temporary festival monarchs, whose rites are basic to the myths of many lands and to the worship of fertility gods who die each winter and are reborn in the spring. But discoveries of other tombs of the Third Dynasty of Ur (circa 2100 to 2000 B.C.), in which many bodies of attendants were found slain with their masters, have confirmed that these were graves of actual rulers. As in the case of King A-bar-gi, the texts maintain a hermetic silence.

With the coming of civilization, such rituals became more elaborate and involved many more people but it would be a mistake to think of them as the trappings of a higher culture. On the contrary, to trace the origins of human sacrifice in one form or another we have to go back very far indeed. Moreover, the stately ceremonies that took place in Ur represent only one kind of human offering—the slaying of the king's attendants—but they are far from being the beginning of the story. Basic forms already existed long before man built cities or came to be ruled by kings.

The remains of Peking Man were first discovered half a century ago in the Dragon-bone caves at Chou-kou-tien, near Peking. The age of the bones was originally put at 500,000 years but they are now estimated to be almost a million years old. In Chou-kou-tien, a number of bodies had been decapitated and buried until the flesh had rotted, while the skulls had been carefully preserved after having been broken open in order to extract the brains, apparently some time after death. The larger human bones had been split mostly in the same way as those of animals found on the site, to make it easier to extract the marrow. The opening at the base of the skull had been enlarged in the exact manner used until recently by Melanesian Islanders, for whom the human brain was a gourmet dish. The split bones had been treated unceremoniously, as if to suggest that Peking Man ate his own kind with as little compunction as he fed upon any other sort of game—though such evidence has to be treated with caution since it is very incomplete. The human head was unquestionably for Peking Man a sacred object. The skulls of Java Man, roughly contemporary, seem to have been treated in the same way and then used as drinking vessels, just as in modern times primitive peoples would still drink from the skull of a warrior in order to imbibe some of his strength.

Further signs of the cult of the human skull and the eating of the brain derive from Neanderthal Man, who lived from about 200,000 to 70,000 B.C. In 1939 at Monte Circeo, on the coast of Italy south of Rome, a Neanderthal skull was discovered in a small chamber placed within a circle of stones and resting on the leg-bones of an ox and a deer. Again the foramen, the opening through which the spinal cord connects with the brain, had been cut away after death, and the brain of this sacred skull taken out and presumably eaten for its life-giving qualities. At Krapina in Yugoslavia the remains of thirteen Neanderthal adults and seven children recalled those of Peking Man; the bones of animals and humans had received the same treatment, having been broken up in order to extract the marrow. In Uzbekistan in southern Russia was unearthed the ceremonial burial of a Neanderthal child, whose skull was surrounded by six pairs of horns of the Siberian mountain goat. All the evidence, therefore, suggests some form of ritual human offering among the Neanderthalers, rather than pure cannibalism. It is very unlikely that these tiny bands of hunters spent their time chasing their own kind simply for food. Other game was not scarce and if early Man had persistently hunted his own species, he would soon have become extinct.

By about 20,000 B.C. such cults had acquired new refinements. In a cave in the Charente in France drinking cups were found made of the upper part of the vault of human skulls. At Offnet in the Jura Mountains two nests of skulls, embedded in red ochre, had been cut off after death and preserved as relics, adorned with shells and necklaces, and placed so that they faced in a westerly direction. At Ofnethöhlen in Germany a mass burial of thirty-three red-coloured skulls was discovered; twenty were of children and it is unlikely that they all died from natural causes. At this time appear signs of that universal form of human sacrifice, the burial of the great with their own attendants, whether family or servants. Again in the Charente a triple burial was found, resting on a bed of ochre. A tall man had been laid on his back with a young woman and a boy facing him on their sides with their arms raised and hands folded together. Both the man and the woman had a flint knife in their left hand, and another knife lay beside the boy's head.

In the Neolithic age, from about 10,000 B.C. onwards, the cult of the head became even more elaborate. In Jericho a whole series of skulls about eight thousand years old had their features moulded in plaster and their eye sockets inset with shells, in which slits were made to indicate the pupils. They appear to be life-like portraits, made to represent dead members of the family for religious purposes. The inside of these heads had been filled with earth or clay in a way that could only have been done after the soft tissues had first decayed. The human head had by then become the centre of a fairly complicated cult, used for the benefit of future generations, and based on a simple form of ancestor worship.[3] By 3500 B.C. skull rituals in Jericho had become more exotic. In several cases the skeletons had been dug up again after the flesh had rotted; these bones were ceremonially burned on a funeral pyre, around which the skulls were laid during the ritual. They were then placed in pots and put into their final tomb, which was filled up with debris. Also dating from this period, in south Germany various burials have been found in which a man and a woman were placed together, sometimes stretched out so that the head of one body lay beside the feet of the other; clearly the woman had accompanied her husband to the grave.

The ancient Egyptians are often looked upon as the originators of civilization, though it now seems that the people of Mesopotamia took this great step slightly ahead of them. Certainly neither Egyptians nor Mesopotamians invented human offering, already practised in the Near East long before the advent of their great dynasties, but they may have devised new forms, and in Egypt written texts offer proof of many kinds of sacrifice, including torture, that subsequently became widespread.

In the Nile Valley the cult of the dead, involving the preservation of the whole body, attained dramatic proportions. The custom became established under the early pharaohs, from about 3000 B.C. onwards, but it was preceded by a more primitive cult of the human skull that recalls the finds in Jericho. At one early site, Nagada, five instances were found where the head had been severed and set up separately on a pile of stones, as in Monte Circeo, while other graves had skeletons that lacked their skulls. The earliest literature confirms that such rites were performed; in the Book of the Dead it is stated, "I am a prince, son of a prince . . . whose head is restored to him after it has been cut off." [4] The brain was taken out through the nose during mummification, but before this process was invented the head was simply severed, and after removal of the brain, filled with spices and unguents to act as preservatives. Extreme care was taken to make sure that each skull was returned to the right skeleton, since it was thought to contain a man's "soul substance" and to put the wrong head on the wrong body would have had horrendous consequences. In Egypt, in this pre-dynastic period, the head was covered with stucco plaster, as in Jericho, and the face carefully remodelled. The practice was only given up when mummification came into vogue and even then permanent models of a dead man's face, made of stucco or resin, were often placed in tombs alongside the mummy; these models paved the way for the full-scale portrait statues that were later used for the purpose. In certain early burials the flesh was found to have been removed from the bones, which sometimes bore the marks of teeth, suggestive of some form of cannibal ritual.

Under the first dynasties of a united Egypt, starting in the third millennium B.C., a radical change took place when the cult of the head was replaced by mummification. The pharaoh was by then regarded as a descendant of the god Osiris, always himself depicted as a mummy. His story is plainly that of a human sacrifice but also represents a protest against such practices. According to legend, Osiris, son of the earth god Seb, was a benevolent king who first gave laws to the Egyptians, taught them to worship the gods, and to abjure cannibalism. Set, his wicked brother, lured Osiris to lay himself in a decorated coffer, which he nailed down and cast into the Nile; it floated out to sea and drifted to Byblos on the coast of present-day Lebanon. Isis, sister and wife of Osiris, recovered the coffer and brought it back to Egypt, but it was again seized by Set, who carved Osiris' body into fourteen pieces, which he scattered far and wide over the land. Isis picked up the fragments, which she buried where she found them, except for the genital member, which had been eaten by fish. Such was the reverence for Osiris that in the course of time his divine limbs, miraculously multiplied, came to possess countless burial places, all looked upon as sacred. Finally Isis, with the help of their son Horus, pieced together the broken pieces of the god's body and swathed it in bandages, as for a mummy. Osiris revived and from then on reigned in the nether world as king of the dead, where he judged the souls of the departed. The resurrection of Osiris gave the promise of eternal life to every man, if only his heirs did for the body what Isis and the other gods had done for Osiris. Hence the rites for the burial of the dead were an exact copy of those performed over the legendary god-king, the forbear of all the pharaohs.

The cult of Osiris marked a turning point in religious ritual. In the first place stress on preserving the intact corpse ran counter to the more primitive system of two burials. For in dismembering Osiris, Set had only followed the custom of the time; separately buried heads have been found in early Egyptian tombs. Any urge towards cannibalism was suppressed though not extinguished. In the tomb of Unas, a ruler of the Old Kingdom, at Sakkarah, the dead king is described as feeding upon his father and mother, even hunting the gods in the meadows of the sky, cutting them up, and devouring their hearts and entrails. The ancient rite of dismemberment as a punishment also survived in symbolic form. Set, the murderer of Osiris, became the god of evil, and was the arch-enemy of Ra, the Sun God. One of the chief devils in his service was the monster Apepi, who appeared sometimes as a serpent and sometimes as a crocodile. The *Book of the Overthrowing of Apepi* recommended the making of a wax figure of the crocodile. The priest would then stamp on the image with his left foot until it became a shapeless mass, uttering the words: "Get thee back, O one hacked in pieces. . . . I slice the flesh from his bones. I fetter his feet. I cut off his hands and arms. I block up his eyes. I tear out his heart." [5]

But not all the older forms of sacrifice were reduced to symbols. The eminent English Egyptologist Sir Wallis Budge cites various texts telling of human offerings made to Osiris himself, presided over by his executioner Shesmn. The Papyrus of Ani shows a picture of Shesmn standing by a kind of stone guillotine; the victim's head was placed between two uprights set in a solid pedestal and then lopped off, probably with a flint knife. Other texts tell of tortures inflicted upon the "enemies of Osiris" and describe in detail the instruments used for the purpose.[6] In the Book of Gates "the enemies of Osiris who are to be burnt" are shown with their arms tied across their bodies and behind their backs in such a way as to cause intense pain; they are doomed to receive in their face the fire which the serpent Khati is about to spit at them, before being burnt and hacked to pieces. Other illustrations depict Osiris, dressed in full regalia, watching a priest-executioner in animal headdress decapitate three kneeling foes. In tropical Africa, many Egyptian rituals took permanent hold, and almost identical treatment was meted out to sacrificial victims in Dahomey in the mid-eighteenth century.[7]

Further evidence testifies to the ritual killing of enemy captives. An ivory plaque found at Abydos depicts Semti, a king of the First Dynasty, in the act of offering up a conquered enemy; a figure of the god Anubis, standing just behind the captive, shows that this is a sacrifice made by the king to honour the god. The immolation of war prisoners did not cease with the early kings; under the Eighteenth Dynasty (1574–1320 B.C.), when Egyptian civilization was at its zenith, an inscription of King Amenhotep II records that he slew seven chiefs with his own club and hung their bodies head downwards at the bows of his boat. When he returned to his capital of Thebes, they were dedicated to the temple of the god Amon. When short of prisoners and other foreigners to use as victims, the Egyptians had to resort to their own people, and on the tomb of Osiris would sacrifice red-headed men (red was the colour associated with Set, the god's enemy). For this rite Busiris, in northern Egypt, where the head of Osiris was supposedly buried, was a favoured centre and every sacrifice in that spot was hailed as a renewed attempt to avenge his death. Another text confirms that red-headed men—an obvious rarity in Egypt—were burnt alive in a number of places. This took place in the dog days of summer, as a precaution against drought or pestilence; the ashes of the victims were scattered to the winds. As the resurrected life-force, Osiris also represented the Nile, whose waters rose each year and brought life to the fields. His worship was therefore closely linked to the vegetation cycle and the seasonal sacrifice of red-headed men was part of the cult. Sir James Frazer has even suggested in *The Golden Bough* that their colouring symbolized the ripe ears of grain.

The Egyptians did not confine themselves to killing the enemies of Osiris but, like the Mesopotamians, also practised the custom of burying retainers in their masters' graves. Hints that men were sometimes slain at the funerals of Osiris' followers occur in Chapter LII of the Book of the Dead, in which the god states, "May these be given to me as victims of my father and mother and as guardians of my door". From about 2300 B.C. onwards, for the next two thousand years, countless tiny figures known as Shabti were buried with the dead; sometimes as many as two hundred were put into a single tomb. The great French Egyptologist Georges Maspero was convinced that this custom could only mean that the Shabti were a substitute for the slaves who, formerly, were buried, dead or alive, with their masters in order to serve them in the next world as they had done in this. In spite of the use of these images, the burying of real humans did not altogether die out and the body of a woman who had been strangled was found in the tomb of a princess of the Eleventh Dynasty. Two women laid out on the floor of the burial chamber of Amenhotep II, of the Eighteenth Dynasty, had either also been strangled or committed suicide.[8] In addition, proof exists of the continued survival of yet another classic form of sacrifice: the burying of children or adults under new buildings. Infants' bodies were discovered in foundations laid as late as the Twenty-second Dynasty (950–720 B.C.).[9]

So although the scale of human sacrifice certainly diminished, any picture of Egypt as a land in which the suffering and death of the god Osiris had taken the place of all the savage customs of the past is not a realistic one. While ancient texts in Sumeria may have maintained an inscrutable silence on the subject, those of Egypt at least offer an inkling of the truth and are supported by the finds of archaeologists. At the same time, the agony of Osiris was a sacrifice with a universal message. As the one who died to save the many, and who rose from the dead, he was the first of a long line that has deeply affected man's view of this world and the next.

Human sacrifice is to be found in one form or another all over the ancient Near East. But in that other cradle of Old World civilization, China, the practice was just as widespread and followed the same patterns to an uncanny degree. The origins of human offering in China are obscure and we know little of what happened between the remote age of Peking Man and the birth of Chinese civilization. The most striking evidence of early human sacrifice comes from graves uncovered in the 1950s and belonging to the Shang Dynasty (1523 to 1028 B.C.). In the Honan Province, eight great kings' burials were found, though the most remarkable of all was in Wukuang, two hundred miles south of Peking. Just as in the Royal Cemetery of Ur, the king was found at a lower level than his attendants, who were buried in chambers grouped around the main tomb, complete with all their arms and equipment. Other resemblances with Ur are startling. Not only were costly treasures piled high in the graves, including fine bronze vessels, together with malachite, jade and turquoise ornaments; in one grave a war chariot, complete with charioteer and horses, was found; other horses, men and dogs were placed on the ramp leading to the king's chamber, the men arranged in the attitude of guards. A feature special to China was a little cavity, hollowed out at the lowest level of all and reserved for the dead man's favourite cat or lapdog or occasionally a favoured human. In the Chinese tombs, unlike those at Ur, certain retainers had been beheaded and their skulls buried separately. These were the gravediggers, who were killed to prevent their telling robbers how to enter the chambers. One instance of thirty-four human skulls, carefully arranged in rows, showed that the more primitive cult of the head was not yet extinct.

In ancient China that other classic form of human sacrifice, the burying of people beneath the foundations of new buildings, was also found. Skeletons, mainly of children, have been unearthed that attest to the popularity of the practice at the time of the Chou Dynasty (1028 to 256 B.C.). It had already begun in the preceding Shang Dynasty and when the Shang capital was excavated, hundreds of bodies were found buried at the entrance to the royal palace. Certain tombs of princes of the Wei State (334 to 286 B.C.) were opened only several hundred years later during the Han Dynasty and, in one case, revealed a hundred bodies, of which ninety-nine were female.[10]

These Chinese finds receive ample substantiation from written texts that suggest that such customs survived for a long time. The great historian Ssuma Chien records that, when the Emperor Wu of the State of Ts'in died in 677 B.C., sixty-six people went with him into the next world. This sovereign was not to be outdone by his nephew Muh, a very successful ruler who died in 619 B.C.: "The ruler Muh died and was buried in Yung. Those who followed the defunct to the next world were one hundred and seventy-seven in number. Amongst them were three exquisite ministers of Ts'in." The account makes it clear that the death of the three ministers was an act of voluntary sacrifice. The Dutch scholar de Groot, in his great study *The Religious System of Ancient China*, lists numerous occasions when the living were buried with the dead, gleaned from his vast knowledge of Chinese literature. A feudal ruler of Chu in 506 B.C., in the act of throwing himself down on a couch in a fit of rage, somehow instead fell on a furnace of charcoal, was burnt and died. "Before he was placed in his grave, five carts and five living men were buried." [12] According to another text of that time, a distinguished nobleman buried two of his own daughters with his sovereign, as a mark of gratitude because the king had once shown clemency to his father. When Madame Fu, the concubine of Mu-Yung Hi, ruler of the State of Yen, died, he howled bitterly, beat his breast, stamped his feet and even tried to have sexual intercourse with her in her coffin. As a consolation to his beloved in the next world, he ordered his own sister-in-law, a woman of beautiful countenance and much worth, to die by her own hand and be buried along with Madame Fu.[13]

China became a unified and stable empire under the Han Dynasty (206 B.C. to 220 A.D.). In the records of this and the succeeding dynasties, burying the living with the dead is not mentioned and de Groot was unable to find a single case of human sacrifice in the great histories of the period or in the biographies of emperors and empresses. Archaeology, however, tells another tale and many tombs have now been opened which show that attendants were buried with their masters as late as the Sung Dynasty (960 to 1260 A.D.). There is even evidence that the practice of burying royal retainers survived into the era of the first Ming rulers in the fourteenth century.

Nonetheless, early recorded protests by certain sages show that people began to have misgivings about the rights and wrongs of human sacrifice as a means of winning the favour of the gods. The philosopher Micius, who lived in the third century B.C., railed against the extravagance of royal funerals in his day. Chen Khien-Sih, a grandee of the kingdom of Tsi, had ordered a coffin for himself large enough to accommodate two slave girls, one on each side of him; but his son said that it was not good to bury the living with the dead, let alone in the same coffin, and suppressed the project. When the three ministers were called upon to sacrifice themselves with the ruler Muh, the people of Ts'in deplored their fate and gave vent to their displeasure in the Lay of the Yellow Birds. Perhaps as the result of such misgivings, the sacrifice of human life was reduced though not terminated. Rather than immolate humans, imitation men and women were often used. Even in the Shang Dynasty bundles of straw, as imperfect models of men, served symbolically as the king's attendants in the next world. Later, under the Chou Dynasty, wooden images with springs to enable them to imitate human actions were often put into tombs. Later still, these became more elaborate and were made of a bamboo framework covered with coloured paper and clothed according to the rank of those whom they represented. Such images were still used at the funeral of the last Dowager Empress in 1908; a large number were carried in the procession and then burned.

This process, however, whereby human beings were replaced by symbols, was sometimes reversed, and a previously harmless ceremony came to serve as a basis for real killings. Confucius (551–478 B.C.) even suggested that the custom of burying living persons with the dead derived from the use in tombs of these wooden images with springs. He may have been wrong in this but one case is known of a man being made to take the place of a beast. In 639 B.C. the Viscount Tsang was sacrificed by the people of Chu in place of an animal chosen for the ceremony, in order to make absolutely sure that the gods would help in a moment of crisis.

Human sacrifice in many of its more common forms has existed from time immemorial not only in China but also in Japan. In early times men were sometimes buried alive in the foundations of castles, bridges or artificial islands. The Japanese had a special name for this custom and the victims were known as hito-bashira, meaning human pillars. Japanese literature tells of slave offerings and, according to the Nihongi, the great collection of chronicles and sagas compiled in the eighth century A.D., many humans died at royal funerals. At the burial of Prince Yamato-hiko, brother of the Emperor, in the year 2 B.C., his vast personal retinue was buried alive; "for several days they died not, but wept and wailed at night". But killing on such an exaggerated scale led to a reaction and even the Emperor grieved at the wailing of his brother's servants and pronounced that the custom was a bad one. When his Empress died in 3 A.D. the Mikado summoned the clay-workers and ordered numerous little images of men and horses to be placed in the tomb. From then onwards it became the custom to arrange effigies of men, animals and objects in a circle round the corpse in royal tombs.

The Shinto religion, which is peculiar to Japan, demanded rich offerings to its rather ill-defined gods. Unquestionably such offerings were at first human, although this was changed at a fairly early stage. Thus the Kojiki, another important eighth-century collection of myths and sagas, tells a story that recalls the Greek legend of Perseus and Andromeda. The God of the Ocean and the Storm was driven out of heaven and came as a human hero to the headwaters of the river Hi, where he found an old man weeping. Originally he had had eight daughters but seven of these had already been given as food, one each year, to the eight-headed serpent of Koshi. To save the last daughter the hero made the serpent drunk with a very special potion; he then cut the reptile into small pieces and threw them into the river. On another occasion, in 323 A.D., a human offering was also avoided at the last moment. According to the Nihongi, the Emperor wanted to sacrifice two men to the god of the Northern River but in the end two calabashes were used instead. A more curious tale of the use of images in place of men comes from an annual feast that was still held in the eighteenth century at the shrine of Kokubo in the province of Owari. The Shinto priests would go out into the highway with banners and seize a passer-by, who was brought before the god together with a wooden butcher's knife and chopsticks for eating flesh. But a rice effigy was then made and placed beside the captive on the block and left for a whole night. After elaborate rites the next day the captive was driven away; inevitably he fell down in a faint and a mound was built on the spot where he collapsed.

In this chapter we have seen how the pioneers of man's progress from the rustic village to the city-state all practised human sacrifice. In Egypt and China it seems to have started as a cult of the human head, recalling that of Neanderthal Man, a hundred thousand years before, and forms of this cult survived into modern times among primitive peoples of Africa and Oceania. So we can say with confidence that human sacrifice was not therefore a by-product of progress, as people are apt to believe. The burial of vast retinues of royal servants at the very dawn of civilization proves the contrary, for such practices are not invented overnight; basic forms of sacrifice were a legacy bequeathed by hundreds of generations of early hunters. But if they were not invented in the cities of Egypt, Sumer and China, in each case the rites there became a hundredfold more lavish, and the victims more numerous, as part of the pomp and ceremony of those mighty monarchs, who were likened to gods or demi-gods, and from whom all life flowed.

Such rituals baffle the modern mind, which questions belief in an after-life that is virtually a replica of the present one. Yet in all that army of retainers who went with the rulers of Sumer to their graves, surely none doubted for one instant that they would live on to serve their masters in their new states; not a single member of Woolley's "gaudy crowd" would have questioned the need for such rites or looked on the whole procedure as a kind of hoax.

3

Of Odin
and Oedipus

All over pre-Christian Europe every imaginable form of human sacrifice was to be found: infanticide, fertility rites, immolation of war prisoners, live burial under buildings, sacrifice of the god or of the ruler in his stead. Even the advent of Christianity did not put an end to these practices, although Christian sacrifices were different, being confined to heretics, disbelievers and witches, who in the eyes of the Church were enemies of Christ.

The Germanic peoples practised all the usual forms of human offering before their conversion to Christianity, among which diverse rituals was the supreme sacrifice involving the death of the god or king in person. The great god of the North was the Scandinavian Odin, or the German Wodan. Odin discovered the secret of runic wisdom by hanging himself on the World Ash. As a result, those offered to Odin were hanged, and he was even known as Hangatyr (god of the hanged). Like Osiris, Odin not only was sacrificed but revived and became god of the dead; in this role he demanded a constant flow of new subjects in the form of fallen warriors. He would select his own victims and then send forth his battle maidens, the Valkyrs, to kill and bring to his kingdom those warriors that he had chosen. Odin himself took part in war and was present at the great battle of Bravalla, in which he personally struck down King Harald. The cult of Odin even produced a literature of its own, including these lines of the Verse Edda[1]:

> The words of the High One,
> I'm aware that I hung
> On the windy tree,

Swing these nights all
Gashed with a blade
Blooded for Odin.

The Eddas also tell the legend of the ritual death of Odin's son Balder, known as the bleeding god. Unlike his father, he was mild and beloved by all. Once he had a dream prophesying his death. To ward off the threat, the goddess Frigg made him invulnerable to all kinds of weapons and missiles. But this immunity became a source of sport for the other gods, who set him in their midst and used him for a kind of target practice; some showered him with arrows and stones, whilst others hacked at him with their swords, all to no avail. But the wicked god Loki found Balder's one weak spot: he was vulnerable to being wounded by mistletoe. Loki therefore cut a branch of this wood and gave it to the blind god Hother, who pierced Balder through and through with the twig, so that he fell down dead. For a while the other gods stood speechless and then they all wept bitterly. Balder's body was burned on a pyre in his ship with that of his wife, who died of grief. The legend, together with the story of his resurrection and return to earth, recalls those other dying gods, such as the Syrian Tammuz, who died ritually every year and were reborn when the seeds sprouted again. Just as the god had originally died, so in his place the king himself was sometimes slain. The Swedes offered up King Domaldi to avert a famine after a sacrifice of ordinary men and animals had been made without effect. Even after the practice of killing the king ceased, he was still held responsible if crops failed and was driven from his throne.

Nine was the gods' sacred number and every nine years a spring festival was held in Uppsala in Sweden in honour of the god Frey. Nine human victims, with nine horses and nine dogs, were hanged. At another ceremony of this kind, held in the winter in Denmark, nine humans and an equal number of horses, dogs and cocks were sacrificed. A legend relates that when King Auun of Uppsala was growing old, he sacrificed nine of his sons to Odin, in order to prolong his life. After Auun had offered up his seventh son, he lived on but became senile and after the death of his eighth son he spent a further nine years lying in his bed. Having sacrificed the ninth son, he survived yet another nine years but had to drink out of a horn like a weaned infant. He then intended to kill his sole remaining child but the Swedes would not let him do so and he finally died.

Both Norsemen and Teutons regularly sacrificed war prisoners to their gods and after a great battle against the Teutons in 105 B.C. Roman captives were hanged upon trees. The object of such rites was more to give strength than to wreak vengeance; the German epic, the *Niebelungenlied*, tells how, many centuries later in 437 A.D., the Burgundians drank the blood of their fallen foes after their victory against the Huns, in order to imbibe their valour. The Teutons observed the widespread custom of foundation sacrifice and would enclose a living person within the masonry of a new building. Children's bodies were inserted into the dykes on the sea coast, to preserve them from the waves. One report from Oldenburg, perhaps exaggerated, states that children were still sacrificed for this purpose in the seventeenth century.[2] The Norsemen had special kinds of sacrifice, performed before a voyage, to guard against storms at sea caused by the sea demon. When setting out on Viking raids, they frequently sacrificed humans to the sea god. More offerings were made if bad weather delayed the departure of an expedition. If no others were available, victims were simply chosen by lot from those who were to take part in the voyage. The Vikings, like the Polynesians, bound victims to the rollers over which a new ship slipped into the sea and reddened its keel with human blood. These seafaring raiders even indulged in torture; they would cut the "bloody eagle" on the back of a Christian captive while he was still alive, and through this incision the vital parts were drawn out, the whole act combining sacrifice and revenge.[3]

Information on the rites of the Ancient Gauls, ancestors of the French, comes mainly from Julius Caesar. He relates that people who were troubled with a severe illness would offer a man to the gods. Like the Romans themselves, they often used criminals as victims; to quote Caesar: "The Gauls consider that the oblation of such as have been taken in theft, or robbery, or any other offence, is more acceptable to the immortal gods; but when a supply of that class is wanting, they have recourse even to the innocent." The Gauls of Caesar's time also sacrificed slaves. Such rites were slow to die out in Gaul, in spite of Roman disapproval; Pliny tells us that the Emperor Tiberius' suppression of human sacrifice in the Province of Gaul was only partly successful, and the custom persisted of hacking pieces of flesh off those condemned to death. Cicero described human sacrifice as a monstrous practice that still disgraced Gaul in his day.

The Romans also provide data on the customs of Celts and Druids in Britain. War captives and criminals were preferred as victims and these, together with animals, would be burned in huge wicker images (simulacra). The more brutal Druid customs were later suppressed by the Emperor Claudius. The historian Tacitus wrote in specific terms about them: "They deemed it indeed as a duty to cover their altars with the blood of captives, and to consult the gods through human entrails." [4] Less is known of the Irish Celts in this respect, but a twelfth-century source states that the Ancient Irish used to offer firstborn children to their great stone idol, Mag Slocht. According to Celtic myth, Ireland was first peopled by the Formorians, a greedy group of gods who exacted from their worshippers a toll of two thirds of the children born each year, as well as two thirds of all supplies of milk and wheat. Saint Patrick is said to have preached against the burning of the firstborn children at the fair of Taillte.[5] One Irish saint was himself buried alive as a foundation sacrifice. The legend forms part of the story of the founding of the monastery of Iona. Saint Columba said to the monks: "It is good for us that our roots should go under the earth here; it is permitted that one of you should go under the clay of this island to hallow it." Saint Oran volunteered for the mission, and the church was built over him; as a reward he went straight to heaven.[6] In another version of the story, Oran had somehow managed to pay a visit to the other world and to return; he was buried alive because he denied orthodox beliefs about what happened in heaven.

Even less is known of the Scottish Celts than of the Irish. Nonetheless headhunting is said to have persisted in the Scottish marshes among people of Celtic descent until the Middle Ages [7] and strange rites that survived until recent times bear an unmistakable stamp of former human sacrifice. The lighting of the Beltane fires which went on well into the eighteenth century is vividly described by Frazer. After kindling a great bonfire, the people prepared a meal and then danced around the blaze. Towards the end of the ceremony the master of the feast would produce a large cake, called the Beltane cake, which was cut into many pieces and handed out. One particular slice bore a curse and whoever received it was known as the Beltane Carline. It was considered a sign of great guilt to hit upon this piece and, when the choice was made known, part of the company laid hold of the Carline and made a show of putting him into the fire. In some places they laid him flat on the ground, making as if they would quarter him. He was then pelted with eggshells and kept his odious title for the rest of the year. The rite is an obvious relic of the annual sacrifice of a scapegoat chosen by lot, probably as part of some fertility or harvest festival.

The Romans freely criticised Celtic customs and said less about what went on nearer home. In fact, the Romans had inherited from the Greeks and others many forms of sacrifice, including ritual suicide. Efforts to suppress them were often half-hearted and they were actually on the increase in the troubled times before Christianity became the official religion. The very laws which the Romans drew up against certain kinds of human sacrifice are the surest proof that they existed. Pliny records that as early as 97 B.C. a decree was passed by the Roman Senate against the killing of human beings to honour the gods. The Emperor Hadrian later saw fit to renew this ban. Hadrian's law is recorded by the historian Porphyry, who wrote in the third century A.D.: "Who does not know that to this day, in the great city of Rome, at the feast of Jupiter Latiaris, they cut the throat of a man?" [8] Other instances may be cited of human sacrifice in Rome, recorded by various historians. Livy states that numbers of people, with heads veiled, would throw themselves into the Tiber during a famine. In 216 B.C., at a moment of dire crisis in the war against Carthage, the Romans revived the old custom of burying alive a man and a woman of the enemy nation. Suetonius writes that Nero, frightened out of his wits by the sight of a comet, offered up a number of Roman noblemen to avert the implied threat to his own life. In 41 B.C., on the Ides of March, Octavian (the future Emperor Augustus) is said to have sacrificed three hundred men on the altar of the deified Julius Caesar.

Such acts might be seen merely as sporadic revivals of ancient and savage customs, but concrete examples of their continuance are quite plentiful, and the records may even understate a case that was found distasteful. Moreover the gladiatorial combats, which claimed countless victims in the course of history, were wholly sacrificial in origin. Their first recorded use was in 264 B.C., as part of the funerary rites of Marcus Brutus; his sons arranged the combat in which three pairs fought to "honour his ashes". Until the establishment of the Empire by Julius Caesar the notion persisted that gladiators fought to honour the spirits of the dead. In 45 B.C. Julius Caesar held the first combat to honour a woman, his deceased daughter Julia. Under the Empire gladiators were employed more to celebrate a victory and fights involving hundreds of pairs were common. Pupils for the gladiatorial schools were recruited largely from war prisoners, criminals and slaves.

Even the antique custom of killing the king or his substitute lived on in Rome into imperial times and is typified by the King of the Wood at Nemi, made famous by Sir James Frazer, who begins the massive text of *The Golden Bough* with this strange rite. The tale is best told in his inimitable language:

> On the northern shore of the lake, right under the precipitous cliffs on which the modern village of Nemi is perched, stood the sacred grove and sanctuary of Diana Nemorensis, or Diana of the Wood . . . where there grew a certain tree round which at any time of the day, and probably far into the night, a grim figure might be seen to prowl. In his hand he carried a drawn sword, and he kept peering warily about him as if at every instant he expected to be set upon by an enemy. He was a priest and a murderer; and the man for whom he looked was sooner or later to murder him and hold the priesthood in his stead. Such was the rule of the sanctuary. A candidate for the priesthood could only succeed to office by slaying the priest, and having slain him, he retained office till he was himself slain by a stronger or a craftier. The post which he held by this precarious tenure carried with it the title of king; but surely no crowned head ever lay uneasier, or was visited by more evil dreams, than his. For year in, year out, in summer and winter, in fair weather and in foul, he had to keep his lonely watch, and whenever he snatched a troubled slumber it was at the peril of his life. The least relaxation of his vigilance, the smallest abatement of his strength of limb or skill of fence, put him in jeopardy; grey hairs might seal his death-warrant.

The grove at Nemi was sacred to the hunting goddess, Diana, and far from dying out, the rites survived for many centuries. The capricious Emperor Caligula (37–41 A.D.) suddenly felt that the reigning king or priest of Nemi had ruled for long enough and hired a ruffian to kill him. And even in the second century A.D., the Nemi priesthood remained the prize of victory in single combat. For Frazer, the story of the king of Nemi is the foundation stone of his central theme, the slaying of priest-kings all the world over, whether in Asia, Africa or America, as man's universal heritage, dictated by the need to safeguard his crops. However much later scholars may regard Frazer as over-obsessed with harvest rites and corn kings, he is probably right to treat the King of Nemi as part of the slain god-king complex, that goes back to Osiris in Egypt and to Dumuzi in Sumer. Diana was goddess of fertility and childbirth as well as of hunting, and the first king of Nemi is the mythical forerunner of a long line of priests who served Diana under the title of King of the Wood and who came to a violent end.

In Rome, the tendency to replace humans with animals or objects set in fairly early, although the origin of the rites, when men not beasts were killed, often remained apparent. An example of this change is the ceremony that took place on the Ides of May, when the Vestal Virgins cast into the Tiber thirty human effigies made of rushes. According to legend, it was Hercules who first threw straw images to river gods in place of men. Another substitute for human sacrifice was the Sacred Spring (Ver Sacrum). When at war with the Carthaginian Hannibal, the Romans—in addition to human offer-ings already mentioned—sought a way out of their troubles by prom-ising to dedicate all the domestic animals born in a single spring and these were duly killed to fulfil the pledge. But originally in Italy the sacred spring also claimed human children, who suffered a curious fate: they were first allowed to grow up and were then driven beyond the borders of their land. This custom, cruel and odd as it may seem, was an alternative to the yet older practice of killing the adolescents. Odder still, in place of these youths beasts were later expelled from the country. Banishment was in effect a form of sac-rifice. In some countries, such as Uganda, it was merely one form of ritual execution. The god would demand a human scapegoat, who would be dispatched, together with a number of animals. They were taken to a spot outside the kingdom where their limbs were broken and they were left to die a lingering death. On the 15th October a strange Roman ceremony took place that also involved animal sacri-fice, but recalls earlier rites of a different kind. A chariot race would be run on the Field of Mars. Stabbed with a spear, the right hand horse of the victorious team was made sacred to Mars. A mock battle took place to decide who should carry off the head. This head was then adorned with a string of loaves, suggestive of an earlier fertility rite with human victims.

But if animals are sometimes used to take the place of men, the change is not inevitable, as we have already seen. In Rome the wheels were put into reverse and human sacrifice staged a partial revival. This came about when foreign cults became popular in Rome under the Empire. Among these new rites was a curious autosacrifice known as the devotio. This was introduced from Spain in the first century A.D. In Rome the devotio became a form of emperor worship, in which high-placed individuals vowed to die on behalf of the emperor, much as in twentieth-century Japan leading citizens still committed hara-kiri to uphold the Mikado's honour. As an early instance of devotio, the Roman nobleman Pacuvius sacrificed himself for the Emperor Augustus. Vows of this kind became more common in later times; when the Emperor Caligula was sick, two distinguished Romans pledged themselves to die so that he might recover. Caligula took them at their word and before they had time to change their minds, had them put to death. Although the devotio was basically foreign, it conformed to certain local traditions. In 362 B.C., a great chasm had opened in the Roman Forum, and the rumour spread that it would only be closed when it received the most precious treasure that Rome had to offer. Thereupon Curtius presented himself on horseback in full armour, prayed to the gods and plunged into the abyss.

In addition to this odd form of hara-kiri, other oriental cults spread to Rome that demanded human victims. For instance, the Emperor Commodus (180–192 A.D.) put men to death in rites that formed part of the cult of Mithraism, which was popular in Rome before Christianity was made the official religion. The period was deeply affected by these mystery religions and human beings were sacrificed fairly frequently, either because parts of the body were regarded as potent charms, or because the spirits of the underworld would not give their aid unless rewarded with the prize of a man's life. Several reports also survive of children being killed in order that the future might be learned from their entrails.[9]

Just as the children of Israel copied the bloody rites of the Canaanites, so the Romans at times adopted those of their Carthaginian enemies, to the extent that the Carthaginian Baal, or Moloch, came to be identified with the Roman Saturn. Child sacrifice was a speciality of the Carthaginians, inherited from their Phoenician and Canaanite ancestors. In honour of Baal, who was both Sun God and God of Fire, the children were rolled down into a fiery pit in the shape of the image of the god; the image was itself known as Moloch. In a site near the modern Tunis six thousand urns containing the charred remains of infants were found. War captives were also sacrificed after a battle and any caught in preliminary skirmishes would be offered up beforehand to Baal as a prayer for victory. Anath, the wife of Baal, was festooned with severed heads and hung human hands on her girdle, as did the Mother Goddesses of Mexico and India. Though Carthage was destroyed by Rome in 146 B.C., it was later rebuilt and in this Roman Carthage, in the fourth century A.D., the suicide was still re-enacted of Queen Dido who, to honour the spirit of her husband, had stabbed herself in the presence of her people on top of a huge funeral pyre, which was then lighted. Carthaginian child sacrifices continued on a reduced scale, though the Emperor Tiberius tried to forbid human offerings in Africa to Saturn, the equivalent of Baal. In earlier times, Baal had demanded the sons of nobles but the latter-day Carthaginians secretly bought and bred poor children for the purpose.

Even Roman justice had a sacrificial element, with criminals executed as offerings to the gods. As in many other places, there was no clear dividing line between sacrificial victims and mere offenders against the law. Julius Caesar in 46 B.C. caused two soldiers to be sacrificed on the Field of Mars as a penalty for mutiny. This might be regarded simply as a legal sentence, but the idea behind the deed was the need to appease the anger of the God of War. An example of expiation for wrong that was both legal and ritual is contained in an old law by which a vestal virgin who had broken her vow of chastity had to be buried alive; the High Priest would himself accompany her to the side of the grave and say special prayers during the burial. In Rome the transgressors were often offered to the god against whom they had sinned, and whose property they were then thought to be. For instance, a corn thief, if he were an adult, was hanged as an offering to the Corn Goddess Ceres.[10]

The distinction therefore became a fine one between victims offered to the law and those offered to the god. Edward Westermarck, in his lengthy commentary on human sacrifice, treats sacrificial execution as the form that survived longest in places where even animal offering had fallen out of use. In advanced communities the gods are still credited with feelings of anger and revenge long after they have ceased to make material demands on their worshippers; they therefore have to be pacified by the death of their enemies. The point is an important one since it helps to account for the savage persecution by the Christian Church of heretics and nonbelievers. Among the Hebrews, an execution was also a religious act, and the criminal was ritually stoned by the whole community. The concept of an execution as quite distinct from a sacrifice is in any case fairly modern. For very often the ruler, if not himself divine, was at least the God's elect, and a crime against the king's realm was also an offence against his god. This was certainly the case in West Africa, where criminals and other victims were often treated alike; for instance, the American anthropologist Herskovits describes how, in nineteenth-century Dahomey, twelve men, together with one alligator and one cat, were offered by the king as a gift to the god. But although the men's only crime was that they were from another tribe, they were dressed, not as typical sacrificial victims, but as state criminals and wore an outlandish version of European prison garb, consisting of a long white nightcap, sewn with spirals of blue ribbon, and calico shorts of quasi-European cut. In general terms, thoughout the history of mankind, sacrifice, vengeance and penal justice were not separate notions but different facets of the same process, needed alike to protect the state against the wrath of the gods.

Roman culture stemmed mainly from Greece, whatever the influence of other conquered peoples on Roman religion. So the attitude of Greeks and Romans was not unlike when it came to the killing of men to please the gods. In Greece too, human offering was attacked by liberal writers but their diatribes often fell on deaf ears; and their pleas serve to prove that men *were* slain to honour the god. Certainly the gods and heroes never ceased to kill and devour each other, and many of the most familiar figures of Greek legend were involved in some act of violence. Zeus, King of the Gods, and his father Chronos head a list that includes Artemis, Dionysus, Thetis, Apollo, Achilles, Agamemnon, Hercules, Peleus, Medea, Demeter, Adonis, Iphigenia, Theseus and Pelops. Greek ambivalence towards human sacrifice is summed up by Westermarck, who writes that the practice was held in horror by the "better minds", though it was treated as "necessary" on certain occasions. The exact frequency of these "necessary" acts is hard to gauge. Greek historians are reticent about this, and readier to talk about such rites among other peoples with whom they came into contact than about those that took place in their own city. For instance, Herodotus describes the funeral of a Scythian king in a way that recalls the scene in the Royal Cemetery of Ur. Cooks, grooms, butlers, and all other members of the royal household were strangled and buried in their master's tomb.

The gods were squarely ranged on the side of those who found an occasional sacrifice "necessary". The original members of the Greek pantheon treated each other with a brutality that makes the gods of Mexico seem by comparison soft-hearted. Like the Mexican Rain God, Tlaloc, and like Baal, they preferred little children as offerings. Greek religion derives from a primaeval couple, Heaven (Uranos) and Earth (Gaia). Their children were collectively known as the Titans. One of these, Thetis, was wedded to Peleus, who was a mortal and could not, according to the rules, beget an immortal son. Thetis was determined to have a child that was immortal; seven children were born to her and one after the other she threw them into the fire or into a boiling cauldron. But at last Peleus put his foot down, and the infant Achilles was rescued from this fate. The tale of child victims continues with Chronos, the most powerful of the hideous breed of Titans. Uranos and Gaia warned him that he would be overthrown by his own children; he therefore swallowed them as fast as they were born. But when the youngest, Zeus, came into the world, Chronos' wife, Rhea, hid him away and gave his father instead a stone wrapped in swaddling clothes. Zeus grew up and made war on his father and his fellow Titans; for ten years the battle raged, but at last the thunderbolts of Zeus triumphed. The Titans were then imprisoned in Tartarus, with the exception of Atlas, whose prodigious strength served for ever afterwards to hold up the sky.

Zeus now reigned supreme in a pantheon that was born of strife and nurtured in sacrifice, mainly of infants. The King of the Gods was himself not averse to child murder; King Lykaion of Arcadia sacrificed his own son to Zeus and he and the god feasted together on the boy's flesh. In Greek legend, the killing of infants, many of whom were eaten, was almost an obsession. Atreus, King of Mycenae and scion of the accursed House of Atreus, seduced the wife of his brother Thyestes, whom he banished from his kingdom. Afterwards he pretended to be reconciled and called Thyestes back; having got his brother in his clutches, he set before him a dish made of his own children and forced him to eat. Another child-slayer was Hercules (the Greek Herakles). After returning home fresh from his famous twelve labours, he was overcome by the mad notion that his wife and children were his enemies and sacrificed them all. Hercules then met his end by being burned alive on a funeral pyre. His jealous lover Deianeira had given him a robe smeared with deadly poison; such was Hercules' agony that he had himself carried to the top of a high mountain, where he was burned alive on a great pile of wood. Garments smeared with a burning venom were a favourite device of Greek gods and heroes and clearly symbolize some ancient rite of sacrifice, or auto-sacrifice, by fire. After Jason had succeeded in his search for the Golden Fleece, he abandoned his wife Medea and married Glauke. Medea sent the bride a robe drenched in a drug that burned Glauke and her father to death. She then killed her own children, preparing them for death in the manner of a priest who prepares an elaborate ritual sacrifice, and escaped from the scene in a winged chariot.

By contrast, Homer's Iliad says little of human offering. An isolated exception is the funeral of Patroclus; Achilles first sacrificed four horses and two dogs on the funeral pyre of his beloved friend, followed by twelve Trojan prisoners, chosen to serve Patroclus in the next world. In another episode from the Trojan war, Polyxene, daughter of King Priam of Troy, is immolated on Achilles' tomb, having been claimed by his ghost. By this act of appeasement, it was hoped to obtain a fair wind for the Greek voyage home. Like the texts of Sumer, Homer does not tell us the whole story, and archaeology offers more evidence of human sacrifice among those Mycenaean Greeks who fought against Troy. A tablet of Linear B writing (a script using an old form of the Greek language) was found at Pylos dating from about 1400 B.C. The text, somewhat hastily scratched, calls on no less than thirteen gods and goddesses, including leading deities such as Zeus, Hera, Hermes and Poseidon. Promised to the heavenly host are thirteen gold vessels, and in addition, to each of the two chief gods the offering of a man, and to each of eight chief goddesses a woman.[11]

The Greek gods set a poor example to their worshippers, though some of their reputed deeds, such as the burning or eating of children, no doubt stem from sacrifices that took place long before classical times. But other forms of ritual killing survived into historical times. The Athenian statesman Themistocles, before the Battle of Salamis in 480 B.C., was driven by pressure of public opinion to kill three Persian captives in honour of the god Dionysus. Annually in Rhodes a condemned felon, especially kept for the purpose, was led outside the city and put to death at the festival of Chronos. At the temple of Apollo at Leucas, a criminal was thrown over the cliff into the sea every year to act as scapegoat for the community; an odd custom of tying live birds or feathers to his body helped to break his fall and he sometimes survived. As late as the second century A.D. a victim was killed once a year in Arcadia.

The Greeks invented democracy, but did not thereupon dispense with human sacrifice. A peculiar institution shows that it was not as uncommon in classical Greece as people suppose. The Pharmakoi were outcasts, kept in Athens and other cities at public expense in case plague, famine or some other disaster threatened. Victims were thus held in constant readiness for use in any emergency that called for an offering. The Pharmakoi were equally useful for annual sacrifices such as the Thargelia, celebrated in Athens in the middle of summer, when two men were led out and stoned to death as scapegoats for the wrongs of others. If one of these Pharmakoi were to be killed, he would first be paraded round the city, in order that he should drain off the impurities of others and take them upon himself; he was then slain in a ceremony in which the whole population took part.[12]

However, the Greeks, like the Romans, were in two minds about such killings and a change from human to animal sacrifice is symbolized by the story in Homer's Iliad of Iphigenia, daughter of Agamemnon, leader of the Greeks. Agamemnon had offended Artemis, the Goddess of Hunting, by boasting of his own skill in the chase; hence, when the Greek force assembled against Troy at Aulis, Artemis prevented it from sailing by abating the wind. A seer declared that the goddess could only be appeased by the sacrifice of Agamemnon's daughter. Iphigenia was duly fetched from home; just as she was about to be slain Artemis relented, snatched away the girl, and put a hind in her place, exactly recalling the ram used by Abraham in place of his son Isaac. But Iphigenia escaped from the role of victim, only to join the ranks of sacrificers. Artemis carried her off to the Crimea, then known as the Land of the Tauroi, where she became priestess of the goddess, who was worshipped in a savage rite in which she claimed the lives of all strangers who landed on those shores. From this baleful office Iphigenia was rescued by her brother Orestes (who had murdered his own mother); together with his friend Pylades, he was taken prisoner in the Land of the Tauroi and handed over to Iphigenia for sacrifice. By a miracle she recognized her brother, and the three of them escaped and made their way back to Greece.

Artemis in former times had claimed many human victims; the flagellation of Spartan boys at the goddess' altar was introduced by King Lycurgus in place of the older custom of killing a man who was chosen by lot. Another story relates to the change from human to animal offering. General Pelopidas, before the battle of Leuctra in 371 B.C., was warned by a spirit in a vision that he must sacrifice a fair-haired girl if he wished for victory. However, a quick-witted seer snatched a chestnut filly that had charged into the ranks of the army and cried out that this was the victim that the gods had called for. The frequency in Greek legend of such stories of last-minute reprieve is significant. Perhaps the most famous concerns Theseus and the Minotaur. Theseus was already the hero of many adventures, including the killing of Procrustes, another slayer of men. With grim humour this giant would lay all strangers on a rack-like bed, and then lop off pieces to make them fit its length, or stretch them out if they were too short. But Theseus' other feat was more spectacular. Athens paid an annual tribute of seven youths and seven maidens to Minos, King of Crete; these he shut up in the Labyrinth, where they either lost their way and died of hunger or were eaten by the Minotaur, half man, half bull. Theseus made his way into the Labyrinth, rescued the latest victims and sailed away, also taking with him Minos' daughter, Ariadne. For some reason, possibly linked with the breach of a tabu, he did not take her to Athens but left her behind on a deserted rock. In this case archaeology supports the myth; Sir Arthur Evans unearthed frescoes at Knossos that point clearly to some kind of bull cult, involving sacrifice.

Greek mythology seems to go out of its way to stress the point that, bestial though the behaviour of the first gods may have been, in Greece at least animals *did* then take the place of humans, so often reprieved in the nick of time by a god or hero. Animal sacrifice was on a generous scale: in Athens horses were offered to Poseidon, asses to Apollo, and dogs to various gods. The throwing of pigs into a chasm also seems to recall an earlier mass human sacrifice. One odd form of animal offering contains a burlesque notion of rebirth. At an annual ritual in Athens, an ox was made to dedicate itself to the gods by eating corn upon the altar. The priest who slew the animal then fled into voluntary exile, while the axe used in the sacrifice was cast into the sea. The ox's flesh was eaten but a mock resurrection of the animal took place in which the hide was sewn together again, filled with hay and yoked to a plough.

The Greeks had their own version of the god who died each year and was reborn when the sun gave new life to nature. The cult of Adonis was already popular in fifth-century Greece and had long been purged of its element of human offering. The comely youth Adonis was adored both by Aphrodite, Goddess of Love, and by Persephone, Queen of Hades. Zeus finally settled the matter by decreeing that Adonis should spend half the year in the upper world with Aphrodite, and the other half with the mistress of the nether regions. Annually, therefore, Adonis had to die, killed by a boar, and the scarlet anemone was said to have sprung from his blood; annually he was then revived and restored to Aphrodite. In Athens the death of Adonis was celebrated at the height of summer; the streets would be lined with coffins and corpse-like effigies and the air rent with the cries of women wailing for the dead god. The name Adonis is merely the Semitic Adon, meaning "lord", and he is the twin of Tammuz, the young spouse or lover of the great Mother Goddess of Syria and Babylon, who each year was rescued from the land of the dead by his divine mistress. Almost identical to Adonis is Attis, who was also killed by a boar; from his blood the violets were supposed to have sprung. His rites, celebrated more in Rome than in Greece, began on the 22nd March. The third day, the 24th March, was known as the Day of Blood, and was marked by savage acts of mutilation in which frenzied men castrated themselves. Significantly, at the end of the third day, Attis' tomb was opened and found empty, for the god had risen from the grave, and thus awakened in his disciples the hope that they too would triumph over death.

Adonis was basically benevolent, being young, beautiful and innocent. Very different was Dionysus, yet another Greek god who started life as a human offering and whose myth is redolent with sacrifice. Originally called Zagreus, he was devoured by the hideous Titans and reborn as Dionysus. In one sense Dionysus was good, since he was linked with the earth and fertility and was God of Wine. But the darker side of his character is brought out in another episode: Pentheus, King of Thebes, fell foul of Dionysus, having declared that the god was an impostor at a time when his votaries were running wild in Thebes. While spying on them from a tree, Pentheus was flung to the ground and torn to pieces, his own mother taking part in his death. Only when her Dionysian frenzy subsided, did she realize what she had done. As described by Euripides in *The Bacchae*, Dionysus first touched Pentheus ritually on the head, shoulder and feet, and the manner of his death became the regular Dyonisian ritual. A beast came to replace Pentheus and in the annual rites of the Bacchanals, a live goat was rent in pieces and eaten raw.

The notion of the one, or the few, as an offering for the many has deep roots in Greek myth, as in the story of Iphigenia or the seven Athenians who served as fodder for the Minotaur, and Ancient Greece was not short of saviours and redeemers, called upon to be scapegoats and wash away the sins of society, whether in the form of Dionysus, sowing panic and frenzy before restoring harmony, or Adonis, the dying and risen god, or Oedipus, the parricide who was exiled to save the city. At once criminal and saviour, Oedipus shows how fine is the distinction between the two roles. He first appears in a benevolent light, having saved the city of Thebes from the Sphynx by solving the monster's riddle. Unwittingly Oedipus had then killed his father, King Laios, and married the widowed Queen Iokasta, his mother. At the beginning of Sophocles' play *Oedipus Rex*, a plague has fallen on Thebes and to save the city Oedipus is banished, the hideous truth about his parricide and incest having been revealed. From being the father of his people and their saviour, Oedipus becomes the universal sinner and is driven out; and although later, in *Oedipus at Colonus*, he resumes the role of saviour, once he has paid for his sins, he is never fully exonerated and remains an equivocal scapegoat, wrongful and yet wronged, part criminal and part victim, embodying the links between the two.

Notwithstanding the latter-day use of animal substitutes, Greek tragedy, epic poetry and history are rich in tales of human victims. The scale in later times was reduced, although probably in both Greece and Rome more offerings took place than their historians admit. But side by side with the old pantheon of playful but pitiless gods, a radically new approach to the supernatural arose with Socrates, the founder of Greek ethics. For Socrates the highest soul, or god, which was the source of wisdom and action, was supremely good. This world spirit had little in common with Dionysus and his frenzied rampages or with Artemis and her insistent demands for human victims. Socrates courted martyrdom by refusing to pay the fine imposed on him for corrupting the youth, and for his lack of respect for the old gods. His death had a profound moral effect and if he did not introduce new gods, he did found a new ethic, one that could not by any stretch of the imagination countenance the slaying of men to honour the gods. Thus two different forces were at work in Greece. The philosophers and their followers made a cult of the supreme good and abhorred sacrifice, whilst the votaries of the old gods still thought these practices "necessary" from time to time. The Greek gods, like most of their African and Asian colleagues, were as eager to destroy as to create and their worship demanded occasional human offerings. But if people once came to believe that the world was ruled by forces that were essentially good —whether in Greece, Israel or even China—the picture was transformed and sacrifice no longer made any sense. Its continuance on a modest scale in Greece was therefore a kind of compromise between two schools of thought.

4

Greater Love Hath No Man

The Hebrews shared many customs of the Ancient Near East, including human sacrifice. In Israel, as in Greece and Rome, it was slow to abate and for a time even increased. When the Children of Ammon made war against Israel, the elders asked Jephthah, described in the Book of Judges as a mighty man of valour, to be their captain. Before fighting the Ammonites, he vowed that when he came back he would make a burt offering of the first living creature to come out of the doors of his house to meet him. The Ammonites were duly routed and the warrior returned home, where he was greeted by his daughter, his only child, with timbrels and dancing. Jephthah rent his clothes but could not revoke his vow. His daughter made a curious request for a sacrificial victim: she asked for a two months' stay of sentence, during which time she "bewailed her virginity upon the mountains" with her companions. Thereafter the daughters of Israel mourned the daughter of Jephthah for four days every year. The Book of Kings relates the story of the defeat of the army of Mesha, King of Moab by the Israelites. So overcome was the king that he made a burnt offering of his eldest son and heir. The story differs from that of Jephthah in that Mesha was an enemy of Israel and his act was prompted by defeat rather than victory, but the message is again clear: a tutelary god demands a human offering as the reward for victory or to ease the pangs of defeat.

A victim was often required, at times the leader's child, at others a wrongdoer, to still the anger of the god and persuade him to turn defeat into victory. When defeated by the men of Ai, Joshua, commanded to find a transgressor to be burnt, chose Achan, who had confessed to stealing war booty on a lavish scale, including a fine Babylonian garment, two hundred shekels of silver and a wedge of gold of fifty shekels' weight. Achan was not burnt but stoned to death and buried along with his whole family. He was acting out the role of scapegoat: arraigned for an impious offence, he died on behalf of the community in order to restore the links that bound them to their god. His story also serves to illustrate the narrowness of the line dividing criminal justice from human sacrifice. Joshua was subsequently able to defeat the King of Ai, whom he sacrificed by hanging him on a tree till eventide; the corpse was placed at the entrance to the city and a ritual mound raised in memory of the act.

Examples can be found in the Old Testament to show that, for all the apologists' denials, human offerings were not uncommon during the whole history of the Jewish state. Samuel, who probably lived in the eleventh century B.C., took his prisoner Agag and hacked him to pieces before the Lord. Much later, after the partition of the kingdom, Ahaz (740–724 B.C.), who ruled in the part known as Judah, sacrificed children by fire and even burned his own son, as did his successor King Manasseh. In the northern kingdom, called Israel, the first king, Jeroboam, set the scene for sacrifice by making an altar to Baal, a god always avid for human victims. Foundation sacrifices, involving even the builder's own offspring, were not unknown. The Book of Kings tells us that when Hiel rebuilt Jericho, he laid the foundations upon the body of his eldest son, while his youngest was buried under the gates. Joshua had prophesied this when he destroyed the city: "Cursed be the man before the Lord, that riseth up and buildeth the city of Jericho. He shall lay the foundation stones thereof in his first born and in his youngest son shall he set up the gates thereof."[1] Archaeology supports the Bible's account of such foundation sacrifices. In the sanctuary in Gezer were found two burnt skeletons of six-year-old children and the skulls of two adolescents that had been sawn in two. At Megiddo a girl of fifteen had been killed and buried in the foundations of a large structure. Excavations show that the practice of interring children and adults under new buildings was widespread and some were evidently buried alive.

When the Israelites first reached the Promised Land, they probably practised sacrifice on a modest scale and offered up single

victims to secure victory or to stave off defeat, as in the cases of
Joshua and Jephthah. Only later, as the Hebrew Yahweh became
confused with the Canaanite Baal, were children burned in "the fiery
pit". As among many peoples, animal and human sacrifice seem to
have existed side by side. The Old Testament abounds in references
to every form of animal offering. The choosing of a beast to become
the scapegoat and take upon itself the sins of the whole tribe is
among the oldest of these rituals and dates from the time of Moses
and Aaron, long before the phase of Baal-worship in Palestine
claimed so many human victims. Aaron, according to custom, chose
two goats; one was killed as an offering and on the head of the other,
the true scapegoat, Aaron laid both his hands and confessed over
him all the sins of the children of Israel. The animal was then led
away "to bear upon him all their iniquities unto a land not inhabited".
Thus among the Hebrews, as among the Greeks and Romans, we
find the strange rite where the victim is exiled rather than killed.

Whether or not the scapegoat in early times was really a human
being, the custom of child sacrifice had deep roots among the Hebrews. The claim of their god Jehovah or Yahweh to the firstborn
is undisguised in the Book of Numbers: "For all the firstborn of
Israel are mine, both man and beast" and in the Book of Exodus:
"The first of thy sons shalt thou give unto me". Undeterred by this
claim on the part of Yahweh, the Book of Genesis insists that even
if human sacrifice existed, the founding fathers of the nation adjured
the practice and with Yahweh's blessing animals took the place of
men. This view is implicit in the story of Abraham and Isaac. The
narrator describes the incident as a "temptation" rather than a mere
act of devotion by Abraham, whom the Lord had ordered to make
a burnt offering of his son. Neither father nor son, however, seems
to have treated the god's command as at all unusual. Abraham knew
exactly how to set about the task and duly took Isaac to the appointed
mountain (children sacrificed to Tlaloc, the Mexican Rain God,
were also taken to mountain tops), built his altar in the prescribed
manner, bound Isaac and laid him on the wood that he had brought;
clearly he was following a familiar ritual. Isaac was to have been
killed before being burned, a privilege not awarded in later times
to victims of Baal and Moloch.

According to the Middle-Eastern scholar E. O. James, the story
as told in Genesis is most probably an eighth-century prophetic Mid-

rash, suitably edited to show that human sacrifice, widely practised in that century, was a foreign innovation long alien to the true tradition of the Jews.[2] The ram caught in the thicket, so conveniently waiting to take Isaac's place at the Lord's bidding, illustrates this point in that it implies that the Israelites renounced all human sacrifice long before they even sighted the Promised Land. But if in its present form the story proceeds from the declared enemies of sacrifice, it perhaps should not be taken at its face value. In fact, the tale rings truer if taken as the report of a sacrifice of his first-born son by an early leader of Israel in order to meet the demands of Yahweh as expressed in the Book of Numbers. Certainly, at the time when the story of Abraham was written, or re-written, the notion of the killing of the leader's son was not unfamiliar; it had been practised by the Phoenicians, first cousins to the Canaanites. In any case the incident seems to conform to the idea, current in other parts of the world, that if one son—or a substitute child—is sacrificed, the gods will then provide many more offspring. After the ceremony on the mountains the Lord said to Abraham, "I will multiply thy seed as the stars of heaven, and as the sand which is upon the sea shore".[3]

Long after Abraham's time, under Canaanite influence such sacrifices became more numerous. For once they had settled in Palestine, the Israelites were caught up in the web of their neighbours' ritual killing on a scale unknown to them before and mainly involving children. In the Old Testament the place where such victims were consumed was called a Tophet, so named because a great din was made with drums (tophim) to prevent the father hearing the cries of his child as it was burnt. According to the Book of Isaiah, "Tophet is ordained of old; yea, for the king it is prepared; he hath made it large and deep; the pile thereof is fire and much wood; the breath of the Lord, like a stream of brimstone, doth kindle it".[4] Exact details of the ceremony are lacking, although we do know of the methods used by the Carthaginians, who were also worshippers of Baal and sacrificed children to him on a massive scale. When faced with defeat in Syracuse in 310 B.C., the sons of five hundred nobles were cast into a fiery pit, or Tophet, from a scaffold shaped in the likeness of the god. At Carthage the local Tophet has been uncovered by archaeologists; it stretches in a narrow belt, several hundred yards in length, along the shores of the harbour and dates from the foundation of the city. The two earliest inscriptions in the Carthage Tophet record sacrifices to Baal that are identical to those of the Canaanites. It seems that in both Carthage and Canaan child burnings took place outside the city, whereas the original Hebrew offerings were made on the temple altar.[5]

There is no mention in the Old Testament of these mass offerings but the records of the eighth and seventh centuries B.C. demonstrate beyond all doubt that the Israelites of the period made burnt offerings of their sons in the Tophet fires lighted in the Valley of Gehinnon outside Jerusalem. Usually the infants were "passed over" or "passed through" the fire, in honour of Moloch (Moloch or Melech simply means "king" and is just another name for Baal). The texts invariably condemn child immolation but such strictures are the surest proof that it existed. The prophet Jeremiah talks of the people as "burning their sons in the fire as burnt offerings unto Baal"; the prophet Ezekiel, just before the Jewish exile in Babylon in 597 B.C., complains that the children of Israel have slain their offspring to honour the idols. Such practices are condemned in the Book of Leviticus: "Thou shalt not let any of thy seed pass through the fire to Moloch". The text further warns that any who transgress in this shall be put to death. The Book of Micah also laments the killing of the firstborn: "Shall I give my firstborn for my transgression, the fruit of my body for the sin of my soul?" Thus by the eighth century, when child sacrifice was at its peak, after the kingdom had been split in two, it seems already to have become a matter of controversy.

It is unlikely that the recipient of these grim offerings, Moloch or Baal, was thought of as distinct from Yahweh himself. The implications of the fulminations in the Book of Jeremiah—"They have built the high places of Tophet, which is in the Valley of Hinnon, to burn their sons and their daughters in the fire, which I [Yahweh] commanded not, neither came it into my mind" [6]—is that the offerings were indeed made to Yahweh. Although made to figure in the Old Testament as the only god of Israel, clearly at times Yahweh became confused with Baal, Sun God of the native Canaanites, known under a variety of names. The cult of these foreign dieties was once so widespread among the Israelites that even Solomon (973–933 B.C.) succumbed. His hundred wives "turned his heart after other gods". He raised a high place within sight of Jerusalem to Chemosh, the Moabite form of Baal in whose honour Mesha had burned his son and heir, and also built a temple to Moloch.

Throughout part of the Old Testament that concerns the time of the kings from Solomon onwards, a contrast is drawn between "good" rulers who obeyed Yahweh, and many others, including Solomon himself, who fell into bad ways and worshipped Baal. Yet in reality the distinction between the two was not at the time very clear-cut. Few rulers could resist the increasing tempo of child sacrifice in the centuries before the exile brought about its subsidence. The prophets who railed against the burning of children that was rife in their day had adapted the ancient story of Abraham and Isaac in order to show that infant offering had been alien to Yahweh since time immemorial, but their campaign was not just a reaction against human sacrifice; they went further and opposed the very notion of killing living creatures as the proper way to placate God. These teachers seem to have been in favour of abandoning tradition altogether, as the only way to free the new ethical god of Israel from past associations with savage sun gods and corn deities. The prophet Amos makes Yahweh say that he hates and despises feast days and that he will not accept meat offerings. These religious leaders pleaded that the people should walk in the way of the Lord and that, if they did not do so, no sacrifice would be of any avail. The offering of animals did continue after the return from exile in Babylonia, and of this the ritual of the Paschal lamb was typical. On the Day of Atonement, a post-exile institution, a sheaf of the first fruits of the barley was offered on the altar, followed seven weeks later by two loaves prepared from the new wheat. Sacrifice ceased altogether after the destruction of the Temple of Jerusalem by the Romans in 70 A.D. Yahweh's claim in the Book of Exodus to the firstborn, both human and animal, had by then been commuted into a cash payment to the priest of a mere five shekels.

By this time the original purpose of the offerings had vanished, since the prophets' teaching had had a revolutionary effect and the Hebrews' view of their God had in a few centuries been changed beyond recognition. Child offering was a thing of the past; it now became absurd to suppose that the all-righteous Yahweh had to be revived or rejuvenated with the blood of bulls or goats, let alone of humans. The fiery Tophet had produced a rapid revulsion and the prophets of the pre-exile era had already begun to speak of God as a moral being whose demands were ethical rather than material. To associate him any longer with the gruesome rituals of the Canaanites was blasphemy to those great teachers. As a result, the rituals underwent a fundamental change; the concept of life-giving was changed into that of self-giving, demanding "the sacrifice of the lips instead of the calves".[7] Accordingly, in Israel sacrifice not merely was reduced, as in Greece and Rome, but ceased entirely. Old and savage rites gave way to a new ethic, whereby people saw God no longer as a relentless tyrant, the price of whose favour was the blood of the innocent, but as good and just. This development is almost unique in man's history. While sacrifice, human as well as animal, went on unabated over vast regions of Africa, Asia and America, in Israel it was virtually abolished in response to inspired preachers at whose instance the Hebrew religion came to be based more on ethic than on ritual.

By the time of Jesus, the fiery Tophet was a memory as distant to the Jews as a mediaeval witch-hunt might be today. Theologians have long argued as to how far Jesus thought of himself as a sacrifice; after nearly two thousand years, they still fail to agree. Nonetheless, his story, as told by the Gospels, shows that in the eyes of others his death was sacrificial. Ciaphas, the Jewish high priest, made this point in precise terms—more precise than those of Jesus himself—when he declared that it was expedient that one man should die for the people to save the whole nation. That, surely, is the noblest form of sacrifice, and the events of the New Testament, therefore, are central to any study of human offering, of whose essence more can be learned from the instance of the one who died to save the many than from mass holocausts that stand at the opposite end of the sacrificial spectrum. The importance of Jesus' death and resurrection in the world history of sacrifice is undeniable in quite another sense. For ritual killing often thrived in remote continents only until it was extirpated by people who were Christians, even if their motives may have been mixed and their Christian principles at times open to question.

Many proofs have been advanced that the story of Jesus fulfilled "traditional" sacrificial concepts. The blessing of wine has been viewed as stemming from early vegetation rituals. Above all, the death on Calvary has been likened to the Jewish atonement for sin; Jesus was the scapegoat on whose head the priest—in the tradition of Aaron—laid both his hands before it was led away into the wilderness. Thus Jesus took away the sins of all men, true to the old Hebrew notion of transferring them physically to some animal or other medium. In the Gospel of St. John, John the Baptist says to Jesus, "Behold the Lamb of God, that taketh away the sins of the world". And, indeed, it seems likely that he died on the day on which the Paschal lamb was slain and that the Last Supper took place on the evening on which the Paschal meal was eaten. Even for the story of the resurrection and ascension, an Old Testament precedent can be found: Elijah ascended to heaven in a chariot with horses of fire and would come again to restore the tribes of Jacob.

Certainly the story of Jesus could not have evolved in a vacuum. Not only the general theme of the dying saviour but even such minor details as the ransom payment of thirty shekels or the descriptions "carpenter" and "shepherd" have antecedents in Mesopotamia. In the many dying saviour cults of the Ancient Near East the despair of the great Mother Goddess, who mourned her lost lover, marked the seasonal decline of nature and the new sprouting of the seed. Typical of them is Tammuz, who originated in Babylon. Every year he died and descended into the nether world, and every year his divine mistress Ishtar, the great Mother, went in quest of him and brought him back to the land of the living. The notion lived on in the stories of Adonis, killed annually by the boar, of Dionysus, torn to pieces and revived from the dead, and of Attis, mourned on 22nd March and risen on the third day. Adonis really represents the wild vegetation, on which the nomad depends, rather than the crops. These cults belong to a single tradition and have a long history. Isis, the sister/wife of the Egyptian Osiris, was also worshipped throughout the Roman Empire. She was supposed to have collected the scattered limbs of Osiris in a winnowing basket that was carried in a procession dedicated to her worship in Rome. But the infant Dionysus was also awakened in a winnowing basket on Mount Parnassus after he had been restored to life. The rites for Osiris in Roman times in Byblos were so like those for Adonis that the two were often confused. Adonis and Attis had been killed by boars and Osiris' and Tammuz' enemies also took the form of a boar.[8]

Not only is the passion of Christ linked to these traditions, the Eucharist itself is also open to two interpretations. A ceremonial meal, held at night, was a Jewish ritual, and in the early days the re-enacting of the Last Supper was probably more a feast of kinship among Christians than a sacrificial act. But other aspects of the Eucharist stem directly from paganism. This central act of worship bears the stamp of sacrifices that marked the eternal return of the divine being, immolated at the beginning of time and changed into food before rising again from the nether world. The broken bread recalls the victim hacked into pieces, whether Osiris in Egypt or the bull who was rent apart and eaten raw in the frenzied rites of Dionysus.

In a sense Jesus is both Paschal lamb and saviour son of the Mother Goddess, whether Osiris, Tammuz or Attis, for at times the two currents merge; not only did the Israelites adopt Canaanite usage but the prophet Ezekiel even saw the women of Jerusalem weeping for Tammuz at the North Gate of the Temple. Taken all in all, the Christian story contains more that is common to the Near East than particular to the Jews of Palestine, whatever native elements may be present, based on Jesus' own Jewish background and up-bringing. The suffering saviour has nothing to do with the militant Messiah, whose destiny was not death on the cross but triumph on the field of battle. A. D. Nock, leading expert on the religions of the Graeco-Roman world, remarks with some truth that the Christian hope has its roots in Palestine but Christian theologians have theirs in Alexandria.[9]

In addition to the more ancient cults of the Mother Goddess and the suffering son, others that became popular in Rome were also based on the yearning for a new life. In the Greek Eleusinian myster-ies, after the "Day of Blood" the novice was reborn and fed on milk as if he were a little child. The rites included a kind of communion in which the initiates gained salvation by death and rebirth. Resur-rection also followed mystic death in Mithraism, which gained a firm hold in Rome before Christianity became the official religion. And if the message of Jesus was to win universal recognition in competi-tion with these mystery religions, inevitably it had also to offer the hope of rebirth. In the words of St. Paul: "We die with Christ when we are baptised, and are then reborn in him and walk in the newness of life." From this to the idea of being born anew as a little child was an easy step for a new convert, and if he knew the Greek mysteries, he would see little difference between the two versions.[10] The ritual pretence of death followed by rebirth was more than a localized cult, limited to the Near East. It was widespread among primitive tribes as part of their puberty or initiation rites. Sometimes the victim had to be dismembered. The Yuin and Murring tribes in Australia worshipped a supreme being called Darumulu, whose name was unknown to women and children. During the initiation, Darumulu "killed" the boys, cut them in pieces, buried them and restored them to life. Their "death" was followed by a spiritual childhood as they were reborn and regenerated.[11] The same pretence of death and resurrection is found in many initiation rites among North American Indian tribes. In the complex Pawnee ritual, the control of crops and the rearing of buffaloes depended on such ceremonies held in spring or autumn. They included the rebirth of a child after ceremonial washing or baptism.

Yet another aspect of the passion of Jesus is basic to the beliefs of peoples, both primitive and advanced, in many lands. All the Gospels stress that he was scourged and spat upon before being crucified and was then mocked upon the cross; and the notion is worldwide that rebirth can only be attained, not by death alone, but by castigation of the victim or by some form of ill-treatment. In parts of south-east Africa novices for initiation rites are beaten mercilessly, and their suffering is essential to their ritual death, prior to rebirth. Similar practices are found among more advanced peoples. The earliest version of the Tammuz myth, current in Mesopotamia four thousand years ago, has been gleaned from a number of stone tablets and slowly pieced together by scholars. In this version, Innana is the Mother Goddess and Dummuzi (from which Tammuz derives) is her beloved husband. Innana in her own sacred city of Erech finds her beloved Dummuzi "dressed in noble garments and sitting on a lofty throne". But Innana is pursued by the Galla, the small and pitiless constables of the land of no return, and is forced to hand Dummuzi over to these ghoulish creatures. They bind, beat and torture him mercilessly in preparation for his descent into the land of the dead; he flees from their grasp, but they recapture him and he is tortured a second and a third time before he finally descends, and returns to Innana in the spring.[12]

Some punishments are linked to the idea that the victim has in some way sinned. Very often the notions of crime and sacrifice are inseparable, and Oedipus is by no means the only man to combine the roles of sinner and saviour. Common to mankind is the complex idea that the sacrificial victim can wash away the sins of others only by taking them upon his own head and thereby himself becoming, temporarily, a sinner. This is also present in Christian doctrine, often to the bewilderment of Christians who, for example, have been puzzled by St. Paul's words in his second epistle to the Corinthians, "For [God] hath made Him to be sin for us, who knew no sin; that we might be made the righteousness of God in Him", and by the phrase in his epistle to the Galatians, "Christ hath redeemed us from the curse of the law, being made a curse for us". In a sense, Jesus did sin, according to the standards of his day. From the Jewish standpoint he was a teacher who flouted cherished conventions and broke ancient tabus. He plucked corn and healed on the Sabbath and voiced the heretical doctrine that the Sabbath was "made for man"; he dined with people who were "unclean" and welcomed them into his fellowship; the Pharisees complained that his disciples ignored the ritual of washing before eating bread. Jesus was a rebel against orthodoxy, of a kind that would have been condemned by the Inquisitors of Spain or by the Calvinist divines of Geneva, just as he was by the Pharisees of Judaea.

The notion that the central figure of a cult must flout conventions and spurn tabus is not confined to Israel or to Europe. In Africa, spiritual leaders had first to commit ritual sins before they gained the power to exorcise those of others. In a vast zone of that continent, stretching from Upper Egypt southwards as far as Swaziland, people were ruled by sacred kings who on occasions such as their coronation or rejuvenation rites "died" and were "reborn". During this process, they were forced to commit incest with their mothers, sisters, and other women, a practice tabu to their subjects according to the strictest tribal law. For the day of the ceremony the king became the sinner, respecting no rules and knowing no shame. For instance, among the Bushong, who regarded rats as repulsive, the king was offered at his coronation a plateful of these rodents. In Ruanda several times during his reign a ruler underwent a mock castigation as a penalty for incest; he appeared in public in a sacrificial ceremony, together with his mother, both bound like criminals; as surrogates for their "incest", a bull and a cow were beaten, ill-treated and killed; then the king and queen mother were sprinkled with their blood. In Swaziland the king retired into a sacred enclosure, took forbidden drugs and committed incest with an adopted sister; meanwhile, the people went about chanting a kind of hymn of hatred against their ruler, threatening to drive him from the throne. After this a battle was fought between his family and his subjects; the king was eventually "killed" and "sacrificed" in the person of a cow that was beaten to death by the warriors of the tribe.[13] Whatever the spiritual gap that separates these tribal scapegoat rulers from the Jesus of the Gospels, parallels do arise in the New Testament. Like the African kings, he breaks local tabus and is "made sin" before he can atone for the sins of others. Like Dummuzi, he is scourged and mocked. He is even decked in the attributes of royalty, forced to wear purple and a crown of thorns.

Even such a brief commentary on the New Testament sacrifice might at first sight seem to be a mere digression which unduly stresses a single act in the face of herds of scapegoats since the beginning of time, whose blood was shed for the gods. And, indeed, if Christianity had not spread beyond its homeland, fewer lessons could be learned from its history. But its very success makes it crucial to the study of human sacrifice. Not only were Christians one day to put an end to ritual killing in many lands; in addition, the expansion of their faith shows up both the strengths and weaknesses of all redeemer religions, based on the god who dies and is resurrected. Christ is the saviour who takes upon himself the sins of mankind. He is the lamb of God who suffers and deflects God's vengeance from the rest of the human race. Osiris did not rise up to heaven but became king of the underworld; yet he too was called to judge the dead.

Jesus in theory banished the need for further bloodshed among his followers; by his command to turn the other cheek, he even forbade it. But his worship was to have side effects of a sinister kind. If Christ were wholly good, then there was no room on earth for his enemies and they too must be pursued without mercy, or the blessing of the Christian redemption would become a curse. Both Christians and Muslims, true to the word of a single prophet, put infidels to the sword. Not only did unbelievers have to perish but Christian dissenters against the orthodox dogma, like the enemies of Osiris, had to be tortured and ritually killed. The Christian version of the saviour-redeemer doctrine brought about, in the words of Arnold Toynbee, "the sinfulness and deadliness of the Catholic-Protestant Wars of Religion in the seventeenth century". As he points out, Pharisaism became the besetting sin of all religions of the Judaic family, including Christianity and Islam: "The fruit of Pharisaism is intolerance;

the fruit of intolerance is violence; and the wages of sin is death".[14]
From this intolerance sprang the excesses of the Holy Inquisition, to
which further reference will be made.

Sir James Frazer, one of the first to stress that Christianity has deep
roots in primitive paganism, used this discovery as a means of de-
bunking the Christian faith. For Frazer, if Jesus' teaching were so
similar to that of pagan religions, there could not be much truth in
it. The author of *The Golden Bough* drew his own moral from the
New Testament: Greek and Roman society was founded on the
citizen's sense of duty to the state, hence the safety of the common-
wealth was the supreme aim of human endeavour; the "oriental religions" (in this context, Christianity) by their "selfish and immoral
doctrine" cherished personal salvation as the only object worth living
for, and by prompting their devotees to spurn public service caused
the decline of the ancient world. But Peter Munz in his book *When
the Golden Bough Breaks* points out that Frazer's argument is un-
sound. If the teaching of Jesus is indeed so universal, and so near to
other creeds, then of necessity it enshrines a profound truth. If traces
of his cult appear not only in Osiris, Tammuz and Oedipus, but even
in the African god-king who was punished for breaking tribal tabus,
died and was reborn, then the Christian claim to a worldwide truth
must be valid. With the Gospels' added message of love, the single
act on Golgotha becomes the culminating point in the saga of sacrifice.
In the words of the Gospel of St. John: "Greater love hath no man
than this, that he lay down his life for his friends".

5

A Use for Statistics

The impact of Mahatma Gandhi's teaching made of modern India the home of non-violence. But peoples often have two sides to their nature; in that same India which produced Gandhi in this century and Guatama Buddha twenty-four centuries earlier, the tale of human sacrifice is long and rich in incident. In devising bizarre ways of offering men to their gods, the Indians showed an inventive genius rare in other lands.

Indeed, in turning to India, we enter a new dimension in terms of sacrifice. Up to this point we have studied principally the peoples of the Ancient Near East and their descendants, the Jews, the Greeks and the Romans, who at least reduced the shedding of human blood, even where it did not disappear. But in most other parts of the world, alien to the Greek and Christian traditions, nothing of the kind occurred. Whether in India, South-East Asia, Oceania, Africa or pre-Columbian America, the slaying of men to placate the gods went on unabated until the advent of Europeans, whose cruelties were of another kind. In many lands, such as West Africa, or Aztec Mexico, sacrifice rose to a crescendo that appalled the first white intruders. The same forces seem to have been at work in India, where the toll of victims had probably reached a low point some two thousand years earlier in the Buddhist era but had risen again to record levels by the time the British came on the scene. The forms of sacrifice which they encountered were so numerous that I prefer to concentrate on a few of the more exotic rites, such as those of the Khonds of the north or the Thugs of Bengal. Suttee, the burning of widows, will be considered in the following chapter on ritual suicide.

The Indian blend of violence and gentleness has bewildered Europeans whose attitude towards the country has swung from one extreme to the other. Indian religion was in the main respected by those English who in the eighteenth century occupied parts of the sub-continent and prepared the way for the British Raj. But in the nineteenth century when the Raj was at its zenith, feelings of respect gave way to a "holier than thou" approach to Indian customs generally and towards the Hindu religion in particular. Though they shrank from the Spanish example of forced baptism in their own Indies, the urge to convert tugged at the conscience of many a Victorian administrator. Their letters home were filled with pious hopes that the Indians would one day "see the light" and abandon their pagan idols and cruel customs. If only they would become Christians, they might even come to believe in the Protestant work ethic and cease to exasperate by their lack of relish for the moralizing materialism of their masters. Scant attention was paid to the virtues of a faith that, at its best, could inspire saintly lives and of a philosophy whose message was universal. The British, as Christians, merely judged by the visible abuses performed by people who kept women like hens, crowded together for life in dark quarters, who thought it a greater offence to kill a cow than a man, who buried young women alive, who married little girls to old men and then threw their offspring to the crocodiles at the mouth of the Ganges.

Only after such excesses were curtailed did the more spiritual and even passive Indian approach to life become the object of praise and envy for Europeans, who were beginning to harbour doubts about the blessings of their own material triumphs. In their hundreds disillusioned Christians flocked eastward, eager to sit at the feet of a guru and thirsting for the nectar of life-denial. Hinduism, no longer spurned as base idolatry, the perfect recipe for ruin, was now the mystic key that would unlock the gates of happiness and the way to freedom from the twentieth-century rat-race. The children thrown to the sharks, the widows burnt on the pyre, the Meriahs killed by a thousand cuts were happily forgotten in the euphoria over a creed whose darker aspects were now eclipsed.

Since sacrifice continued for so long under British rule, many details were minutely filed and the numbers involved recorded: a rare instance of the use of government statistics for documenting human sacrifice. The variety of the rites involved and the fullness of the data make India an absorbing case to study. In addition to British statistics, we have Indian religious texts from earliest times that write of human offering in explicit detail. The Vedas were written in about 1400 B.C.; one of these, the White Yajur Veda, opens with special incantations suitable for such offerings. Various gods are named, together with the kind of victim suitable for each, such as a priest for Brahma, a musician for the god of music, a fisherman for the god of rivers; other parts of the text contain further details. One early form of sacrifice that could gain for a man supremacy over all created beings required eleven humans and eleven barren cows to be offered. The horse-sacrifice, designed to give wealth, also demanded the killing of a man. It would be unjust, however, to imply that the offering of humans to the gods was an Indian monopoly among the countries of Asia. Suttee, for instance, as the Europeans styled the sacrifice of widows, was a Chinese as well as an Indian custom, and in South-East Asia ritual killing assumed many forms. Until recent times Burmese kings had victims buried alive at the gates of their capital "so that their spirits might watch over the city".[1] In Thailand, when a new city was being built, officers of the king would lie in wait and seize the first four or eight passers-by, who were then buried under the gate-posts to serve as guardian angels.

Whilst Indians indulged in most forms of sacrifice, they rarely ate their victims. Only hints of this practice survive from the dim past. For instance, among the remote Ooryah tribe, the priest, when he offered a human being to the war god, would say: "The sacrifice we now offer, you must eat".[2] An isolated case of cannibalism in muted form can be found in parts of north-eastern India. In the early nineteenth century an annual victim was offered to the Mother Goddess Kali, who was the wife of the Hindu god Shiva and was always thought of as living off raw human flesh. Dressed in new clothes and bedecked with garlands, the voluntary victim sat on a raised dais in front of the goddess' image reciting prayers. When he made a sign with his finger, the executioner cut off his head, which was placed before the goddess on a golden plate. Only the lungs were cooked and eaten by such Yogis as were present, and the local royal family ate a small amount of rice cooked in the victim's blood. In 1832 one rajah, short of volunteers for this ritual, kidnapped people from outside his own state and, as a result, his realm was annexed by the British.[3]

At times rites to honour the Mother Goddess assumed the proportions of a mass sacrifice. In Assam, in north-eastern India, when Rajah Nara Narayana rebuilt his temple in 1565 A.D., he celebrated the occasion by sacrificing one hundred and forty men, whose heads he offered to Kali on copper plates since he did not have enough gold to go round. The choice of volunteers and conscripts to provide heads for Kali was rather haphazard. The volunteers were known as Bhogis; they were loaded with favours, and until the annual festival of the goddess ended their days, every woman was at their disposal. But when willing victims were lacking, any man of sound health and body caught abroad after midnight might be snatched away for the purpose.

The Indians often added special refinements, but almost all the basic forms of sacrifice were present and most of them were an integral part of Hindu rites. For instance, in the great temple of Shiva at Tanjor, a male child was offered every Friday evening, until the British forbade the practice in the mid-nineteenth century. In the city of Jaipur as late as 1861, when a rajah was crowned on the death of his father, a young girl was killed in honour of the goddess Durga, also Shiva's wife. The universal urge to bury people under new buildings survived into the present century; people still believed in many parts of India that lives were needed for this purpose and were careful not to wander out at night when building was in progress for fear of being used as victims. When Sir George Grierson, who published eighty years ago a book called *Bihar Peasant Life*, wanted to photograph a Bihar peasant house, the grandmother of the family refused to allow any of the children to appear in the picture; she said that the Government was building a bridge across the River Gandak and needed children to bury under its foundations. Sacrifices to water spirits and rivers were frequent, since river demons were greatly to be feared. Until 1828 the Rana of Mewar in southern India, before crossing the Mahi River, invariably sacrificed a man whose body was then thrown into the stream.[4]

To swell the ranks of voluntary victims for different forms of sacrifice in India the net was cast wide. War prisoners, slaves and criminals were an obvious choice, as well as itinerant merchants, and the risk of being kidnapped for this end added to the hazards of their calling. Even the highest in the land were not exempt. The chronicles of Tippera tell of a king in the sixteenth century who offered some slaves to the "fourteen gods" but the gesture was ill-received and the high priest declared that Shiva demanded the blood of the leaders of the king's army. The ruler therefore sacrificed eight of his best captains; his successor, however, offered only prisoners to the fourteen gods.

In India forms of child-sacrifice were many. A macabre custom was the killing of children of humble parents in order that the wife of an exalted person should conceive. Even royal infants were sometimes offered as single victims to ensure that a copious flow of offspring would follow. The tale is told of King Somaka in northern India who for some time could not get a single son out of his cohort of a hundred wives. Finally one boy was born but the king wanted not one son but a hundred and the family priest advised: "O king! let me set on foot a sacrifice, and thou must sacrifice thy son, Jantu, in it. Then on no distant date, a century of handsome sons will be born to thee. When Jantu's fat is put into the fire as an offering to the gods, the mothers will take a smell of the smoke and bring forth a number of sons, valorous and strong. And Jantu also will once more be born as a self-begotten son of thine, in that very mother; and on his back there will appear a mark of gold." The son was sacrificed; the wives smelt the smell of the burnt-offering, all of them became pregnant, and when ten months had passed one hundred sons were born to Somaka, of whom Jantu was the eldest, being born of his former mother. But the family priest died and was grilled for a certain period in a terrible hell as a punishment for what he had done.[5] This story may be little more than a legend but evidence exists of similar rites in much later times.

In the 1860s infants were still offered to Shiva in Lower Bengal to ward off famine, and the strange custom went on of killing one child in order to obtain more. William Sleeman, famed for his fight against the Thugs, informs us that barren women would promise their first born son to the God of Destruction, Mahadeo, in the hope of being given others. The mother would rear this first child and then tell him of his fate when he reached puberty. From that moment he was pledged to the god, and at his annual festival would cast himself from a rock five hundred feet high. The grimmest infant sacrifice was the throwing of children to the sharks at the point where the

River Ganges met the sea, as an offering to the Water Goddess. This rite was among the first to come to the notice of the British, who made a law against it in 1802.

Another practice that soon began to weigh upon the British conscience was the systematic killing of unwanted young girls. If this infanticide was not a sacrifice in the strictest sense of the term, since no ritual took place, it was a direct outcome of Hinduism and of its ever more rigid caste system. Marriage of a girl outside her own caste was out of the question, while to remain single was unchaste and a disgrace. As the rules became more elaborate, the choice grew narrower and narrower. By the early nineteenth century matters were at their worst in the Punjab, where the supply of bridegrooms of the right caste fell far short of the demand. Sons were given to the highest bidder and the dowry for a single daughter could completely ruin her parents. The birth of a girl among the poor but high caste Rajputs was by then nothing short of a calamity. The easiest way out was to kill the infant by pressure on the neck, underfeeding, or other means, such as rubbing the mother's nipples with opium. Sir John Shore, Governor-General of India, brought the matter to the attention of the Asiatic Society in 1794. Due to the seclusion of women, it was hard to ascertain the number of female births; the simplest way was to count the survivors and keep a watch on the ratio of girls to boys, just as methodical statistics were also compiled for suttee sacrifice at the time, complete with charts of age, caste, and income bracket. In some villages, no girl babies were found at all; in a total of thirty others, there were 343 boys to 54 girls. Progress was made slowly; in Bombay, the number of girls alive in 1834 was 603, but by 1841 the figure had risen to 1370. However, not until the 1870s was the evil eradicated and the numbers became approximately equal.[6]

Of all the human offerings that survived into the nineteenth century, among the most bizarre were those of the Khonds of Orissa, an ancient tribe descended from the Dravidian peoples who had lived in northern India before they were pushed southwards by the Arians in 1500 B.C. Their ritual has been immortalized by Frazer, whose vivid account was gleaned from the reports of British officers.[7] These rites were plainly linked to harvest or fertility, and served as a perfect example of Frazer's own theories. The Khonds offered men to the Earth Goddess Tari Pennu. In particular they were thought necessary to ensure good crops of tumeric; without the shedding of human blood and the planting of human flesh in the fields, the dye made from the plant would lose its deep red colour. The victims used were known as Meriahs and the goddess demanded that they should either have been bought in early infancy or have been destined to this fate from birth, as sons of future victims who were kept alive specially in order to breed more Meriahs. Those children not born as Meriahs were usually bought from the Pans, a weaving tribe, who kidnapped infants from the plains for the purpose. During the long years that the Meriahs were kept before they were given to the goddess, they were pampered and shown every kindness. They were even given lands and wives, with whom they had the children who in their turn were one day to be sacrificed.

Ten or twelve days before the annual ceremony, the chosen victim had his hair shorn. Several nights of revelling followed, after which, on the night before the great event, he was dressed in a new robe and led forth from the village with music and dancing in solemn procession to the Meriah grove, a clump of high trees situated at a short distance and untouched by any axe. Great crowds gathered to see the sacrifice; as in Ancient Mexico, no one stayed at home; everyone, men, women and children, had to be present. In the grove the Meriah was tied to a post, anointed with oil and tumeric, adorned with flowers and revered as a god throughout the day. The crowd danced round the post, addressed the earth and said: "Oh god, we offer this sacrifice to you; give us good crops, seasons and health". During this time people struggled wildly for the tiniest relic from the Meriah's person, including even a drop of his spittle. In some villages, before reaching the grove, he was taken round from door to door and people would pluck a single hair from his head. The mode of the Meriah's death varied from one village to the next, though everywhere the principle was the same: it had to be slow and painful; as in Mexico, he must not make a show of resistance and was often dosed with a potent drug. Some of the methods used are described by Frazer:

> One of the commonest seems to have been strangulation, or squeezing to death. The branch of a green tree was cleft several feet down the middle; the victim's neck (in other places, his chest) was inserted in the cleft, which the priest, aided by his

assistants, strove with all his force to close. Then he wounded the victim slightly with his axe, whereupon the crowd rushed at the wretch and hewed the flesh from the bones, leaving the head and bowels untouched . . . In Chinna Kimedy he was dragged along the fields, surrounded by the crowd, who, avoiding his head and intestines, hacked the flesh from his body with their knives till he died. Another very common mode of sacrifice in the same district was to fasten the victim to the proboscis of a wooden elephant, which revolved on a stout post, and, as it whirled round, the crowd cut the flesh from the victim while life remained. In some villages Major Campbell found as many as fourteen of these wooden elephants, which had been used at sacrifices. In one district the victim was put to death slowly by fire. A low stage was formed, sloping on either side like a roof; upon it they laid the victim, his limbs wound round with cords to confine his struggles. Fires were then lighted and hot brands applied, to make him roll up and down the slopes of the stage as long as possible; for the more tears he shed the more abundant would be the supply of rain. Next day the body was cut to pieces.[8]

Immediately after the Meriah's death, a portion of the flesh was rushed to each Khond village by relays of runners; as soon as it arrived, the priest split it into two parts, one of which was given to the Earth Goddess and burned in a hole in the ground. The other part was cut up into as many shares as there were heads of households. Each of these rolled his shred of flesh in leaves and burned it in his favourite field, placing it in the earth behind his back without looking round.

Accounts of the suppression of the Meriah rites are taken from the reports of Major (later Major-General) John Campbell, whom Frazer mentions. Extra details come from the official reports of the government of India, together with those of the provinces of Madras and Bengal, published in 1854 as part of a general account of the campaign against the custom. Confronted with the Meriahs, in addition to suttee, Thuggery and other forms of sacrifice practised not in isolated cases but all over the country, the British were in something of a quandary. As stressed by Philip Woodruff in *The Men Who Ruled India*, everyone agreed that the English should be wary of using their power to interfere with the religion of the people. British rule at that time depended on tacit consent. A tract of land might have been wrested by naked violence from its Hindu master, yet within a few months the English magistrate who took the rajah's place was able to go without escort anywhere in the district, alone among a million of his subjects. They would not have put up with him, if they had not felt that on the whole he was better than any alternative; but this preference would have melted overnight, the very moment he began to meddle with their religion.

To such a man as James Thomason of the North-West Provinces, the enforced restraint was agonizing. Thomason was a devout Christian, son of a missionary, and ward of an evangelical preacher. To live among heathens without attempting to convert them disturbed his conscience. As an official he must stand aloof and as a private citizen could help the missionaries only by prayer, and no more. He and his fellows, even the less devout, consoled themselves with the belief that since the British Raj allowed people to think more freely for themselves, light would one day conquer darkness. To try to hasten that day by short cuts would only delay its coming. Such was the general attitude to Indian religion. But at the same time the policy of turning a blind eye had its limits. Could they countenance so many acts done in the name of the gods but which to a Christian were nothing less than bestial murder? Of these, the Meriahs, carefully raised and tended by the villagers, as other men keep and fatten pigs, were only one example, and the British were not even aware of this particular practice until 1830. But in 1836 George Russel of the Madras Civil Service sent in his first report. He wrote ably and at length, citing the facts but advising against hasty action. The government of Madras studied Russel's report with intense and painful concern. Major Campbell was then sent to find out more, but the authorities made it clear—so cautious was their attitude—that his escort was to be used only to protect his own person and not to rescue Meriah victims from their fate.

Campbell, however, was a man ready to take risks. He summoned the Khond chiefs and leaders, who already knew him well, since he had commanded the troops in the war against the late rajah. Campbell reasoned with them and told them of the horror with which the "Great Government" viewed all forms of human sacrifice, adding that it was the habit of that government to demand a life for a life, and that it would do just this if they persisted in their evil ways. Campbell made another practical point: did their crops grow more abundantly than those of other people who did not sacrifice human beings? The chiefs retired to talk the matter over, and Campbell waited with anxiety for their answer. He had already turned down a compromise suggestion of a single sacrifice each year for a whole group of villages and had gone too far to hold back from using force in face of a rebuff. But at last the leaders came back. Killing the Meriahs had always been their practice and the rajahs had never objected, but they were now the subjects of the Great Government and they must do as they were told. That government would be to blame for their ills if they gave up killing men and offered animals instead. They would tell their goddess: "Do not be angry with us; vent your wrath on this gentleman, who will be able to bear it". And so it was done. The Khonds brought in their Meriahs, and Major Campbell went on working in the region for another sixteen years, during which time he rescued the amazing total of 1506 intended Meriah victims. These had been bought or bred before his arrival and were therefore stock in hand for ceremonies in coming years. But if the gods lived on, their bloodier rituals could not be expected to cease overnight; time was needed to suppress them even after the rulers decided to take the plunge. By the beginning of the twentieth century, however, the commoner forms of killing had become a thing of the past wherever the British Raj held sway. Only isolated cases still cropped up, such as two children killed near Bombay in 1909 by a neighbour in need of blood to cure his wife's barrenness.

The gods of the plains claimed human victims as avidly as those of the hills; their rites merely came sooner to the notice of India's masters, even if they reacted but slowly. Some of the frontier peoples, far more remote than the Khonds, managed to cling to their tribal customs, which survived into modern times and often involved head-hunting. These were bound up with a belief in the magic properties of the human head as seat of the soul; among Indian hill tribes such notions differed little from those found in Borneo and New Guinea, where headhunting was a national industry. Among the more fervent supporters of the cult were the peoples of the Naga Hills in Assam, in north-eastern India. Naga girls would refuse to marry a man who had not taken a head from a neighbouring village, on the grounds that a man who brought in no surplus soul-matter from outside was unlikely to be fertile and to beget sons.

The tribes had many ways of treating the enemy heads they took. The Lhota hung them on the village head-tree; the Tangkhul put them on a pile of stones (recalling the skulls some 100,000 years old found at Monte Circeo in Italy). The Konyak who lived across the Burmese border hoisted their heads on bamboo poles. Signs are few, however, that in India headhunting went hand in hand with cannibalism, though part of the head of a British official killed at Khonoma in 1880 was tasted by the young warriors of the village. T. C. Hodson, writing in 1880, tells of a visit he paid to tribes of the Naga Hills. He took a military escort and arrived just after two heads had been taken; by an unlucky chance, one head belonged to the nephew of one of his escorts, and Hodson had a difficult task in persuading the Nagas to restore it to its owner's relatives. The custom was by then already on the wane. An old man told Hodson that he remembered headhunting raids on a larger scale but was not clear just why the heads were needed, except that they played a vital role in burial rites, since their owners became slaves of the village chief in the next world. Other Nagas said that they took heads because they brought riches to their captors.[9]

Cristoph von Fuerer-Haimendorf, leading scholar on the peoples of northern India, confirms that by the 1940s ritual killing of humans by the hill tribes had ended except for isolated cases in backward areas. Only among semi-independent groups between Assam and Burma did the practice linger on. In 1936 von Fuerer-Haimendorf met an intended victim who had somehow eluded his fate as well as some boastful and unrepentant partakers in such rites. Among the Reddis and Koyas he found positive signs that ritual murders had been carried out in the recent past, and a belief in human sacrifice still had a powerful hold. On another tour in 1941, he found that the Reddis and Koyas of the village of Chodavaram were still frightened of kidnappers, in spite of the establishment of a police station nearby. The village headman admitted that on a mountain about twelve miles to the north heads were still offered to the goddess Maveli. She would not accept animals in their place and, if she were not given a human head every three years, would come among the people and spread disease. The victim's head was severed at a single stroke;

a cloth soaked in his blood was then placed before the goddess for the years to come, if no new human victim could be found. The Reddis were still too afraid of Maveli to bring the practice quite to an end.[10]

Another curious rite survived until very recently among the Khasis of Assam. The Khasis were a by-word for atrocities and their habit of kidnapping children to offer to their snake goddess, Thlen, provoked an angry telegram from the Associated Press of India to the *Calcutta Daily Englishman*, dated 19th June 1924. It had little effect and on 19th May 1929 a Khasi living in a village near Shillong, the capital of Assam, went missing. His wife told the police, who investigated the matter very thoroughly and found that he had been sacrificed to the snake deity. The trial shed new light on the prescribed rites. The victim was dispatched with a wooden club, a usage that probably derived from the Stone Age. His hair and the tips of his fingers were cut off with a pair of silver scissors. It was stated at the trial that three or four people were killed in this way every year. People believed that when a Thlen took up its abode in a family, there was no way of getting rid of it. So long as the snake was supplied with its favourite food, the family prospered, but when it felt a lack of human blood, sickness would break out and mishaps become frequent.[11]

While other forms of ritual killing lived on into the twentieth century, the very scale of Thuggery, once discovered, prompted drastic action, and it was stamped out long before then. When the Prince of Wales, later King Edward VII, visited India in 1876, Thuggery was a thing of the past. The Prince was taken to the gaol at Lahore, where he spoke to an aged and notorious Thug, whose life had been spared when he turned Queen's evidence and betrayed his fellows. The prisoner calmly told the Prince of Wales of the two hundred and fifty murders which he claimed to have committed. The august visitor, though enthralled by such an unusual tale, was himself more intent upon dispatching animal victims; after hearing the old man's tale he killed six tigers on a hunting expedition, in which a thousand elephants were used.

The Thugs were no ordinary bandits murdering people for mere profit. Their victims were strangled according to an elaborate ritual and were dedicated to the grim Kali, wife of Shiva, leading Hindu deity. The killings were therefore in every sense a sacrifice—one of a number of forms dedicated to this goddess. We have already mentioned the Koch king who in the sixteenth century decapitated a hundred and fifty men and presented their heads on copper platters to Shiva's consort. At that period sacrifices to Kali were already widespread, particularly in Bengal, though her temples were to be found in many parts of India. The "Song of Manik Chandra", a well known Bengali folk ballad of the time, tells how war captives and criminals, among others, were offered up to the goddess Chandi, who was simply Kali under another name.

Kali, said to have first come down to earth on the banks of the River Hooghly, on which Calcutta stands, is the most popular deity of Bengal and has been revered throughout the ages under many names. Although some scholars insist that Kali worship is more recent, she is already mentioned in the Puranas, the great collection of myths and religious stories dating from the second century A.D. onwards. A celebrated hymn to the goddess was composed in about 800 A.D. by the great philosopher, Shonkaracharya, who was her fervent votary. In the first stanza he praises her as the life-giving Mother Goddess: "Whatsoever breathes, does so by me". But in the very next stanza the philosopher describes her as the life-destroyer. In her four hands she holds the symbols not of plenty but of death: the iron hook which drags a man to his doom and, significantly, the noose with which he is caught and strangled—the precise way in which the Thugs killed the victims they offered to Kali.[12]

Hindu beliefs, and the actions they inspired, perplex the Westerner. Kali's beloved husband, the great god Shiva, is a bundle of contradictions: he is the creator and sustainer of life and at the same time the destroyer of the world. In the south Indian temple of Perur his image, like those of Kali, wears a garland of skulls; one of his four pairs of hands bears her gruesome weapons, the hook and the strangling noose. In Kali the dark side is more prominent than in Shiva himself. Another Hindu poem describes her birth. She emerged from the forehead of the Divine Mother and became black with anger as the demons came to attack her. She had a large hideous face and carried a sword, in addition to the inevitable hook and noose. Many stone images of her survive, to which animals are still sacrificed, and folk-songs describe the goddess as she has been known in Bengal for the last few centuries. In her most popular form she has four hands and a gruesome face and is black as night; she wears a garland of human heads; her body is smeared with the blood that oozes from them; two corpses hang as pendants from her ears; she holds in her two left hands a severed head and a sword; she is surrounded on all sides by howling she-jackals and blood trickles from the corners of her mouth as she smilingly chews raw flesh. In the form known as Siddhakali, her body overflows with nectar dropping from the moon, emblem of childhood and fertility, but even this more benign Kali drinks blood from a skull held in one of her left hands. As Guhyakali she is covered with a black cloth and has sunken eyes and fearful teeth, but a smiling face; to her left is Shiva in the form of a child. In her fourth form, Bhadrakali, she is wan with hunger; her face is once more black as ink; she weeps and says: "I am not satisfied. I shall swallow the whole world at one gulp".

Such was the gruesome goddess whom the Thugs adored. Legend relates that she assembled them and showed them the method by which groups of travellers were henceforth to be strangled to satisfy her thirst for blood. She herself names them "Thugs", meaning "deceivers". As long ago as the thirteenth century A.D., the Sultan of Delhi arrested about a thousand of their number. Thévenot, a French seventeenth-century traveller, complained of Thugs on the road from Delhi to Agra. Their favourite trick at that time was to send pretty women out on to the road, weeping and dishevelled, on whom the traveller would then take pity. So secret were their ways that the British, during the earlier part of their presence in the sub-continent, were blithely unaware of what was going on. Only in 1799 did they come to suspect anything when two Indian soldiers mysteriously vanished on their way back from leave. Sepoy soldiers of the British army going on leave had become favourite victims, for they always carried money to their family; in addition, they would not be missed for a long time, since their relatives did not know that they were coming home and if they failed to report back for duty, their officers assumed that they had deserted.

The Thug bands would set out in the autumn after the rains; by the next spring, a single group might have dispatched as many as a thousand people. Sometimes victims would be lone travellers; at other times whole parties were swept into oblivion in the twinkling of an eye. An entire band would be strangled together, with minute attention to the ritual. It was essential that none survived to tell the tale; care was even taken to kill dogs along with their masters. Events would follow a consistent pattern. The gang camped near a town or village and a few of its members, chosen for their good appearance, went to the shops and wandered about the streets. As soon as they saw a small band of travellers of the right kind, they found an excuse for getting into conversation. Invariably the dangers of journeys without escort would crop up, and sooner or later someone would propose that the two parties join forces for safety's sake. The leader of the gang would then make a great show of resistance, but in the end matters were settled and the two groups would ride peaceably side by side for a few days. Around the camp-fires at night there was much merriment and laughter.

Then one night the talk would be livelier than ever and the stories even funnier. In such congenial company, people would hardly notice in the shadows a little man who sidled up to the side of the leader of the second group. The jovial chief leaned back and whispered in a special slang: "Is it ready?", to which came the answer, "Yes, it is dug deep and wide". Suddenly the leader cried in a loud voice, "Bring the tobacco", which was the last sound on earth that the travellers would hear. In a matter of minutes they were expertly strangled and their corpses tumbled into the prepared grave. Deep gashes were made in their sides to prevent them from swelling in the shallow pit, and to fit its cramped dimensions their legs were doubled back against their bodies.[13]

The recorded confession of a Thug, taken from A. J. Wightman's book *No Friend for Travellers*, describes in detail how they set about their work and the lengths to which they went to win over the most suspicious of their prey. Three times, in three different disguises, a party of Thugs attempted to engage the confidence of a Moghul officer travelling across the Ganges Plain on his way from the Punjab to Oudh, accompanied by his butler and syce. But each time they failed to allay his suspicions and to persuade him of the advantages of their travelling together. The Thugs, however, were undaunted by this setback.

The next day saw the officer and his servants, still alone, crossing a boundless plain, where he knew he could hope for no help, if attacked. . . . He was still congratulating himself on having shaken off risky companions, when his attention was drawn by a rather pathetic group huddled by the side of the path: six Muslims, crouched down, weeping and wailing by the side of a dead companion. He reined in and demanded to know what was the matter.

The spokesman for the party replied that they were soldiers from Lahore on their way to Lucknow, worn out by fatigue in their anxiety to reach homes and families once more after long and hard service. Their unfortunate comrade, who had been the sole support of a large family, had been unable to withstand the rigours and strain of travel and, when he died suddenly, they had dug a grave for him in this part of the plain. Unfortunately they were all uneducated men, unable to recite the funeral service from the holy Koran, and, unless they found someone able and willing to perform the necessary rites for them, they had no means of laying the man to rest. Would it be possible for his Highness to spare a few precious moments? Would he be willing to speak the words of the last rites? If he would do so he would, without doubt, find his reward not only in this world but in the next.

His Highness agreed. He dismounted. The body was placed in the proper position, head towards Mecca, and a carpet quickly spread as the Moghul removed his many weapons and laid them on the ground nearby. After calling for water with which to wash his feet, hands and face so that he would not officiate in an unclean state, he knelt down on the carpet and began to intone the funeral service in a loud, clear voice. Two of the soldiers had knelt down by him, one on either side, while their companions begged the khidmutgar (butler) and the syce to move a little way off so as not to interrupt the good Samaritan at his devotions.

At last all was ready. The signal was given, handkerchiefs were swept about throats and drawn tight and, in a very few minutes, all three—the Moghul, his khidmutgar and the syce— were dead and lying in the grave in the usual manner, the head of the one to the feet of the next below him.[14]

To become a Thug was a long and complicated process. Boys were first allowed to accompany a gang when they were ten to twelve years old, and they were often sons or near relatives of a Thug. A boy then had to work through the various stages of his tuition, first acting as a scout to get news of unwary groups of travellers. Then he was used as a gravedigger: according to tradition, this work was not needed in earliest times, when the goddess Kali swooped down to earth and herself ate up the corpses. Out of respect for this legend, a strangler must never turn and look back on the scene of his act; once a novice, in defiance of this rule, had glanced over his shoulder and spied the Black Kali crouched over a corpse; from then on she ceased to come in person and left it to her servants to hide the evidence of their handiwork in graves of their own digging.

The initiation ceremony for the novice was elaborate. The candidate was bathed and dressed in new unbleached clothes and then led by his master, or guru, to where the head of the gang was seated on a clean white cloth. If the answer came that they were ready to receive the youth as a Thug, he was taken outside by the entire band. Once in the open, the guru raised his hands and eyes to the sky, calling, "Oh Bhowani! Mother of the World, whose votaries we are, receive this thy servant and vouchsafe him thy protection". Next a handy victim for the blooding of the novice had to be found, which was not difficult in pre-twentieth century India. An old man camping in a nearby grove would have been an ideal subject. First the guru took the boy away and waited for a sign from Kali, such as a crow flying into the branches of a nearby tree and starting to caw—an especially propitious omen. They then returned to the grove where the unsuspecting old man was being charmed by convivial companions, a signal was made, the trembling youth cast his noose about the scraggy neck and death was instantaneous. Far from remorse or pity, the killer could only feel delight that he was now privileged to strangle for Kali, the Black Mother. To end the ceremony, a small piece of coarse sugar was handed to the new member to eat and the guru made an impassioned speech, urging him to strive to secure the greatest number of victims in the shortest possible time—excluding women, lepers and certain castes that were under the goddess' special protection.

A vital part of the new strangler's training had been the precise technique of the lightning-quick kill. This depended on expert handling of a piece of yellow silk tied at one end to a silver rupee, which made a grip for the left hand. Yellow was Kali's sacred colour. In former times other methods had been used, when some Thugs travelled about on horseback and killed with a long string with a running noose, rather like a cowboy's lasso. The slaying, whether done by a novice or by an old hand, was followed by the ritual eating of coarse yellow sugar. This would be laid out on the ground, where a pickaxe (of the kind with which the graves were dug) and a piece of silver (part of the noose) were placed upon it, as offerings to Kali. After fervent prayers by the assembled company, the signal for strangling was given, just as if they were really about to kill; the sugar was then handed out and eaten by those present as consecrated food; only those who had strangled with their own hands could partake.[15]

Of all this, almost nothing was known to the British. Though suspicions had been aroused twenty years earlier, not until the 1820s did Lord William Bentinck, Governor General of the East India Company, order Captain William Sleeman to devote his whole time and energy to the task of suppression. Sleeman had already studied for some years the activities of the Thugs, but was given little support by his colleagues; scornfully, he was nicknamed "Thuggee". And while his companions shrugged their shoulders, local rajahs tended to obstruct his work, and he could not even count on the help of the British official residents at their courts. Many Indians of high rank were themselves involved; when one of his provincial chiefs had arrested a Thug gang, the Maharajah of Gwalior sent a brigade of troops against him. Richard Cavendish, Resident at Gwalior, turned a blind eye when the ruler gave shelter to stranglers, and even wrote a letter to the government in Calcutta, opposing Thug-hunting parties. Sleeman made slow progress; by 1827 only some three hundred Thugs, two large groups, had been convicted and Thuggery went on unabated. Then, to hasten matters and to win sympathy for his work, in 1830 Sleeman sent an article to the *Calcutta Literary Gazette* which was published on 8th October. He pointed out that Thuggery was still a scandal; Kali's temple near Mirzapore on the Ganges was thronged with stranglers from all quarters of India, who went there to give the goddess a share of their spoils.

A breakthrough came shortly after this when a notorious Thug, Feringeea, was caught and turned King's evidence. The Governor General, in a letter to Sleeman, authorized him to spare the strangler in return for full disclosure of every killing of which he knew, together with the name, caste and residence of all the Thugs involved. Feringeea further had to promise to assist with all his might in bringing to justice all those guilty of Thuggery; should he fail in any of these conditions, the pardon would be null and void. The Thug agreed to the terms, remarking to Sleeman, "My family have been Thugs for eleven generations. My grandfather, Tula, was a great chief among them. He had eight sons, of whom my father, Purasrah, was the youngest, and hung for murder at Gwalior. I am the last of Tula's descendants. Turah and Bowanee were seized by you at Bhilsa when I fled and they have been hanged. Maharaj and Gunesh you have taken and have in custody. Me you have purchased for five hundred rupees and I will serve you freely and faithfully and no one knows so much of Thugs as I do".[16] Feringeea believed that his misfortunes stemmed from having strangled women, in defiance of the Thugs' strict code. After this coup, Sleeman's campaign made rapid advances. By the end of 1832 he had arrested and sent for trial a further 389 Thugs; 126 were hanged and 177 transported for life. Thuggery went on for some years in certain places, but total suppression was not far off.

The work of rounding up the Thugs was full of excitement and adventure. Their pursuers had to be as wily as the gangs themselves. For instance, one young British officer came up with a big band when he had only a dozen orderlies with him. He dared not accuse them of being stranglers, since he was vastly outnumbered and might easily have ended up as a choice offering to the Black Goddess. At the same time, he dared not let them go and risk never seeing them again. So he ordered the group to come with him to the nearest headquarters to answer a trumped-up charge that they would easily be able to disprove. Under strong protest they complied; not until they were surrounded by superior numbers was anything said about Thuggery. There were many such tales as this, but much routine investigation was also involved. Sleeman's young assistants had the painstaking task of building up lists of members of each gang and of incidents in which they had taken part. Evidence was hard to piece together, for the culprits had killed so many people that they had lost all count of who had been strangled in what year; therefore, when called to the witness stand, they contradicted each other as to the facts.

By 1837 Sleeman's uphill struggle had come to a successful end; more than three thousand Thugs had been convicted, although two thousand were still at large; probably in all about ten thousand had been at work before Sleeman's net was drawn tight. One has only to recall that a single Thug could boast of two hundred and fifty victims in his career to realize that the total number of killings must have been staggering. The Thugs who confessed made it plain that to destroy life, not just to rob for their own gain, had been the first aim. They explained how although, for the Hindu, God was both creator and destroyer, the goddess Kali, seeing that the forces of destruction were losing, came down to earth to teach the Thugs their craft and to promise to act as their guardian. Their personal share of the booty was merely the goddess' earthly reward for their work and came a long second to the blessings she offered in the next world. They believed that their mission was divine and would be rewarded by a place in their own special heaven.

A sprinkling of Muslims was even recruited into the ranks of the Thugs, though it remains a mystery how they were brought to do the dirty work of the great Hindu goddess. The Mohammedan Moguls ruled over much of India before the British but Muslims as a whole obeyed the Koran and steered clear of rites involving human sacrifice. This does not mean that they were always kind to their Hindu subjects; the Emperor Jehangir (1605–1627) liked to watch criminals being trampled underfoot by elephants; to deal with lesser offences, he maintained in his capital of Agra a squad of forty hangmen. Persia, from where the Moguls stemmed, was the home of the nearest equivalent of the Thugs, the Assassins (Assassin is a corrupt form of "Hashishin", and derives from a narcotic made out of the Indian hemp). But unlike the Thugs, their deeds scarcely amount to a true human sacrifice for, in spite of being an Islamic sect, they killed for motives that were as much political as religious and were required to assassinate anyone whom the head of the order marked out for death.

The practices which appalled the nineteenth-century British were intrinsically Hindu, though some of them lay on its fringes. The human killing was stamped out but many of the ceremonies survived with animals taking the place of men. At an annual feast among the Konyak tribes, a puppy was hurled from the roof of a high building; the animal was given human attributes in the form of a spear and a piece of cloth, and it requires little imagination to see what form the ritual once took. In place of the human Meriah, who was tied to the wooden elephant, a goat or a buffalo was tethered to a post in the sacred grove and hacked to pieces in the same way. Kali still claims her victims. On 17 March 1980 the *Times of India* described how the thirty-two-year-old Shanmuga Gramani, a week earlier, had taken his daughter Rajakumari into their local village temple and there slit her throat, as a human offering. This was no single instance. According to the *Süddeutsche Zeitung* of 21 March 1980, ritual killings are not infrequent among fanatical Hindu sects who believe that the gods can only be appeased by fresh human blood, preferably that of children. In Cooch Behar, according to the *Indian Express*, a father cut down his four children, who were all under seven years old, with an axe, in front of the picture of the "Black Goddess", Kali. Another case caused an uproar in the Parliament of the State of Karnataka. Lakshman Singh Giri was supposed to have killed at least three young children, performing his sacrificial rituals at the temple of Kali next door to his house in order to master evil spirits and to help childless parents. Protesting against these and other instances, in a recent article the *Times of India* asks "how is it possible that in the industrial age children in our country can be slaughtered like cattle, in order to appease some deity?" However, Kali's victims are now more often goats, sheep and buffaloes, whose heads are severed with the single stroke of a scimitar; even this practice is being modified, and pumpkin gourds and cucumbers are being used instead. Nonetheless, the tradition of Kali's claim to human victims is far from over. Today in Bengal and elsewhere popular representations of the goddess are on sale, pasted on wood and gaudily coloured. In these she is still portrayed with a garland of human heads; in one hand she holds a bloody sword and in another a dripping severed head.

Changes were made under duress, at the instance of reluctant foreign rulers. The case of India is therefore of special interest since we do not have to rely on scant references in ancient texts, as in Egypt or even Greece, that seldom tell the whole story. Instead, the fullest accounts survive both of the rites themselves and of the reactions of those modern observers, who saw them with their own eyes. In the end changes were enforced after the advent of British officials of a kind who took their Christian principles more seriously and were no longer content with a policy of leaving well alone.

The earliest settlers had not themselves been very squeamish about human life. In the mid-eighteenth century a woman who incited her lover to kill her husband was burned alive under British auspices in Calcutta. Also in that city, in 1789 some robbers were tied down, their right hands and left feet burned off, hot butter dripped onto the stumps and the men left to die.[17] The story is also told of Elihu Yale, governor of Bombay, who, when his butler left his service without due notice, directed that he should be hanged. His legal advisers queried what the charge should be since hanging, though by English law the punishment for a whole series of petty crimes, by some odd oversight did not apply to butlers who left without notice. Yale announced that piracy was the charge, and hanged the servant duly for piracy. Even in the nineteenth century, the British could suddenly cease to behave as humanitarians: the quelling of the Indian Mutiny in 1857 was followed by savage reprisals. It is not perhaps surprising, in any case, that for so long the new rulers of India turned a blind eye to sacrifice when they were confronted with so many other examples of violence and arbitrary killing. For instance, a party given by the Mogul governor of Surat, the very first British settlement, was rudely interrupted when the host fell into a sudden rage and ordered all the dancing girls to be decapitated on the spot, to the stupefaction of his English guests.

Doubtless most Indian forms of human sacrifice would have ceased in the end in any event and the British merely hastened the change. Many Hindu divines and scholars went to Europe and these were the very people who took the lead in the campaign against widow-burning and other such rites, and who pressed the authorities to act. As long ago as 1830, the Indian teacher Ram Mohan Ray, whose Hinduism was deeply tinged with Christian ideals, went to England with the chief motive of fighting the threat that the law against suttee would be suspended to appease the anger of orthodox Hindus.

The obvious question remains as to *why* Indians were so extravagant in giving humans to the gods, long after such killings had been reduced to a tolerable minimum in the Graeco-Roman world and had vanished for a time in the Christian West. Civilization is a hard word to define, but nonetheless India will pass almost any historian's test as the home of a "higher" civilization; Arnold Toynbee, in *A Historian's Approach to Religion*, does not hesitate to name Hinduism as one of the world's "higher" religions. However, when he refers to India in another passage of the same book, he expresses horror "at the pandering to Nature's lust by the sacrifice of living creatures in an ascending scale of agony, in which the most efficacious victim is the sacrificer's only child".[18] But nothing whatsoever can be understood of human sacrifice in India or, for that matter, in Africa, Polynesia or Ancient America, unless it is first grasped that the concepts behind the acts were the opposite of our own. Europeans, whether Christian or ex-Christian, are imbued with the idea that good is good, and bad is bad. The two forces, locked in never-ending conflict, are not thought of as two halves of the same deity. For the Christian, God is love and the devil is his enemy. The notion that God and the devil can be one person is alien to Western thought.

In India Shiva, husband of the loathsome Kali, forms with Krishna and Vishnu a kind of trinity at the summit of Hindu worship. But Shiva is at one and the same time the creator-sustainer and the destroyer of the universe. Not only can the skull, symbol of death, and the crescent moon, standing for birth and growth, be found on the same image of the god; Shiva is pure contemplation, merged into the void of the absolute, where all tensions are at rest, but he is also total activity, frantic and playful; these opposing attitudes can be seen side by side in his sanctuaries. A myth well illustrates this wickedly playful side of Shiva, as the conqueror of a great demon, who had taken the form of an elephant. The god forced the elephant to dance until the animal fell down dead; Shiva then flayed his victim and, wrapped in this bloody trophy, executed a horrendous victory dance.[19]

Even Vishnu, who is usually painted in more benevolent colours, has a dual nature. The Bhagavad-Gita, the Song of the Lord, is the great classic of Hinduism and presents the god Vishnu as the supreme deity. The poem takes the form of a dialogue between Prince Arjuna and his charioteer, who is Vishnu in disguise. On the eve of battle, Arjuna hesitates to plunge into action, filled with horror at the slaughter that will follow. In the dialogue between the two, Arjuna becomes aware of the identity of his companion and begs him to reveal his true self. Vishnu consents, and Arjuna is granted a vision of the benign creator. He is filled with awe, but feels that he has not seen all and that there is another side to the god. He is warned not to ask to be shown this but persists in his demand and is granted the terrible truth; he now beholds all forms of life passing swiftly to their ruin in the awful mouths of Vishnu, their one-time creator.

At the crucial point in India's great epic, the supreme deity is thus revealed as facing both ways, being both the creator and destroyer of all that exists. To those nurtured in the Christian tradition, this Indian view of eternity may seem strange and disturbing, but goes a long way towards explaining their attitudes to death and their readiness to destroy human life. For if God is both good and bad, man does not have to try to be good, but is perfectly free to copy either side of God's nature. The Hindu ascetic may aim at passive withdrawal from the world; but the Christian ideal of following in Jesus' footsteps of actively loving one's neighbour as oneself loses its point. If anything, the cruel side of the gods was easier to copy and the results more spectacular. Why should anyone have qualms about killing a fellow human being in a colourful ceremony, when the great Shiva himself and his wife Kali delighted in destruction, bore in their hands the instruments of death, and fed on human flesh?

Krishna, the more benign member of the Hindu trinity, is made to say in the Bhagavad Gita: "One shall not absolve oneself from an obligation consequent on one's birth . . . . even if it involves evil. For all undertakings are surrounded by evil, as fire is surrounded by smoke".[20] In another passage, Krishna says that the world has no meaning and is merely a play that God acts with himself, making all living creatures spin round like marionettes on their stage. But having placed God beyond good and evil, and made of man his plaything, traditional Hinduism was bereft of an all-embracing ethic; in its creed the ethical and non-ethical live side by side. Only dimly present are that respect for human life and love of mankind, preached by Christ, Confucius, Socrates and Buddha. Indians, like their gods, are creatures of paradox, and can at times be cruelly violent and at others insistently non-violent; the Jain sect strictly forbade the killing of insects, and tender-hearted Hindus would implore the newly-arrived British at Surat not to shoot down pigeons, even offering them money to spare the poor birds. However no principle offered the same degree of compassion for humans as for gnats.

In India, particularly, to sacrifice a man was no act of cruelty and certainly no disfavour. The victim stood to gain more than he lost. For firmly embedded in their dogma was the idea of reincarnation— that endless cycle whereby the individual, after death, merely takes on a new form and returns to earth. The doctrine assumes that animals and even plants may have souls like ourselves, and are subject to the same iron law. For anyone holding this belief—including the victim himself—the importance of slaying a man, or for that matter a goat, is secondary. Death loses its sting when the departed comes straight back to this earth and the end of a life marks the beginning of another.

In 563 B.C., India produced a kind of saviour, the Buddha, although the great teacher did not regard himself quite in this light. Firm in his belief in the doctrine of reincarnation, the highest aim was to reach a state of perfection, Nirvana; only those who could attain this state were freed from the doom of eternal rebirth and instead were snuffed out, like the flame of a candle. Buddha did not pose as a true saviour and merely told his disciples, when about to die, that he would depart, never to return, and that they must fend for themselves and find their own way to Nirvana in the light of his teaching. But these abstract notions had too little popular appeal and in the first and second centuries before Christ Buddhism was revamped and a new version arose known as the "Greater Vehicle". From being a teacher or philosopher, Buddha was now exalted to the rank of saviour, and it was taught that he had not been snuffed out after all, but laboured on in heaven in order to save others. Like Jesus, this new Buddha no longer strove for escape from life's toils, but entered the fray and took upon himself the whole mass of human suffering. Buddhism thereby became a redeemer-religion, but in this guise was summarily expelled from India, after it had taken root in China and Japan.

The Indians accordingly preferred to do without the services of a saviour, and from about 800 A.D. onwards, instead came to adopt popular Hinduism, based on the gods and beliefs of the pre-Buddhist era. So India, having been the home of the world's most tolerant religion, chose to go back to the worship of gods whose own destructive nature demanded human offerings. The underlying conditions did not alter: lack of any benevolent redeemer, absence of a truly humane ethic, and, finally, belief in a ceaseless cycle of rebirth that turned the death of a man into a trivial incident.

Out of respect for the higher reaches of Hindu philosophy, it may be reasonably argued that the religion from which these sacrifices sprang was not that which we know today. Shorn of such killings, and with some of the rigours of the caste system relaxed, Hinduism has much to contribute to the world. But this latterday version owes a good deal to European liberal thought and to the original message of Jesus. To quote Mahatma Gandhi: "Though I cannot claim to be a Christian in the sectarian sense, the example of Jesus' suffering is a factor in the composition of my undying faith in non-violence, which rules all my actions." [21] But until modern times with their alien influences, the Indians remained the captives of gods who had a thirst for blood and whose victims were legion.

6

Burn the Bride

The early Christians often sought to end their lives as the only sure way to escape from sin, and although for the past 1400 years the Church has taught that suicide is damned, the practice was extolled by writers in India and China and hallowed by tradition in Ancient Rome and Japan. Often the very gods set their seal of approval on self-slaughter, disregarding any technical snags involved in the death of an immortal. In a hymn of the Indian Rig Veda, "The Lord of the Creatures offered himself as a sacrifice"; the Scandinavian god Odin had ended his own life, swinging on the windy tree; in Mexico, when all was dark, two gods leaped into the fire, and emerged as the new sun and moon, making the Fifth World, the era of the Aztecs, owe its very existence to divine self-immolation.

True to the basic notion that the one should give his life to save the many, the victim may in certain cases be his own executioner; our original definition of sacrifice must therefore include suicide, provided that it be in pursuit of a defined religious end. The principle remains the same, whether a man dies at the altar by his own sword-thrust or by someone else's. Indeed, far from excluding self-slaughter from human sacrifice as a whole, it could even be regarded as its highest form; for the greater the degree of compulsion in ritual killing, the less pleasing the act to the gods, and the less noble in the eyes of men. Of no sacrifice is this truer than of Jesus. In practice, a dividing line cannot always be drawn between a death that is freely undertaken and one that is imposed; some rites combine elements of both. For instance in India, if a widow willingly climbed onto her husband's funeral pyre, she was clearly committing suicide. If, however, religious and family pressures were so strong that the woman was left with no choice, and was even then tied by ropes to her husband's body, the act was a ritual killing, whatever the pretence that she acted of her own free will.

Not only suttee but many forms of religious suicide were rife in India. The early Hindu scriptures write of the practice, though it suffered an eclipse with the spread of Buddhism in the sixth century B.C.; people were then denied the right to kill themselves, even though Buddhist writings at times condoned the act. Only with the decline of Buddhism and the return of the Hindu gods did ritual suicide take a full hold. The Puranas, religious texts from the early centuries of the Christian era, take a new attitude, and praise self-slaughter if carried out in sacred places with the appropriate rites.

These writings, however, insist that suicide was not a right but a privilege; it was not an escape for the impious but a reward for ascetics who had attained a level of perfection. The motive was to end at a stroke the eternal cycle of birth and death to which every Hindu was condemned, since suicides were held never to return to earth. The rule applied also to suttee; the widow who shared her husband's funeral pyre lived on with him in Paradise and neither spouse came back to this life. An odder pretext was the desire to avenge a wrong. Spirits of suicides aroused terror, and would haunt forever those who had offended them. If a creditor fasted outside the house of his debtor, he was forced to pay up, lest the creditor die and he be then plagued by his ghost for ever after. A particular sect in Rajisthan, the Bards, were experts in such tactics. They had a way of making people comply with their demands known as Traga. The Bard would shed his own blood or that of a member of his family, while calling down the wrath of heaven upon the offender, whose obstinacy made this sacrifice necessary. At times Bards would form a cordon round the recusant's house, start a fast and force the inhabitants to fast as well, until their demands were met. The ghost of a suicide Bard was sacred and held in peculiar dread. Traga thus came to be a means of protest against unpopular acts and a method of extracting money. The literature of the Gujarati region abounds in chilling tales of its use, until banned by the British.

The appointed places for self-sacrifice were many. One of the Purana texts states that whosoever abandoned his body at Pehoa, on the north bank of the River Sarasvau, after repeating the prayers laid down for the occasion, would never again suffer death.[1] Other Puranas specially recommend suicide at Kasi, in the region of Benares, and many texts record such acts. This ancient city was a Mecca for pilgrims from all over the country, who believed that if they ended their lives in Kasi, they crossed the stream of the world and broke away from the grim cycle of rebirth. The god Shiva gave salvation to all who went to die there and whispered a magic verse into the right ear of those on the point of death; they would thus never be reborn. Another sacred spot was the point where the Rivers Ganges and Yamuna met, regarded as the best place to cut one's own throat.

The choice of ways to commit ritual suicide was wide and included drowning in a river, leaping from a height, burning and starvation. Death by exhaustion was another method; a man would set off towards the Himalayas, and go on until he collapsed; others died by burying themselves in snow. The Jain sect specialized in slow suicide and death by fasting was a favourite method. An even better way of prolonging the agony was to die on a slow-burning cow-dung pyre or to hang head-downwards over the fire and drink in the flames. Other Jains cut off pieces of their own flesh and offered them to birds of prey. All these practices were highly recommended in religious texts written between the thirteenth and seventeenth centuries.[2]

Of the great men who committed ritual suicide, a few examples may suffice here. Already in the period of the Gupta Empire (founded in 320 A.D.) a poem describes King Aja drowning himself at the confluence of the holy rivers, the Ganges and the Sarayk, and immediately going to heaven. King Kumaragupta, a later Gupta ruler, entered a slow fire of cow-dung in 554 A.D. Anandapala, son of the ruler of the Punjab, jumped into the fire in 1065 A.D., after he had been defeated in battle. According to one tradition, the great eighth-century philosopher, Kumarila, also burned himself on a pyre; and the scholar and statesman Hemacandra starved himself to death in 1172. Countless other stories tell of men and women who abandoned life, contemplating the divinity and taking no food and water until they died. By the fifteenth century all barriers against suicide had fallen. Formerly it had been confined to high-caste Brahmins, but now the right was granted to all castes alike. Mass suicide became the fashion, and when the King of Narsynga, in the Central Provinces, died in 1516, five hundred men and women threw themselves on to the fire.[3] Another mass suicide is recorded on a pillar at Halebid in Mysore State in the south of India; it commemorates the death of the general Kuvara and of a thousand warriors who showed their devotion by sharing his end. Sculpted on the pillar are men with swords in the act of cutting off their own arms and legs and even their heads.

The rite of Jauhar, where a whole tribe—both men and women— became extinct in a matter of hours to avoid the horrors of captivity after defeat, is an ancient one and can be traced back to about 1000 B.C. Nearly seven hundred years later, Alexander the Great on his Indian campaign routed the Agalassai but the survivors, said to number twenty thousand, set fire to their capital and cast themselves with all their wives and children into the flames.[4] A number of cases of Jauhar occurred when India was invaded by the Moguls. The city of Chitore was attacked in 1533; after the bravest had fallen and defeat was certain, the signal was given, gunpowder was strewn in hollows in the rock, and the flames of the blast consumed thirteen thousand ladies, led by the mother of the King.[5] Heroines of Jauhar, like certain suttee suicides, were worshipped in temples. Their deeds were recalled in the religious festivals of Rajisthan and pilgrims thronged to their shrines. In many places of that region the ashes of Jauhar heroes and heroines are marked by memorial stones.

Many forms of ritual suicide went on unabated into the last century and were described by British witnesses. The most famous was the Juggernauth ceremony, held every year at Puri in Orissa in honour of the god Vishnu, also known as Jagganatha; a British eye-witness observer, H. T. Colebrooke, relates that in the early nineteenth century many people still plunged beneath the wheels of the huge car on which the image of Jagganatha was dragged from its temple to a distant garden. The rites survive, but the suicides were frowned upon by the authorities and have long since ceased. Not only were children cast into the sea at the mouth of the River Ganges, but men also drowned themselves there of their own free will until in 1802 a law was passed "to prevent the practice of suicide on the island of Sagar, where, in pursuance of vows, not only were children cast into the sea to be devoured by sharks, but grown-up persons voluntarily underwent the same fate". Unlike sacrifice by burning, this custom was confined to the lower castes. People also sprang into the stream from other sacred spots on the Ganges, such as Allahabad, in order to acquire merit that would redound to their advantage in the next rebirth. A man who chose to die in this way first made the prescribed ablutions and repeated certain mantras, or prayers. He then jumped from a boat, or waded out of his depth, with earthen vessels tied to his limbs, which dragged him down when they filled with water; it was an especially good sign if a crocodile carried off the victim before he drowned.

There is an island in the Narbada River in the Central Provinces where annually, until 1824, devotees threw themselves onto some rocks which were thought to be the abode of Kal Bharaiva, consort of the goddess Kali, who fed on human flesh. People also threw themselves from a precipice in the mountains south of Narmada, in fulfilment of vows made long before. A. B. Keith describes this strange rite; for both the perpetrators and the spectators, it was a matter not for sadness but for rejoicing. "Great concourses gathered at the place on the new moon of phalguna, the day appointed for the ceremony, and it is significant of the passion for public recognition as part of the motive of such suicides that the man meditating this fate was wont to proclaim his intention publicly, and attended by a band of musicians to promenade in the neighbouring towns collecting alms." [6] Another custom that survived into the nineteenth century was the live burial of lepers, who thereby gained the right to a proper funeral that was otherwise denied them.

British interference in all these practices was gradual, but in the end they adopted the principle of making a crime of ritual suicide and the acts then lost much of their religious character. In the early years of this century, however, Jain monks and nuns occasionally fasted to death and certainly where suttee was concerned the British were to have an uphill struggle. The word *sati*, written as *suttee* in English, in ancient Sanskrit means "a chaste woman". But the term has long been used for women so chaste that they chose death beside their husband's body, usually but not always by burning.

Widow sacrifice became so popular in India that the corrupted form of the local word for it came into general use to describe the same practice in other lands. Starting in the Stone Age, it is to be found in every continent. Pharaoh Amenhotep II (1450–1425 B.C.) was accompanied to the other world by four of his wives. In Greece the wife of Capaneus, a hero of the Legend of the Seven against Thebes, was burned with her husband. The custom was observed by the pagan Scandinavians and by the Slavs of eastern Europe. In pre-Christian Poland, as late as the tenth century A.D. spouses often died with their husbands; Arab visitors recorded that in southern Russia, if a man had three wives, the favourite one would be first strangled and then burned on the man's pyre.[7]

In Asia, suttee was not limited to India. In Bali, widows were accursed if they shirked their duty to join their husbands in the next world. For the Balinese, the very source of all evil was a witch widow called Rangda, who was believed to devour children; hence widowhood itself came to be a monstrous state.[8] Widows died with their late spouses among the New Zealand Maoris, in Fiji and in many parts of Africa. In Dahomey, in West Africa, the funeral rites of King Adanzu in 1791 claimed hundreds of victims. His many wives took poison after placing themselves in a circle round the king's body, seated according to their rank at court—whether head wives, birthday wives (those whom the king married on his natal day) or those known as "leopard wives", the youngest and prettiest of all.[9]

In China the custom of suttee is reported from an early date and it survived there even longer than in India. Large-scale burials of the living with the royal dead, dating from the Shang period (1523–1028 B.C.), have already been mentioned. Written texts support the archaeological record and show that mass burials in royal tombs had not ceased by the time of Confucius. A horrendous case concerns the death not of a king but of the daughter of Hoh Lü, monarch of Wu, who committed suicide in 510 B.C.

> She was buried outside the Chang gate, to the west of his capital. Tanks were dug, and the earth piled up; a crypt of veined stone was built and an accumulation of wood constructed therein, and gold tripods, cups of jade, silver goblets, and most precious clothes stitched with pearls were sent along with the maiden into her second life. Thereupon they played with white cranes in the shop-streets of Wu, so that the crowd followed to look at them; and then receding, they caused men and women to pass with the cranes through the gate which opened upon the road which led into the crypt. Engines, now suddenly set at work, shut the gate upon them. This slaughter of living persons to accompany the deceased was disapproved of by the denizens.[10]

In the last centuries B.C. concubines were still interred with kings, and the burial of the living with the dead was so common in China that a special character exists in Chinese script to denote self-destruction to accompany the dead and is constantly to be found in ancient and even in more modern texts.

J. de Groot states that in writings of the Han Dynasty (206 B.C.– 220 A.D.) and its immediate successors, so many cases are cited of wives and daughters killing themselves in order to follow the defunct into the next world, and they are so alike, that he finds it tedious to quote examples. Nonetheless he gives a few samples of the custom and shows that it continued into early Ming times in the fourteenth century. Madame Kao was wife of Tih-O-sien. One month after their marriage her husband died, and his widow, her arms clasped about the corpse, wailed piteously for three days. As her family was not rich the body was cremated, not buried. When the pyre was already blazing, she leapt into the flames. Her mother-in-law, however, rushed to her rescue and dragged her out. Determined to follow her husband into the underworld, Madame Kao chewed up his scarred bones and that same evening hanged herself. The first Ming Emperor died in 1398; we do not know the fate of his widow but great numbers of court ladies and concubines are stated to have followed him to the grave. There are also many cases where one suicide has led to another, as when devout wives were followed by their women slaves, who voluntarily shared their fate. Many widows ended their children's existence along with their own. Some took their own lives while holding the "soul-tablet" of their dead spouse or strangled themselves with the remains of the linen used to swathe his corpse in the temple devoted to the worship of his ancestors.

The deliberate way in which widows in China acted in their thousands indicates that such suicides were not prompted by a fit of despair or by fear of penury. If such were the case, all these acts of self-destruction would not have been faithfully put on record by historians as deeds worthy of the highest praise. That suttee was carefully premeditated is shown by the care sometimes taken not to die until all duties to the defunct had been punctiliously performed. The books extol numerous suttees who stayed alive until they had, in obedience to the laws of filial devotion, provided for their parents or their husbands' parents to the end of their days.[11] The belief was firmly held that widows and even daughters were the property of the dead man, and logic demanded their sacrifice as an act of devo-

tion to him and to the gods. A Chinese suttee widow formally invoked her ancestors before dying and prayed to them to receive her
soul; she put on her best clothes so that she would be appropriately
attired when she greeted them after death. The act was favoured by
public opinion and moralists were lavish in its praise.

The methods of self-sacrifice adopted by Chinese women were
more varied than those found in India, where immolation by fire was
the rule. The majority hanged themselves or cut their throats; but
others took poison, or leaped into a chasm. Cases have been recorded
of wives who threw themselves into burning buildings in which their
husbands or parents were trapped in order to perish with them and
of others who cast themselves into a fire that had been kindled to burn
up the chattels of the dead man. Widows could also drown themselves. De Groot tells of an instance that occurred as late as 1886
and at less than fifty paces from his own home on the Island of
Kulangsu, opposite Amoy. An employee of the office that regulated
dealings with foreigners died and his wife drowned herself in her
own well in order to join him; a few days later de Groot saw the
two coffins being loaded onto a steamer that took them away to the
man's place of birth.

At that time, barely a century ago, the most fashionable form of
Chinese suttee was death by public hanging, but the expense involved
was so great that only rich families could afford it. The date of such
events was announced by placards posted round the town. To quote
de Groot's account:

> Pending the arrival of the great day, the principal actress in
> the drama dons her finest garments and, seated in a palankeen,
> makes a round of calls on her family, friends and acquaintances,
> allowing them to regale her sumptuously. She is much con-
> gratulated by all, and extolled to the skies. By order of the
> authorities, but at the expense of the family, a platform is raised
> in due time on the chosen spot, and beautifully decorated with
> flowery canvass and lanterns. Each mandarin who arrives at
> this place with his usual escort of underlings, is received with
> the customary honours due to his dignity. Forthwith kneeling
> down, he knocks his head a few times against the ground before
> the suttee who, seated on a chair upon or near the platform in
> her choicest costume which she desires to wear in the grave and

in the Realm of Shades, receives motionlessly the highest homage ever paid in China by proxies of the Son of Heaven to commoners.

When all are assembled and tea and dainties have been served, the highest mandarin present gives the signal for the woman to ascend the platform. In a few moments she adjusts the fatal noose around her neck, and launches herself into eternity by kicking away a stool upon which she stands; the mandarins then leave, and the large crowd of spectators, attracted by the scene, disperse. A number of notables from the environs, who have arrived in palankeens to shed lustre over the heroic suicide by their presence, throng round the family to offer their congratulations, flattering them about the imperial distinctions of honour which are to be expected.[12]

Notables and mandarins were amply rewarded for their presence. For several days they were invited to festive meals, which drained the coffers of the woman's family. By honouring such scenes with their presence the authorities set their stamp of approval on the deed. Even foreign newspapers reported a case that took place in 1879 near the port of Fuh-cheuh-fuh. Sometimes such acts received formal recognition and temples were dedicated to wives and girls thus honoured. An order from the governor-general of Hukwang Province issued in 1832 lays down clearly the official nature of the rite. For, like the British in India before they had summoned up the courage to suppress suttee, the Chinese Imperial Government laid down that a permit was needed. The widow must first apply in writing to the Board of Rites; if the application was approved, the local officers were charged to pay out thirty taels of silver for a memorial gate in her honour. In practice, assent was given rather grudgingly and the mandarins were apt to turn down women's petitions to kill themselves, except those of a favoured few, mostly the families of their own colleagues.

In India suttee has a long history. It was found in the Punjab by Alexander the Great in 326 B.C. and the Greek historian Strabo also writes of a suttee of that time. The earliest instance described in an Indian text took place in 316 A.D., when one of two wives of a Hindu general was led by her brother to his funeral pyre; she is portrayed as having been "all gleeful", even when the flames licked her body.[13]

By 400 A.D. widow-burning had come into general vogue, above all in Bengal. Its progress was encouraged by the Hindu scriptures, and the Brihad-dharma Purana, written between 1200 and 1400 A.D., recommends it in glowing terms: "A devoted wife, who follows her husband in death, saves him from great sins. Oh twice-born, there is no greater exploit for woman, because by this she enjoys in heaven the company of her husband." [14] Protests were not to come until much later and by 1200 A.D. suttee was entrenched in the Hindu religion: legend even records that four wives of the god Krishna burned themselves on their husband's pyre.

Bengali literature grew even more lavish in its praise of suttee. The great sixteenth-century lawgiver of that province, Raghunandan, recommended it to every widow without reserve. He laid down exactly how the rite was to be performed: the fire was first to be applied to the funeral pyre, and only after it had blazed forth could the widow chant hymns and climb on to it. There was no question of the victim being held down with ropes, as sometimes occurred later on; the point of the rite was that she acted of her own free will. Nowhere do we find any suggestion of force being applied at this time.

The lure of eternal happiness as a reward for suttee stemmed directly from the Hindu belief that the husband was a living god; if the wife burnt herself they would be reunited in Paradise and live happily ever after. Since it was not supposed to be compulsory, families would boast of the number of suttees to their credit; sometimes, as in China, little pyramids or mounds were put up to honour them. In later times social pressures mounted and darker motives crept in; many widows thought it preferable to perish than to lead the desolate life that had become their lot. If their mother consented to be burnt, sons were relieved of the expense of keeping her and came at once into the whole estate, of which she would have had a life share. Furthermore, a widow was held to bring bad luck and was not even allowed to attend family festivals. She was still a member of her husband's family and could not return to her parents. These relatives watched her closely to see that she did not break her vows of chastity and thereby endanger the dead man's spirit. Even the servants shunned her as unlucky.

Zakiuddin Ahmed, writing of suttee in eighteenth-century Bengal, describes a typical ceremony. On the death of her husband, the widow would declare her intent of being a suttee. This done, she was dressed in her best attire and carried in a procession, accompanied by a tumultuous musical band. As a pathetic gesture of farewell to her home, she would dip her hand in red ochre and leave its imprint on the outer wall. On her way, she handed out parched paddy and other fruits that were eagerly snatched away by the crowd as relics. The pyre would normally be set on the bank of a river, preferably the Ganges; on arriving there, the woman first bathed in the stream and changed her dress. She then gave away her valuables to the presiding Brahmins and put on a new white garment. The priests rubbed lac on her feet and applied cotton dyed with lac to her hands, tying it on with red thread; a recital of prayers then followed, during which she would call on the eight Lords of Regions, the sun, the moon and the Fire God to witness her death. Lastly she walked round the pyre three times, while the Brahmins chanted hymns and verses, extolling her sacrifice. After speaking the final words of farewell she mounted the pyre. She sat down with her husband's head on her lap, and her eldest son applied the first torch. While this was going on, the thunderous noise of the crowd and the beat of drums made sure that her cries of agony could not be heard.[15]

An eye-witness account of a British officer, published in the *Calcutta Gazette* of 10th February 1735, adds some vivid details taken from his view of a suttee ceremony at Chandernagore near Calcutta. In spite of the vast crowd, he was able to approach the victim:

> I went ashore, and walked up close to the girl; she seemed about twenty-one years of age, and was standing up, decorated with flowers; pieces of silk were tied upon her wrists. Two of her children were near her, the eldest, about eight or nine years of age, was mixing up rice in a large pan, some of which, with many ceremonies, he put into his deceased father's mouth, who was laid upon his back on the pile: this was composed of straw and dry wood, and about four feet high; close round it were six bamboo stakes drove into the ground, about seven feet in height, to keep the pile from giving way too soon after the fire was lit. I asked some persons present whether bhang or opium had not been given to her; they declared not, but that the loss of her husband was the sole cause of her dejection. I however perceived from the redness of her eyes that she had been

drugged; she seemed not in the least ruffled, but surveyed the crowd with great composure, nor did the dreadful preparations appear in the smallest degree to disconcert her. The Brahmins took her down to the Ganges: she sat on the edge of the water and was bathed, while prayers were repeated. Her clothes were then taken off, and a red silk covering [a saurry] put upon her. When she returned from the river, fresh flowers were again put round her neck and arms.

At this point, the Brahmins asked the girl if her sacrifice was made of her own free choice, and whether any force had been used. She merely bowed her head and said nothing. The account continues:

She afterwards sat down, and threw several handfuls of cowries among the crowd, which were scrambled for with great avidity. She then took leave of her children and relations in a very affecting manner. The Brahmins afterwards fixed several combs in her hair and led her six or seven times round her husband's corpse. I perceived, as often as she came to his head, she bowed, and some words were repeated by those who attended her which I could not understand; she then was lifted upon the pile and laid herself down by her deceased husband, with her arms about his neck. Two people immediately passed a rope twice across the bodies and fastened it so tight to the stakes that it would have effectually prevented her from rising had she attempted.

During the final act of the drama, a great quantity of straw and wood was laid upon her, and tar thrown on top of it. The victim died a thousand deaths, since these preparations, after she was tied to the pyre, took some time to complete. She could hear the demands from people around her to bring up more fuel, and the final order to hand over the brand, with which the eldest child set fire to the straw, that was soon ablaze. Two men kept a long pole pressed against the bodies, but the heat was so intense that several people had to pour water on the heads of these two men.[16]

There were many variants of suttee rites, although the burning of a wife on the same pyre as her husband remained the standard ritual. Another form existed for use in cases where the man died

Pharaoh Narmer inspects the bodies of slain prisoners with their heads between their feet. (Plaster cast, *British Museum*)

Chronos swallowing his children (Francesco Goya, *Prado, Madrid*)

The Assyrian king Assurbanipal holds up the head of a decapitated Elamite
prisoner. (Relief, *British Museum*)

Abraham prepares to sacrifice Isaac. (Mosaic, *Palatine Chapel, Palermo*)

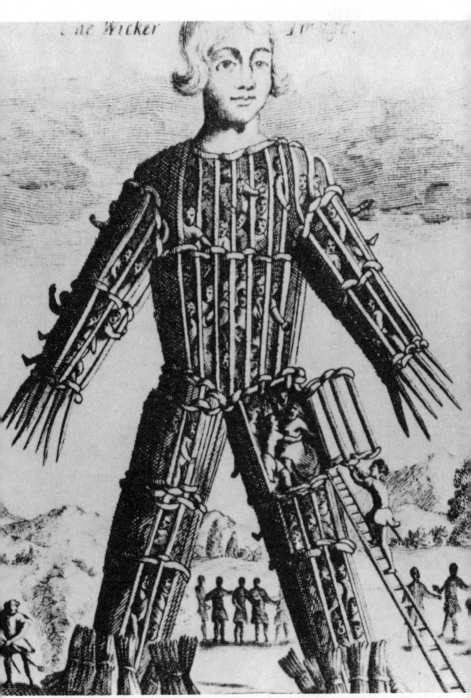

A Druid wicker image filled with victims about to be burned (Engraving from *Britannia Antiqua Illustrated*, Aylett Sammes, 1676)

Ritual strangling by Thugs (From *Collections on Thuggee*, Captain James Paton, *British Museum*)

Chinnamasta, the goddess "whose head has been cut off," a form of the mother goddess in Bengal, holds her head in one hand and a Bengali curved sword in the other. (Courtesy of Dr. Volker Moeller, *Berlin*)

An eleventh-century skeletal reproduction of Camunda, another form of the mother goddess. The ten-armed figure bears the same regalia of death as the goddess Kali. (Eleventh century, Indian, *Museum für Indische Kunst, West Berlin*)

Tibetan gods eating human hearts (*Museum für Völkerkunde, Hamburg*)

Tree sacrifice (above) and cannibalism (below) in the Andaman Islands
(From *Le Livre des Merveilles; Bibliothèque Nationale, Paris*)

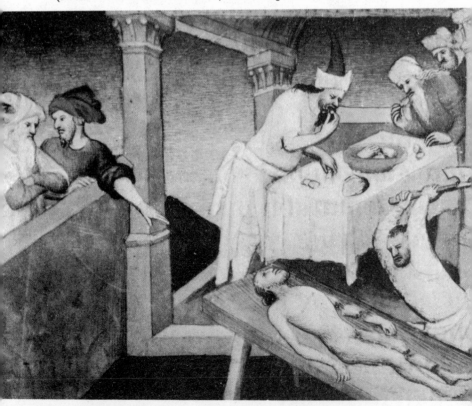

Rangda, the Witch Widow of Bali, triumphs over a victim. (*British Museum*)

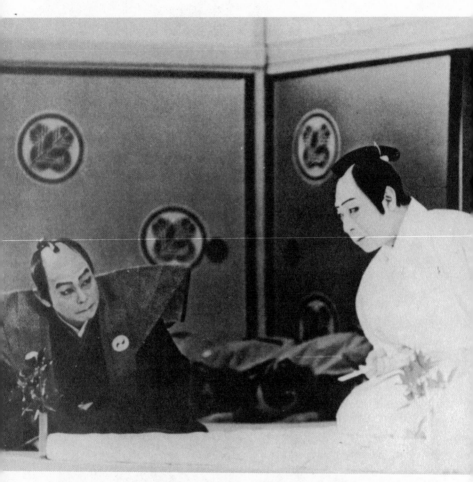

A scene from the famous Kabuki play *Kanadehon Chushingura* or *The Forty-seven Ronin*, showing a Daimyo committing hara-kiri upon the orders of his liege Shogun (Courtesy of the *Tsubouchi Memorial Theatre Museum, Wasada University, Tokyo*)

when away from home or where the wife was pregnant at the time of death. She would then be burnt on her own, holding some chattel of her spouse, such as his turban. A few widows faced the flames as many as fifteen years after their husband's demise. Other misguided wives dreamed that their spouse had met his death while away on a journey and burnt themselves a few days before his safe return. At times not only legitimate wives but also concubines who had lived with the dead man for some time and even male slaves perished in the flames. At others a mother was burned with her son. Women of the weaver caste were occasionally buried alive with their husbands. In such cases the grave was usually dug by the side of a river. The widow went down into the pit containing the corpse and the eldest son threw earth upon her until she vanished from view. Suttee was open to females of all ages; in 1820, a four-year-old girl was burned with her husband; on the other hand, in 1825 a hundred-year-old woman staggered onto her consort's pyre in Midrapore, north of Calcutta.

As the custom tightened its grip in the late eighteenth and early nineteenth century, particularly in Bengal, the abuses grew greater. Some small children were left as orphans, while others were themselves burnt, as child brides, tied to the putrefying corpse of an elderly spouse. From being a single sacrifice, suttee became at times a massacre. This was because parents sought to gain status by a marriage alliance with the high-caste Kulins of Bengal. Males of the Kulin families made a profession of marriage, selling themselves to a number of girls and women. Few of these wives ever lived with the man, or even set eyes on him after the wedding until the dread day when the order would come and they would be hauled on to his funeral pyre. In 1799, for example, thirty-seven women were burnt alive with the remains of a Brahmin at Nadiya, near Calcutta. By the time the fire was first lit, only three of the women had been found but it was kept burning for three days, while relays of widows were dragged in from a distance.[17]

While suttee was supposed to be voluntary, this characteristic lost its vigour as the custom took ever stronger hold. In Bengal by this time it was usual to bind the victim with ropes, and her relatives, together with amused spectators, stood by to push her back, in case her bonds burnt and, scorched and maimed, she struggled free. The poles used for the purpose were of green bamboo that resisted the fire. Once on a dark night an unfortunate victim did escape from the pyre and hid in the bushes, but she was soon caught and her son threw her back on the blaze; on another occasion, when a suttee struggled free, her irate father called on those present, who struck her down with the bamboo poles. The British reaction to such excesses was at first one of apathy, but in the end their conscience was stirred. The East India Company by the early nineteenth century ruled most of India from its capital of Calcutta in Bengal, the very centre of the suttee cult, though it had spread all over the subcontinent and in particular to the big cities of Bombay and Madras.

The Marquis of Wellesley, an outstanding governor-general and the Duke of Wellington's brother, wanted to prohibit suttee but was warned that any ban might spark off a mutiny in the native army and so let the matter drop. Nothing was then done until 1812, when the question was referred to the Supreme Court. As a result, in 1813 orders were issued that, far from stopping suttee, gave it legal status. A widow could no longer be burned without a government permit; once the right forms had been completed and permission given, an Indian police officer then had to attend the burning and certify that the victim was not drugged, that she was not a minor nor pregnant, and that she acted of her own free will. In this respect, as we have seen, the British were merely taking a leaf out of the book of the former Muslim rulers of India, who also decreed a system of licenses for the rite. Shortly after this, another British regulation forbade the practice of suttee in the centre of Calcutta, confining it to the suburbs only.

Suttee, however, continued to increase and such measures of control merely ensured that meticulous records were kept of the annual suttee count in the best Whitehall fashion. Details were also kept of the number of widows buried alive, which in 1817 reached a total of nine. Between 1815 and 1828, 8134 widows were burnt in Bengal alone, including 511 in the city of Calcutta. The statistics listed the victims and their spouses according to their age and rank; in 1825, in the Hughly district, 26 of the deceased husbands were rich, 52 in middling circumstances, and 26 were poor; of the 575 widows who committed suttee in Bengal in 1823, 32 were below twenty, while 188 were over sixty years old.[18]

In isolated cases, British officers had intervened to prevent or interrupt a suttee. As early as 1679, the famous Job Charnok, one of the founders of Calcutta, had snatched a beautiful Brahmin lady from the pyre of her husband and married her; they lived happily together for the next fourteen years. But this unusual incident had no sequel until 1806. Charles Harding of the British Civil Service, who was stationed in Benares, was faced with the acute problem of a Brahmin woman who had been goaded into burning herself with a relic of her husband, twelve months after his death. The pile was raised two miles upstream from Benares, on the opposite side of the Ganges. She was not well secured and as soon as she felt the fire, jumped off and plunged into the river. The people ran after her along the bank, but the current drove her towards Benares, whence a police boat put off and took her in.

> She was almost dead with the fright and the water, in which she had been kept afloat by her clothes. She was taken to Harding; but the whole city of Benares was in an uproar at the rescue of a Brahman's widow from the funeral pyre. Thousands surrounded his house, and his court was filled with the principal men of the city, imploring him to surrender the woman; and among the rest was the poor woman's father, who declared he could not support his daughter; that she had, therefore, better be burned, as her husband's family would no longer receive her. The uproar was alarming to a young man, who felt all the responsibility upon himself in such a city as Benares, with a population of three hundred thousand people, so prone to popular insurrections. At last the thought struck him suddenly: "The sacrifice was manifestly unacceptable to their God—that the sacred river, as such, had rejected her; she had, without being able to swim, floated down two miles upon its bosom, in the face of an immense multitude; and it was clear that she had been rejected. Had she been an acceptable sacrifice, after the fire had touched her, the river would have received her". This satisfied the whole crowd. The father said that, in face of this unanswerable argument, he would receive his daughter; and the whole crowd dispersed satisfied.[19]

Not until 1829 was widow-burning officially forbidden in Bengal on the orders of Lord William Bentinck, the first governor-general who was willing to risk a crisis on this score. But the change came about slowly, and suttee lingered on in the states ruled by Rajahs and subject only to indirect control by the British. In many such states a prince's success in this life was judged by the quantity of women burnt alive at his funeral. The number of empty guns fired when he went to visit the governor-general was a tame substitute. Matters came to a head in 1833 after British public opinion had been shocked by the funeral arrangements of the Rajah of Idar, whose body was burnt together with seven wives, two concubines, five female slaves and a personal man-servant. The British Resident for both Idar and Ahmadnagar was determined to stop another slaughter when he heard that the Rajah of Ahmadnagar had also died. But only after five widows had already been burned, and some fighting had ensued, did he send for artillery reinforcements and extract a promise from the Rajah's son to renounce suttee forever both for himself and his children.

The Japanese form of ritual suicide, highly dramatized in Kabuki plays, has become world-famous. In the West it is called hara-kiri (meaning literally "cutting of the stomach"), a word of which any Samurai warrior would have been ashamed; the correct term is *seppuku*. For the Japanese, seppuku has a special mystery since it is tied to the ancient notion that the mind exists in the stomach. Therefore in committing seppuku a man is purging his sins and dying at the same time. But while Japan is noted in this respect, a kind of ritual suicide belt runs across northern Asia, of which Japan merely forms a part. Certain tribes of east Siberia were strangely addicted to killing themselves; of these, for instance, the Samoyeds held that self-slaughter was "an act pleasing to god", [20] and the Chuckchis, who live on the eastern tip of Siberia, facing Alaska, and whose religion is very primitive, were also willing suicide victims in case of national emergency, such as a plague.

Shintoism, which later brought forth hara-kiri, flourished long before the Chinese brought Buddhism to Japan in the sixth century A.D. This early Shintoism was based on ancestor and nature worship. Over a thousand years later, after it had suffered a long eclipse due to the triumph of Buddhism, Shintoism staged a revival. Its creed was founded on two basic principles: mystical devotion to the Emperor, and the pursuit of high moral values and virtues, handed down by the departed ancestors. The two principles were intertwined, since these moral values depended on the cult of the Emperor, who was not only God's representative on earth, but was placed, along with his family, half way between God and man. Shinto traditions further demanded that the Emperor should hardly ever appear in public; of those privileged even to hear his voice, few could understand him since he spoke to them in a sacred form of ancient Japanese.

The unrelenting pursuit of virtue led to a disdain for this life and a conviction that if a man were brave and good, he would join his ancestors in Paradise. During this great Shinto revival the Samurai evolved, a tightly organized society established by the Tokugawa Shoguns, who first came to power in the early seventeenth century and then governed Japan until 1867. Their rule is known as the Edo period, named after their capital, the present-day Tokyo. The Samurai ethic rested on the twin pillars of Shintoism: Emperor-worship and a rigid code of honour; this code came to be known as Bushido (the Way of the Warrior). The essence of Bushido was the fervent resolve of the young warrior to sacrifice his life, but only after he had killed as many of the enemy as possible. The Samurai, distinguished by his hair, which was shaven in front and with a top-knot behind, and by his kimono, which was marked with the clan badge, devoted his entire life to the art of fighting. At all times he carried two swords, one long and one short. These swords had a special mystique; the large two-handed weapon served for legendary exploits, while the short one was used to decapitate the fallen enemy —perhaps a relic of ancient headhunting. In the last resort, the short sword was also used for self-destruction, and every Samurai was taught how to commit hara-kiri, as part of his basic training. This gruesome form of auto-sacrifice was first practised in the eighth century A.D., but later became intrinsic to the Samurai code, based as it was on Shintoism. A Samurai was obliged to perform hara-kiri to avoid capture or as a penalty for any kind of dishonour.

In its original form, the act of hara-kiri required tremendous will-power since it involved the making of two inter-crossing cuts in the stomach and then a sharp final thrust into the vitals. In practice, the self-chosen victim often failed to cut deep enough and was finished off by a faithful companion, who, as part of the ritual, stood at his side and, after the stomach had been rent open, beheaded him with one deft stroke of the longer sword. In the Edo period, the short sword was only stabbed once into the left side of the stomach and drawn across to the right; again the cut was usually too superficial and the trusted friend ended the man's agony by cutting off his head. At that time warriors were forced to commit hara-kiri as a punishment for deeds thought to be shameful. However, for the Japanese, the principle was the same: as long as the proper ritual was observed, the deed was in every sense a religious sacrifice, whether self-inflicted or imposed from above, and the same word served for both varieties.

Hara-kiri survived in the modern Japan that came into being with the advent of foreigners and fall of the Edo regime in 1867. Although the Samurai were abolished as a relic of feudalism, ritual suicide was still carried out on a number of occasions. The Samurai spirit lived on and the Kamikazi suicide pilots of World War II—as we shall see in Chapter XI—were also imbued with the Bushido code. Sir Ernest Satow, a British diplomat, was an eye-witness of a hara-kiri ceremony in 1864. A Japanese officer, Taki Zenzaburo, was obliged to take his life because he had incurred dishonour by firing on the recently-arrived foreigners. One member of each legation was taken to a Buddhist temple to witness the ceremony and the envoys were even given the chance to put questions to the victim. He entered the principal hall of the temple from the left side, accompanied by his two kai-shaku, or best men, and followed by two others; he squatted on the dais, which was covered in a red cloth, was given the sword on a wooden stand and then requested all present to be witnesses.

He next divested himself of his upper garments by withdrawing his arms from the sleeves, the long ends of which he tucked under his legs to prevent his body from falling backward. The body was thus quite naked to below the navel. He then took the dirk in his right hand, grasping it just close to the point, and after stroking down the front of his chest and belly inserted the point as far down as possible and drew it across to the right side, the position of his clothes still fastened by the girth preventing our seeing the wound. Having done this he with great deliberation bent his body forward, throwing the head back so as to render the neck a fair object for the sword. The one kaishaku who had accompanied him round the two rows of witnesses to make his bows to them, had been crouching on his left hand a little behind him with drawn sword poised in the air from the moment the operation commenced. He now sprang up suddenly and delivered a blow the sound of which was like thunder. The head dropped down on to the matted floor.[21]

Taki had obviously committed the later and slightly less atrocious kind of hara-kiri. In other accounts of such rites, gruesome details are not lacking, including cases where men stuck their fists into the stomach opening and tore out their own entrails.

In one earlier form, a man who committed hara-kiri would pull out his sword after cutting his bowels and then apply it to the right side of the neck to sever the artery. This method became rarer, but was used once more in 1912 when Emperor Meiji died. General Count Nogi, hero of the capture of Port Arthur in the Russo-Japanese war, resolved that he would follow his master to the grave; not only did he first make the diagonal stomach cut, but he then thrust the sword into the jugular artery, a feat that required unflinching courage. His wife followed her husband's example and died by putting a sword through her throat, in the manner laid down for Samurai women. After the triumphant end of the war against China in 1895, a number of people committed hara-kiri, not to celebrate but to protest that the peace terms were too lenient and therefore dishonourable. The last hara-kiri wave came after the surrender of 1945, but those who took their lives then were a fairly small group, mainly confined to senior officers.

Self-slaughter for religious reasons was, if anything, an Indian and Japanese speciality, but it was not confined to Asia. Ritual suicide was not uncommon in Hawaii when a king died, and even the Druids approved of it: "There is another world, and they who kill themselves to accompany their friends thither, will live there with them".[22] Whatever the abuses of latter-day Indian suttee, suicide was meant to be a voluntary act, dependent on the consent of the victim. The deed—whether hara-kiri or suttee—involved a cruel death, and the will to undergo such an ordeal sprang directly from an unshakable faith in rebirth. For those who lack that faith, the spirit of such acts is hard to fathom. It is obvious, however, that ritual self-slaughter is the very opposite of the present-day non-ritual suicide, in which the very last aim to be pursued is an immediate return to earth.

As heirs to the Christian tradition, we instinctively shrink from suicide. But the ban did not exist among early Christians, and it was only in 533 A.D., under the influence of St Augustine, that the Council of Orleans denied funeral rites to anyone who killed himself while accused of a crime. Thirty years later funeral rites were refused to all suicides, who then came to be known as "martyrs of Satan". In contrast, the early Christian attitude towards death and self-slaughter was closer to that of the Romans, for whom death itself was not important; what mattered was to die in a dignified and proper manner. But the Christians went further and even courted a violent end. Roman persecution of Christians was at times half-hearted; many judges would have been only too happy to let them escape after being condemned, but they refused to do so and thousands of men, women and children were beheaded, burned alive, flung from cliffs, roasted on gridirons and hacked to pieces, all more or less because they chose to be. One bored Roman proconsul in Africa, surrounded by a mob of Christians baying for martyrdom, shouted to them: "Go hang and drown yourselves and ease the magistrate". [23] The Romans may have thrown them to the lions partly for sport but little expected to see the victims greeting their ravagers as the instruments of glory and salvation. Typical of this attitude was St Ignacio, who said that he wished the lions were even more cruel, and declared that if they did not attack him, he would provoke them to do so.

For these early Christians death was a deliverance eagerly awaited. Why go on living when divided from eternal bliss by a single sword-thrust? The early fathers spoke in raptures of the joys that lay in store for martyrs and offered incentives to what was, in effect, ritual suicide. Like the pagan Vikings, the Christians were given a passport to Paradise in return for a violent death. The only difference was that they were passive victims, not warriors.

The urge to end one's life as a martyr became more desperate with the rise of the Donatist sect in the fourth century; their acts drew from St Augustine the remark: "To kill themselves out of respect for martyrdom is their daily sport". Edward Gibbon has elegantly described their weird death-wish.

> The rage of the Donatists was enflamed by a phrensy of a very extraordinary kind: and which, if it really prevailed among them in so extravagant a degree, cannot surely be paralleled in any country or in any age. Many of these fanatics were possessed with the horror of life and the desire of martyrdom; and

they deemed it of little moment by what means or by what hands they perished, if their conduct was sanctified by the intention of devoting themselves to the glory of the true faith and the hope of eternal happiness. Sometimes they rudely disturbed the festivals and profaned the temples of paganism with the design of exciting the most zealous of the idolators to ravage the insulated honour of their Gods. They sometimes forced their way into the courts of justice and compelled the affrightened judge to give orders for their execution. They frequently stopped travellers on the public highways and obliged them to inflict the stroke of martyrdom by promise of a reward, if they consented—and by the threat of instant death, if they refused to grant so very singular a favour. When they were disappointed of every other resource, they announced the day on which, in the presence of their friends and brethren, they should cast themselves headlong from some lofty rock; and many precipices were shown, which had acquired fame by the number of these religious suicides.

The Donatist argument was impeccable: the fuller the life, the greater the temptation to sin, and the only sure way to heaven was to die as soon as possible. But St Augustine saw the flaw in the theory: if suicide was allowed as a way to avoid sin, then it became the logical course for all fresh from baptism, and there would soon be no more Christians left alive. Hence their frenzied search for martyrdom forced the church to declare the Donatists heretics. Today the ban on suicide remains, though without the harsh penalties of the past and the denial of a proper burial. Barely a century ago, anyone who made an unsuccessful attempt to commit suicide in England was hanged after he had recovered.

7

Cities of Blood

On a Saturday evening in January 1948, Mochesela Khoto sat in a hut drinking beer with Dane Rachakana and a number of other people who had come to a wedding feast in Moloi Village in Basutoland (now known as Lesotho, an independent republic within the territory of South Africa). In the course of the party, the Chieftainess of Mochesela's ward arrived with a number of her men and told certain of those present: "I want you to kill Mochesela for me, because I want to make a medicine horn which I will use to get a place for my son. Anyone who disobeys this order will be killed."

One of the Chieftainess' men drew Dane Rachakana aside, explained the situation and told him that all was ready for the execution of the plan. Dane then got up and said to Mochesela: "Cousin, let us go outside for a while." The latter followed to where sixteen men were waiting for them, together with the Chieftainess and two of her women attendants. She greeted Dane, reminded him that he already had her orders, and told the men to seize Mochesela. As one of them caught hold of him, he cried out, "My father Pholo, are you going to kill me?" and, when Pholo did not reply, continued, "Let me free and I will give you my black ox." "I am not your father, and I want you, not your ox", replied Pholo. Mochesela started to shout, but they gagged him and marched him off from the village, while Dane threw stones to drive away some boys who had been attracted by the shouting. When they reached an isolated spot, they stripped Mochesela and held him naked on the ground. An oil lamp was produced, and by its light they cut small circular pieces of flesh from his body with a knife. Pholo took a portion from the calf of his left leg, another man cut the biceps of his right arm, a third carved a piece from his right breast and a fourth from his groin. These morsels were laid on a white cloth in front of Mosala, the native doctor who was going to make the medicine, and one of the men held a billy-can to collect the blood from these and other wounds made later. Dane then took the knife and with it removed the entire face of Mochesela; he cut right down to the bone, beginning at the forehead and ending at the throat, the tongue and the eyes. The victim died only when his throat was cut. The Chieftainess, who had watched the proceedings, graciously thanked those present and gave orders for the disposal of the body.[1]

This summary of evidence for the British Crown in High Court criminal case 27/48, Rex versus Mamakhabana and fifteen others, is a fair example of a form of ritual killing that had reached alarming proportions in the colony. The sole purpose of the rite was to make a medicine called *diretlo*; this could only be done by cutting flesh in the prescribed manner from the body of a living person; the victim had to be a member of the tribe, who had been designated by the witch doctor as having those magic qualities needed to produce a potent mix. Often he picked a relative of some of the participants in the rite; exact details of the choice of victim were never explained, since those questioned at the trials simply said that they didn't know.

To make diretlo, the flesh not only had to be cut from the body of a living man; he had to die afterwards and his corpse be hidden for a time and then left exposed in a remote spot. The manner of killing was also carefully laid down. In the various trials, the uses to which diretlo was put do not emerge very clearly. Strictly speaking, it was more charm than medicine; to cure illness—or to make others sick—was only one of several of the purposes which it served. In case 27/48 it came to light that the Chieftainess was not really seeking to obtain a "place", or appointment, for her son; on the contrary, she was out to prevent his being named as chief of the Paete ward since she would then have lost her own position as its regent. Case 42 of 1948 concerned another killing to make a second batch of diretlo, purely to act as an antidote to the earlier charm.

Diretlo had formerly been called ditlo, and in the nineteenth century had only been made from the flesh of strangers, especially war captives. The authorities, rightly or wrongly, believed that even the making of ditlo was not an ancient custom, but rather the by-product of the internecine tribal warfare which plagued the region in the early nineteenth century and which created a constant need for protective potions, made out of enemy prisoners. Diretlo, the substitute for ditlo, came into being when these wars stopped and the supply of captives dried up. The 1949 report attributes the brisk demand for the product to "the increased stress and anxiety of modern living", though life in tribal Basutoland was in most respects the very opposite of "modern". Ditlo and its successor diretlo were made in the same way; pieces of flesh were burnt with herbs and other ingredients over a fire until they became a charred mass, which was pounded and mixed with animal or human fat to form a black ointment. This ointment was kept in a small horn from a buck or a goat, called a lenaka, a name at times used for the medicine itself. These lenakas had once been the property of powerful chiefs. One, known as the Horn of Mosesh, was the national fetish of the Basutos; its contents had been used to fortify warriors before battle, to protect the chief's village and to ward off the spells of enemy magicians.

The Basuto trials are remarkable because, unlike many earlier reports of African sacrifice, they describe what took place in the most minute detail, and bear witness to measurable changes in ritual. The ending of tribal warfare did not kill the demand for a charm made of human flesh; it merely debased its uses. No longer an arm to bring victory in war, it became a device to promote personal intrigues. In place of enemy warriors, the victims were now members of the tribe, a rare feature of older forms of sacrifice, which claimed only aliens, or slaves, who had no tribal rights. The writer of the official report, perhaps judging it wise to play down the scale of the killings, took the view that they were not wholly "ritual" and hence, by implication, were not a true human sacrifice. But the choice of victim, the mode of slaying and the disposal of the body show that elaborate ritual accompanied every stage in the making of diretlo. It was not really thought to heal sickness by its physical properties; benefits, such as the obtaining of a chieftainship, were sought that depended on the magical power of the tribal gods and those who died in the process were victims of those gods. A parallel case may be cited. The belief in the efficacy of human flesh and blood in southern Africa was not confined to Basutoland. In Swaziland in the 1930s a number of similar killings had taken place where the flesh was made into a charm which not only benefited persons of high rank, but was also calculated to induce the gods to provide good crops.

In the days of tribal warfare, the making of courage-boosting charms from captives' flesh was very widespread. Diretlo in its original form, ditlo, was an elaborate version of the more direct practice of devouring an enemy warrior's heart to imbibe his valour, current, for instance, among the Ashantis of present-day Ghana. Their approach was pragmatical and the stimulant was reserved for those faint-hearted braves who had not yet killed an enemy. The Dyaks of Borneo too, according to official reports from the beginning of the century, still ate raw hearts of enemy captives to instil courage. In certain parts of Africa, enemy hearts were pulverized to make a potion, and this method of preparing medicines from parts of the body also existed outside Africa. Tribes on the River Orinoco in Venezuela would hang corpses for a week in a hammock; with the fluid that dropped to earth they prepared a potent magic drink, reserved for medicine men. Probably the most dramatic example of its kind, if not the most factual, concerns a king of Arakan in Burmah, whose life was wholly dedicated to Buddha's Eightfold Path of Compassion. He ascended his throne in 1634, but his peace of mind was shattered by a prophecy that he would die soon after his coronation. The time came when he could put off this ceremony no longer; a seer then told him that he could be saved—and also made invisible at will—if he drank an elixir concocted from two thousand hearts of white doves and six thousand human hearts. The story has a sad ending; the magic did not work and the king died soon after his coronation, leaving a greatly depopulated kingdom to his heir.[2]

Perhaps the most singular rituals for making medicines out of human entrails are to be found in the Leopard Societies of Sierra Leone, on the coast of West Africa. These also survived until recently and court proceedings revealed eye-witness accounts of the events.[3]

As long ago as 1607 a visitor to Sierra Leone wrote of fierce man-eating tribes who lived in the interior of the country and dressed as leopards, though other travellers two hundred years later heard nothing of them. In 1807 coastal Sierra Leone became a British colony, but the Leopard Societies acted with such secrecy that only in 1891 did the British first gain an inkling of what was going on inland. It was hard for them to find out much more, since these activities were hidden not merely from the eyes of Europeans but also from other Africans. However, news began to filter in of numbers of people being burnt to death, which came as a severe shock to the colonial government. Ritual killing was known to exist but no one realized that it had reached such proportions. The first precise reports arrived in the form of complaints by prospective victims in the vicinity of the town of Bogo not about the bizarre leopard rites that later caused such a commotion, but about a "game" called Tongo Play; as a finale to one such "game", no less than eighty people were thrown onto a huge fire and burnt to death. The official reaction took the form of a government proclamation forbidding Tongo Play "whereby people had been unlawfully burnt to death". Tongo players were to quit the colony (the order did not specify where these sportsmen were to go).

The authorities then became aware of an even more sinister kind of killing in the depths of the forest. It was the work of a secret organization that was to become notorious as the Human Leopard Society. To combat this extraordinary state of affairs, the government drafted drastic laws. A bill entitled "The Human Leopard Ordnance" was passed by the legislature as Ordnance No. 15 of 1895. Having stated in its preamble that "whereas many murders have been committed by men so dressed as to resemble leopards and armed with a three-pronged knife commonly known as a leopard knife", the bill made it a crime for anyone to have in his possession a leopard skin shaped so as to make a man wearing it resemble a leopard, a three-pronged knife and a native medicine known as "Borfima". The police were given powers to search for such trophies without a warrant.

The human leopards created a veritable furore throughout the colony and even its boundaries had to be changed. To combat the evil, the government established a protectorate over the hinterland, which had previously been left to its own devices. The chiefs of inland tribes were henceforth subject to draconian penalties if they failed to report Leopard Society activities. But the human leopards showed scant respect for the might of Britannia; the situation even worsened and in 1901 a Human Alligator Society was discovered, working hand in glove with the leopards. A new ordnance duly added alligator skins shaped to fit the human form to the list of proscribed menswear.

By 1903 it had become clear that many chiefs were themselves involved up to the hilt. In the ensuing crackdown, four hundred people were arrested, some of them highly placed, though few were brought to trial at this stage for lack of evidence. Then in 1907 the government strengthened its hand by bringing in two more bills. In introducing the first of these, the Attorney General of Sierra Leone warned the legislature that the Leopard Societies had previously confined their activities to lesser people, but had now become so powerful that even the "paramount chiefs have been drawn into it and are now the leaders". [4] The second anti-leopard bill added yet another list of forbidden regalia: a dress made of baboon skin, commonly used by members of an unlawful society; a whistle commonly used for calling together members of an unlawful society; an iron needle commonly used for branding members of an unlawful society. A special court of three European judges was also set up to try offenders; their sentence had to be unanimous. Backed by these measures, the government succeeded in bringing the Leopard Societies' activities to a virtual halt within a few years. By 1912, seventeen cases had come before the court; 187 people were charged with murder, of whom 87 were sentenced to death. To drive the lesson home, many of these were executed at the scene of their bizarre crime.

To obtain such positive results, the court had to overcome peculiar obstacles. The object of the Leopard killings was to obtain Borfima, a special medicine normally kept in a tight leather package. Its ingredients included the white of an egg, the blood of a cock and a few grains of rice, but the key elements were human fat and blood, only to be obtained by a strange and elaborate ritual. Borfima, made in the prescribed manner, was a potent instrument in the hands of its owner and could help him become rich and powerful. It had, moreover, a unique quality: it was the ideal protective charm for anyone who had the ill luck to be hauled before the white man's court, with its outlandish notions of justice. Administered with due ceremony, an oath upon Borfima was also a sacred pledge and bound a man to absolute secrecy. Because most witnesses had sworn a solemn oath on Borfima, the court, therefore, could not get anyone to talk. The only way around this problem was for the court interpreter to make his own invincible medicine, compounded every Monday out of salt, pepper and ashes, mixed with water. A spoonful was given to each witness who then took his oath on the court's medicine: "I swear by this medicine to speak the truth, the whole truth, and nothing but the truth. Should I tell a lie, if I go to the farm may snake bite me, if I travel by canoe may the canoe sink, and may my belly be swollen. I swear by my liver, my lungs, my kidneys, and my heart that, should I tell a lie, may I never be saved, but may I die suddenly." [5]

The manner in which the Leopard Societies set about their business is well described in Garry Hogg's book on cannibalism. The victim had to be a freeborn girl (as opposed to a slave or captive) and over fourteen years old. Preferably she should be the eldest child of the family who provided her. Initiation into a Leopard Society was a complicated ceremony, and the initiate had to produce a sacrificial victim from his own or his wife's family. In later years a man or boy could be used, but a girl was still preferred.

As among the Thugs in India, the first killing by a novice was a dramatic step. Two members of the society would accompany him on his quest for the appropriate offering. Notionally they had to "beg" a family to provide a victim but the request was not one that left scope for argument. The "beggars" would corner the mother or father of their chosen candidate in a lonely place and stress the need to make the sacrifice for the wellbeing of the tribe. Tradition demanded that the parent or guardian should begin by turning down the demand but after this symbolic gesture matters were soon settled, since the family knew that they had no choice and might themselves figure on the leopards' list if they baulked. When there was no novice to find a candidate, the choice was made in the same way by whomever the society members named for the task. He normally picked one of his relatives.

Once the choice had been made, the human leopards retired to the forest and all through the night would roam about, imitating the animal's roar. This roaring had to be kept up during the whole period from the naming of the victim until her death; during the actual sacrifice, she too was expected to roar. The man who did the killing bore the special name of Yongolado. The leopard-skin used by this slayer was always kept by the chief of the society and was handed under cover of darkness from one member to another until, rolled round the special knives, it at last came into the hands of the Yongolado. Other members of the society present at the kill also wore some part of the insignia of the leopard and had their own leopard knives. The victim had by this time been sent forth on her eerie quest, walking alone on a particular track leading to the forest, as a prelude to capture and sacrifice, which had to take place in darkness. The leopard men kept watch on both sides of the track for the girl's approach, lurking behind the dense wall of creepers that flourish in this humid jungle.

After the victim had passed the first leopard men, the silence would be shattered by a deep-throated growl. The Yongolado leaped from his hiding place, sprang onto the girl's back like a leopard, and with a lightning movement tore open her throat. His companions then closed in and bore her off into the depths of the undergrowth. Meanwhile, one of the party carried out the curious rite of simulating as many leopard tracks as possible, in the form of a number of trails running into the trees in opposite directions to the route of the sacrificers. For this purpose, he was shod with pieces of wood, carved to imitate the claw marks of a real leopard. At an agreed point in a clearing the Yongolado threw the girl's body on the ground. The head was hacked off and the liver, heart and entrails torn out. The liver was examined for signs that the body would make a good brew of Borfima. The corpse was then divided into four quarters, which were carved up, wrapped in banana leaves and given to all present. The face was cut away so that the uninitiated could never recognize the remains.

This was the most common form of the ritual, but it differed from place to place. In one grisly variant, the girl was not killed immediately but forced to sit on the ground beneath a tree. The chief who presided, and for the welfare of whose people the sacrifice had been devised, then came forward and sat astride her shoulders. Those present laid a hand either on the chief or on the victim herself so as to make a chain of contact. After this the Yongolado, praying that good medicine should come from the offering, gashed the girl's throat. Next the body was opened and other participants tore out the intestines. The victim occasionally survived such mutilations; alive or dead, she was then taken to a platform outside the chief's hut and left there, tethered to a post. The body was taken back to the jungle and cut up the following morning. The chief received the hands and feet; a small portion of the flesh was given to the mother and father of the victim.

In the trials of the human leopards, yet further variants to the standard practice were described, such as those relating to the Kabati case. In 1911 a leopard sacrifice had taken place at the village of Kabati; only three of those involved were charged, the paramount chief (known as the Mahawa) and two sub-chiefs (known as Mahawuris). One of these sub-chiefs had been named to preside over a human leopard ceremony at a meeting of the local branch of the society held in Kabati. This meant that he had to provide the victim, so he proposed his niece Mini, whom he stated to have a devil in her. Then, after working out the detailed arrangements for the sacrifice, the meeting broke up. Mini was duly set walking on a path into the jungle and dispatched in the prescribed manner. The paramount chief received the scalp, together with finger- and toe-nails, while the heart was set aside for an important member of the society who did not want to be present in person. The blood was taken off to make Borfima and the body was cut up and mostly eaten on the spot, part cooked and part raw. The matter came to light because some non-members of the society accused the sub-chief of having sacrificed his niece and a search party discovered her scattered bones in the forest. Witnesses admitted that the paramount chief had been present; his quarters were searched, and many tell-tale sets of human finger- and toe-nails were found.[6]

The Sierra Leone trials provide copious details about a form of human sacrifice that survived well into this century. They tell us little. however, of the gods in whose honour the acts were performed, since the courts were not concerned with this. Indeed, to put it in more general terms, a lack of knowledge of African religions has distorted the picture of human sacrifice in that continent, and of the attendant cannibalism, confined to certain places. For human sacrifice and its offshoot ritual cannibalism are by their very nature religious acts, and can only be understood in the light of the cults that they are designed to serve. For people who ignored these cults, African sacrifices were in effect murders.

Though most accounts say not a word about this, the very act of behaving like a beast of prey, whether wolf, bear or leopard, has a universal religious meaning. It betokens that one has ceased to be a mere mortal, that one has become a magic force incarnate, and in some sort a god. For primitive peoples, the beast of prey often represents a mode of existence superior to man. Moreover, the leopard skin was a form of communion with the divine in another sense, for in the sweltering jungle the garb made its wearer extraordinarily hot, and excessive body heat is a characteristic mark of magicians, shamans, mystics and even healers all over the world and proclaims the attainment of a godlike state of being. Thus the bare narrative of human leopard activities in a British court is a façade behind which lies concealed a complex web of religious beliefs and superstitions that neither the court nor its witnesses sought to bring to light. As in the case of the Basutoland killings, the suspicion is often voiced that the customs may be fairly "new". But they conform to rites that are both ancient and universal; in America the earliest civilizations of Mexico and Peru had as their main deity a local version of the leopard; in pre-Conquest Mexico, warriors who sought captives for sacrifice used to dress as ocelots.

Accordingly, the elaborate rituals of Sierra Leone, far from being a kind of savage charade, were an essentially religious act, even if we are only dimly aware of the beliefs that lay behind them. In his classic study of African religion, E. G. Parrinder justly remarks that African religion has been despised because it has no mighty stone temples as relics of its former status. But as he also points out, their absence indicates no lack of respect for the gods. There is little soft stone in much of Africa, and mosques and churches are today built of clay. African temples were also made of perishable clay and were usually small and crude, because acts of worship often took place in the open air. Most Africans in one form or another worshipped a supreme being, whose nature is hard to understand because they seldom portrayed him. Many of the brightly painted wooden temple images in western and central Africa did not represent this chief spirit but merely his assistants, who were human figures.[7] Parrinder stresses the importance of ancestor-worship and insists that this cult is fundamental to African religions. In one form or another, it provided the motive for both human sacrifice and cannibalism. The great sacrifices of Dahomey that so shocked travellers in West Africa were the outcome of a pious, if exaggerated, concern for the soul of the dead king, who, year after year, had to be provided with a constant flow of new retainers.

Sacrifice in Africa took many forms but few were peculiar to that continent. The same urges as elsewhere inspired the same kinds of offering. Much emphasis was placed on fertility and harvest rites, especially on rain-making and rain-stopping. Parrinder tells of a friend, a university graduate, who employed a rain-stopper to sit in his compound during his wedding festivities. Often pleas for rain, or rain-stopping, were addressed to ancestors as much as to the gods; for instance, among the Bagangwato of southern Africa, in times of drought "rain songs" were chanted not to the gods, but to the dead chiefs.

If human sacrifice was widespread in Africa, the annual toll of victims was not particularly large and, contrary to common belief, cannibalism was restricted to specific regions, more particularly the Congo and Niger river basins. Throughout Africa killing on a large scale was the exception rather than the rule. For instance, in Uganda, single human scapegoats were sent to die in exile whenever the king was warned by the gods that his enemies were working magic against him. A man and a boy would be chosen, or a woman and her child. Accompanied by a cow, a goat, a fowl and a dog, they were sent off to die a lingering death in enemy territory; their limbs were broken so that they could not return. The scapegoat principle also prevailed in Nigeria, where, in certain parts, a young woman would be sacrificed to take away the iniquities of the people. Victims for the occasion would be bought from neighbouring tribes and anyone who was known to have committed a gross sin during the year, such as witchery, theft or adultery, was expected to pay a fine for this purpose. The scapegoat was made to suffer. In 1858 the Rev J. C. Taylor witnessed one of the ceremonies: at Onitsha on the Niger, the victim was dragged alive face downwards from the king's house to the river while the crowd remorselessly shouted "wickedness! wickedness!" The body was drawn along the ground, as if it represented all their iniquities that were thus being carried away.

In Africa, apart from the element of ancestor worship, sacrifice is notable for the paramount role played by the king himself. Not only were people offered as retainers to dead monarchs, but in many regions the rulers themselves became the victim. Among the Shilluk in southern Sudan the king's life was precarious. Not only was he killed at the first sign of decrepitude; even when in the prime of health he might be challenged by a rival and had to defend himself in combat to the death. In West Africa the king-killing custom was also to be found. Among the Tukun, the king was allowed to rule for only seven years; if during that period he fell ill, or even sneezed or coughed, or fell off his horse, he might be put to death; it became the head councillor's duty to strangle him.

The same notion prevailed at the opposite end of the continent. The great German anthropologist, Leo Frobenius, describes how in what is now Zimbabwe the king, or Makoni, used to be condemned to die after a mere four years' reign. The sentence had to be carried out by his head wife, who would throttle him with a special cord, made out of the tendons of an ox on the night of the new moon. The corpse was then taken to the top of the nearby mountain. The priests visited the body every day and performed the most elaborate ceremonies; brain, liver and entrails were one by one removed and put in a leather bag, while their place in the king's body was taken by herbs and leaves. It was eventually wound round with cloth like a mummy and placed in a seated position in such a way that only the nails emerged from the bundle, which was then enveloped in the hide of a bull, specially reared for the occasion. One year later the remains of the king were taken by the priests out of the bull's hide and put back in the leather bag; special care was taken to see that none of the nails were missing. On this occasion, at sunrise after the night of the new moon, the king's favourite wife, the Mwiza (not the Wahesi, or head wife, who had throttled him) was also strangled, having been ceremonially stripped of all her finery and left naked. After several other leading people had been sacrificed, the king's mummy was immured in a cave, in which only a tiny opening was left. A priest kept perpetual watch there until a snake, worm, tortoise or beetle, thought to be the soul of the defunct monarch, should come out. As soon as this creature had emerged, the hole was filled in.[8] Writing in 1929, Frobenius states that these rites had not taken place within living memory. As late as 1928, however, a king's daughter had been sacrificed to bring rain. The drought must have gone on for a long time, since she first had to be kept for two years, until she reached puberty, before she was ceremoniously strangled.

In the Zimbabwe royal rituals lies the essence of African sacrifice, which required the ceremonial death of one person rather than mass immolation. The likenesses between rites in Africa and elsewhere are striking: widows are strangled, scapegoats exiled, bodies buried alive under buildings, offerings made to river gods and at harvest time, and messengers sent to the next world to provide gods and ancestors with current items of news. In addition to victory in war, particular emphasis is placed on rain-making and fertility, which may even involve the killing of the ruler himself, who re-enacts the death of the god whose living representative he is. This survival of royal and ritual immolation suggests that even in this remote part of nineteenth-century Africa we are still near to the very origins of human sacrifice; Egyptologists have often pointed to parallels between the ceremonial death of the king in different parts of Africa and that of Osiris, both ruler and god, who five thousand years earlier was killed and dismembered. The notion of king-sacrifice may have spread to the rest of Africa via Ethiopia, where it was common until the third century A.D. for the Meroe ruler's life to end in this way. Those other African rituals, previously described in Chapter IV, in which the king was not killed but forced to break tabus and suffer humiliations at the hands of his people, surely also derive from earlier rites when the monarch was actually slain. In some cases the ruler had to die for his people while in others he merely "sinned", in order to expiate their wrongdoing. In certain lands, such as Uganda or the Niger Delta, single scapegoats took the king's place and were immolated to lift the load of sin that weighed upon both the ruler and his people.

In one region of West Africa the situation was different. The principles remained the same—the king played a focal role in religious observance and the cult of his ancestors was all-important—but in place of rituals that elsewhere claimed one single scapegoat, whole cohorts of victims were offered to ensure the king's wellbeing, both in this world and in the next. This region was centred upon the Kingdom of Dahomey, corresponding to the present day Republic of Benin and stretched eastward to include the kingdom known as Edo, lying some hundred miles inland. Mass sacrifices in these places were witnessed by European visitors over the course of several centuries, and were a never-ending source of shock both to these visitors themselves and to readers of their accounts. In their vivid detail and their extended time-span, these chilling reports are unique in the annals of human sacrifice. Spanish descriptions of similar rites in the New World refer only to ceremonies in use in the early sixteenth century.

The story begins with the city of Benin, the capital not of Benin but of Edo. Portuguese ships first reconnoitred that part of the coast of Africa in 1469 and 1475, but left few records of what they saw. However an early attempt to convert the natives must have taken place, since three missionaries sent there by King John III of Portugal in 1538 discovered traces of Christianity. The ruling king, known as the Oba, had himself been baptized in 1516, but this concession to the white man's god left his morals, education and beliefs untouched. His house was crammed with idols and the letter sent to him by King John was cast unopened into a box to the left of his throne.

The Portuguese who came in the 1470s had been only dimly aware of the existence of human sacrifice in those parts. King John's mission gives, for the first time, concrete instances of offerings on behalf of this "Christian" king. Alan Ryder, in his book on Benin, hints that the baptism of the Oba might itself have acted as a spur to human sacrifice, as a tribute to his enhanced status as a Christian monarch. But as in the case of other rituals among Africans, treated by Europeans as latter-day perversions of the kind and noble savage, I suspect that these rites were really very ancient. Nonetheless, however limited its effect on his spiritual life, the European presence did prompt the Oba to seek material gains on a European scale, and he set out to conquer the peoples that separated his kingdom from the coast. To their credit successive Obas spurned the thriving trade of selling slaves to the Europeans and thereby spared their subjects quite as much suffering as they inflicted by the scale of their ritual killings.

Things were different in neighbouring Dahomey, where king Adahoonzou, who died in 1789, told a British visitor that he sometimes spared sacrificial victims in order to sell them as slaves. Adahoonzou, in saying this, was making a very important point, seldom stressed in accounts of West African sacrifice. At the time of this monarch's reign, the slave trade was still booming and was not banned throughout the British Empire until the Abolition Act of 1833. The search for slaves to sell to Europeans and the need for captives to sacrifice to the gods both complemented and conflicted with each other. Lured by the profits to be made out of the slaving and armed to the teeth by Europeans, the rulers of West Africa would send expeditions hundreds of miles inland to seize human merchandise for the slave traders who at this time had their own settlements on the coast. Some of these were imposing forts. Cape Coast Castle, for instance, could accommodate 1,500 slaves at a time in its dungeons. Hence, it always has to be borne in mind when reading these accounts of sacrifice, that in doing homage to his father and to his gods, the king was in effect depriving himself of liquor, arms, court uniforms and other material blessings to be gained in exchange for slaves for the American and West Indian market.

After this first glimpse of Benin, the records remain silent for two centuries until the visit of a French sea captain J. E. Landolphe, who saw an Oba crowned in 1750—almost certainly Akenbuda. He did not witness the funeral rites of the previous ruler but merely reports routine sacrifices performed in honour of a new trading agreement signed with the French. In the Oba's presence two executioners, masked and dressed in long grey robes, clubbed a man unconscious and cut off his head. Before his death, the victim was told to go to Olokun, god of fertility and of the sea. On another occasion, Landolphe saw three men dispatched, probably as part of the annual great yam festival.

Dahomey, with its capital, Agbomey, was visited by the British Captain Snelgrave in 1727. From then until 1890, we have eye-witness accounts of a whole series of visitors to that city. Victory celebrations after a successful campaign seem to have claimed many victims, but most of the ceremonies described by travellers were of another kind: they served to provide the late king of Dahomey with a ghostly retinue of servants, whose numbers were swelled by annual sacrifices on the anniversary of his death. Far from concealing this blood-letting from the squeamish Europeans, the king commanded that all visitors to his capital should attend. The ceremony that marked the death of a Dahoman ruler was called the "Grand Custom". It was often delayed for as much as two years after his demise since it took a long time to muster the required horde of victims, whether captives or slaves. The annual sacrifice, which served to dispatch a fresh batch of retainers to the late king, was called the "Annual Custom".

The ceremony witnessed by Captain Snelgrave in 1727 seems to have been a Grand Custom, though he describes it as a celebration of victory over the neighbouring Wydahs. More probably it was this victory that had provided the numbers of victims needed before the Grand Custom could be properly performed. His account of four platforms for sacrifice erected outside the town exactly matches later descriptions of the Grand Custom. Snelgrave and a Dutch companion were led by priests to a place about a quarter of a mile from the settlement, where four small stages had been set up. They insist that they saw four hundred victims dispatched but only describe the death of the first. He was a comely old man, on whose head the fetish man first placed his hand and repeated some words of consecration; an executioner then severed his head with one blow. Women and children were also sacrificed and uttered "piteous cries". Snelgrave maintains that some victims were killed by boys only seven or eight years old and suffered prolonged agonies, because these children could barely lift the ceremonial sword. He states that altogether four thousand prisoners were sacrificed, but this figure derives from hearsay and, to judge by other accounts, is an exaggeration.

To gain a clearer picture of Dahoman rites, one must first divide the various accounts into those that relate to the Grand Custom and others that tell of an Annual Custom. Among those privileged to witness a Grand Custom was a British governor of Fort Appolonia on the Gold Coast; this was the Grand Custom held for Adanzu II in 1791, at which five hundred victims are said to have been sacrificed, though this British visitor left no description. The ceremony was probably little different from that held for King Gezo in July 1860, described in detail by a French eye-witness, M. Lartigue:

> The 23rd I assist at the nomination of twenty-three chiefs and musicians, who are going to be sacrificed in order that they may enter into the service of the deceased king.
>
> The 28th, immolation of fourteen captives, whose heads are carried to different parts of the town, to the sound of a big bell.
>
> The 29th, they are preparing to offer, to the memory of King Gezo, the customary victims. The captives have a gag in the shape of a cross, which must make them suffer terribly. The pointed end is put into the mouth, and presses upon the tongue, which prevents them from doubling it, and in consequence, crying out. Almost all these unfortunates have their eyes starting out of their heads. In the coming night there will be a great massacre.

Lartigue goes on to write of the huge crowd, which he puts at 40,000, and of the smell of the putrefying corpses. On 30th and 31st July the ceremony reached its climax, when about five hundred victims were dispatched. The bodies were thrown into trenches, to be eaten by vultures and wolves. As a finale, the late king's wives placed themselves in order of rank round his body—interred in a great vault —and drank poison. Lartigue says that this "voluntary" sacrifice brought the number of victims up to about six hundred. The next two days witnessed the death of fifteen more female prisoners, stabbed in the breast. On 5th August, another important sacrifice took place:

> The 5th day reserved for the king's offerings. They form a collection of everything that is required by an African monarch: fifteen women and thirty-five men, gagged and bound, the knees bent under the chin, and the arms tied to the ankles,

each one held in a basket which is carried on the head. The defile has lasted more than an hour and a half. . . . Behind me were four magnificent blacks, acting as coachmen around a little carriage, which was intended to be sent to the deceased. . . . one of them had two large tears which glistened on his cheeks. They were all four killed like chickens, by the king in person.[9]

The same Grand Custom was still in full swing in October of that year and its closing scenes were witnessed by the Rev. Bernasko, a native Wesleyan missionary. He states that he saw ninety heads severed on 16th October. He also saw a curious assortment of fresh gifts that were to be sent to the late king: two chariots, one glass wheel, seven plain wheels, three solid silver dishes, three solid silver tea pots, one silver sugar pot, one silver butter-pot, and a large wheelbarrow drawn by six females from his Amazon retinue.[10] These Amazons played an important part in the ceremonies. When a king died they would smash his furniture and utensils and then destroy themselves. On King Bossa's demise in 1774, 285 women died in this manner before the new ruler could break into the palace and stop the carnage. Bossa was buried seated in a sedan chair that another British visitor, Robert Norris, had given him.

Norris describes the sacrifice that he attended in 1772, after presenting King Bossa with his cherished sedan chair. It must have been an Annual Custom for the previous king, and involved far fewer victims than the Grand Custom. On 6th February he saw seven men fastened by their wrists and ankles to tall posts fixed in the ground. They seemed indifferent to their fate and tried to beat time to the music that was being played. An equal number of horses were tethered in like manner to stakes and were to share the same fate as the men. At the entrance to the market-place Norris saw two gibbets, with a dead man hanging naked by the ankles from each; their private parts had been cut off, to spare the sensibilities of the ladies of the court. On 16th February the final sacrifice of the series took place. A large stage had been built against the palace wall; the crowd stood below, separated by a thorn fence. A man, a muzzled crocodile and two pigeons with clipped wings were thrown down from the dais. A great scramble took place to seize their heads, which were valued as a great prize.

Nearly eighty years later, in 1850, Commander Forbes of the Royal Navy saw a version of the Annual Custom that had evidently changed little in the meantime. Twelve men, eight of whom were trussed up in baskets, as in Lartigue's account of the Grand Custom, and four lashed in small canoes, together with one crocodile and one cat, were thrown from the platform. The victims were held high above the heads of their bearers, in the exact manner illustrated in Sir Richard Burton's account of the same ceremony a few years later (see the illustration). The king himself tipped the first basket over the edge. The heads were then cut off, the bodies brutally mutilated and left for the birds of prey to eat. Captain Wilmot R.N. witnessed the same ceremony in 1862, when the procedure only varied by the inclusion among the victims of fowls tied to long poles and a few goats trussed up like the men in baskets.

The most vivid report of an Annual Custom comes from the great English traveller and explorer, Sir Richard Burton, better known for his exploits in the Near East. He saw the ceremony at the beginning of 1863 and describes it in his book *A Mission to Gelele, king of Dahome*. By then it was no longer held by the palace wall but in a "victim shed", just outside one of the gates of the town; Burton describes this shed as being not unlike an English parish church, complete with barn and turret. It differed merely in that the whole roof was covered by a tattered cloth, blood red.

Burton offers perhaps the most detailed account ever given of the circumstances of a human sacrifice, including even the dimensions of the shed and the height of the posts on which it rested. Inside the barn Burton found twenty appointed victims. All were seated on stools and tightly lashed to the interior posts; each had an attendant squatting behind him to keep off the flies. They were fed four times a day and were loosed at night to sleep, since the king wanted to keep them in good humour. They were dressed in the oddest garb— a long white nightcap and a calico shirt with a crimson patch on the left breast and shorts of quasi-European type. Since Lartigue's time other changes were only minor; he had also seen twelve men lashed in the same manner. The last king, however, had invented the turret, and the present ruler had added a second storey to the victim shed. The sacrificial ceremony itself does not seem to have altered much over the years. Burton mentions additional features such as a special tent, larger than the king's shed, that housed the relics of the old king. His ghost was supposed to be present and all bowed and prostrated themselves to it before noticing the present ruler. Burton also writes of the presence of Amazon warriors; a group of these were squatting beside the king, with gun barrels bristling upwards.

Perhaps the most gruesome part of Burton's account concerns the disposal of the victims after the sacrifice: "The approach to the Palace was not pleasant. . . . Four corpses, attired in their criminals' shirts and nightcaps, were sitting in pairs upon Gold Coast stools, supported by a double-storied scaffold. . . . At a little distance from these, on a similar erection, but made for half the number, were two victims, one above the other." Burton next describes a gallows, not unlike that seen by Norris in 1772, with corpses similarly mutilated lest they offend the modesty of the king's wives. The account continues: "We then passed the south-eastern gate of the Komasi House, where the palace shed [i.e. the victim shed] was also untenanted. In front of sundry little black dolls, stuck in the ground at both sides of the entrance, lay a dozen heads. These were in two batches of six each; their faces were downwards, and the cleanly severed necks caught the observer's eye. Around each heap was raised a rim of white ashes." [11] Burton counted in all twenty-three bodies exhibited as a result of what he calls Gelele's Evil Night. He also mentions the concluding ceremony of the Annual Custom, accompanied by interminable speeches of congratulation to Gelele on having so worthily performed the Customs in the presence of white men. Burton remarks that these people were "as practised in the art of public speaking as any American politician".

Burton adds many interesting comments. He states that the king purchased victims from his soldiers for months before the ceremony and suggests that in an ordinary year, when the Annual Custom was held, the total number of people sacrificed would amount to about 500, a figure that rose to 1000 for a Grand Custom year. The Annual Custom in the reign of the late king involved some 36 deaths (out of a total for the year of 500), but the present ruler had raised this to 39 or 40. Burton says that the missionaries had tried to hoodwink him about this and given higher estimates. This is his only reference to their presence in Agbomey, where their restraining influence was clearly small. Burton incidentally states that a missionary called Duncan had described the city of Benin as "that saintly place of so many converts", at the very time when men were being sacrificed daily.[12] (When Burton visited Benin City in 1862, he saw three violent deaths in three days and the large open space before the palace was strewn with human skulls and bones.) He admits that for the Dahoman Grand Custom, the total of additional deaths may have been higher than 500, due to the unseen killing of a number of females by the Amazons inside the palace. Nonetheless he stresses that the numbers had from time to time been grossly exaggerated in Europe, and dismisses as "grisly nursery tales" the stories of two thousand men being killed in a day and of canoes paddling in a pool of gore. The accuracy of Snelgrave's original figure of four thousand victims had been questioned ever since 1793, when Archibald Dalzel first published his *History of Dahomey*.

The British explorer puts the annual total at five hundred in an ordinary year, because there were so many other forms of sacrifice in addition to the Annual Custom. The king's constant relay service of messengers to his paternal ghost cost countless lives. Any event, however trivial, had to be faithfully reported, whether the invention of a new drum, the move of the court from one palace to another, or the visit of a white man; a report that the late king's ghost had been seen bathing in the sea required the dispatch of a series of messengers. According to another traveller, a single message to the late ruler could result in several deaths; after one victim was beheaded to carry the news, the king would suddenly remember that he had forgotten some minor detail. In order to add a postscript to his letter, another courier was slain and sent on his way to the next world; he was first given a piastre for travelling expenses and a bottle of rum as provision for his journey.

As a man of the world, Burton takes a most matter-of-fact view of the proceedings and maintains that human sacrifice in Dahomey and its neighbours had been greatly misunderstood by the press, though he fully admits that the cost in human life was heavy. He goes so far as to call the great Dahoman rites "a touching instance of the king's filial piety, deplorably mistaken but perfectly sincere", and insists that the offerings sprang from no mere lust for blood nor delight in torture. The king had to perform a disagreeable task over his ancestors' graves and his subjects would deem it impious were he to curtail or omit the performance; to suddenly suppress it would be as if a European monarch were forcibly to abolish prayers for the dead. In Burton's view, the sacrifices were carried out without brutality—a statement only belied by Lartigue's report of the excruciating pain caused by their gags. In stressing the prisoners' extreme nonchalance, he is probably nearer the truth than Snelgrave, with his description of the weeping lackeys who attended the late monarch's coach. For whatever the attitude of Dahoman victims, in neighbouring Benin City in the nineteenth century favourites and servants still positively competed for the privilege of being buried alive with the late ruler. After the choice had been made and the tomb closed over the dead and the living, sentinels were set to watch it day and night. Every day the sepulchre would be opened to enquire whether any of the entombed men had yet gone to join their master. The same question was put daily, until there was no further answer.[13]

Burton is often more ready to condone than to condemn the mass sacrifices of West Africa. He says that to abolish human sacrifice would be to abolish Dahomey, and predicts that European pressure will merely cause the number of victims to rise. As a final justification he recalls that in 1864 four murderers were hung on the same gibbet in Liverpool before 100,000 gaping souls. He even comments that the Meriahs of India were hardly grateful to General Campbell for saving them from their grisly fate and compares Dahomey favourably with the massacres of Mexico and Peru, and with the burnings of the Druids. Before leaving Dahomey, his only comment on the subject to King Gelele was a tactful hint that he should spare sensitive Europeans the shock of seeing nude and mutilated corpses rotting in the sun.

The eminent American anthropologist Melville J. Herskovits regarded Burton's figures as reasonably accurate. Based on information from a range of sources, he shares Burton's view that a wide variety of events, quite apart from the Grand and Annual Customs, claimed their victims. All the more standard forms of offering are present. Killings occurred when the king went to war; when he built a new palace, men were buried under its foundations or their blood was mixed with the earth of the walls. Moreover, the Grand Custom involved the death of between a hundred and two hundred of the king's wives, and this mass suttee—coupled with the slaughter of other women within the palace—probably brought the full toll to well above Burton's figure of five hundred. The scale is at all events impressive, when measured against estimates for the population of the town of Agbomey of about twenty-five thousand. If correct, this means that deaths by sacrifice there were as numerous as the total of babies born in any given year! Herskovits makes the important point that human offering was a royal privilege in Dahomey, strictly forbidden to commoners. A wealthy man could merely offer a goat or a sheep, while the poor made sacrifices of beans and corn.[14]

The rich variety of reports on Dahomey and Edo bear directly on the general problems of human sacrifice. In particular, major changes over the centuries are conspicuously absent; if anything, sacrifice was on the increase; while sixteenth-century visitors have little to say on the subject, the report of the Niger expedition of 1841 states that the Oba of Benin City offered up three men every day, one in the morning, one in the afternoon and one at night. Crucifixion trees, not seen before 1838, became a common sight in the late nineteenth century.

If early travellers said little, it was probably because they saw little, but those writers who look upon human offering as a decadent innovation are surely mistaken. In the Customs of Dahomey, we are clearly in the presence of rites that have ancient roots. The practice of sending a huge retinue of servants to follow their king to the next world is proven, as we have seen, from the time of Ur five thousand years earlier. The Dahomans merely added a new touch with their dispatch of a fresh set of attendants each year; even the ruler's obsessive decapitation of slaves to keep his royal father abreast of current events has precedents in other lands. As in the rest of Africa, the status of the Dahoman monarch was godlike and, though here the king was not himself the victim, the sacrifices were centred upon his person.

To many minds, black Africans were people who were in the habit of eating each other for dinner and on special occasions added a missionary to the menu. But in that part of West Africa notorious for mass sacrifice, it has been seen that the victims' bodies were not eaten but left to rot on gibbets or abandoned to the vultures. Even the Leopards of Sierra Leone devoured only single victims from time to time. Human sacrifice on a less lavish scale also existed in southern and eastern Africa, but in both regions cannibalism was rare; in Moslem North Africa it was non-existent. On the other hand, William Arens of the State University of New York at Stonybrook is writing sheer nonsense when he maintains in his recent book *Anthropology and Anthropophagy* that cannibalism never existed at all but was simply invented by native informants to please the people who questioned them. Arens may be right to insist that anthropologists should be less gullible and should evaluate their data on the subject most carefully. However, not only in Africa but in every corner of the globe factual accounts and concrete evidence of man-eating survive. To name but a few: the Sierra Leone trials discussed above; Captain Cook's personal discovery of the remains of a cannibal banquet in New Zealand; the New Guinea trials of people who ate corpses; Fray Sahagun's description of Aztec rites, complete with the method of cooking the human flesh; accounts of Fijian cannibalism with the modes of cooking and even the actual cooking pots that were used. To deny cannibalism is to deny part of the basis of human sacrifice which often, though not always, involved the commemorative act of eating the god, personified by a fellow human.

In Africa man-eaters were mostly to be found in the Congo and Niger river basins. Garry Hogg summarizes the customs of the tribes of the Niger basin, who—with the exception of the Yoruba—were mostly cannibals and ate their tribal enemies. He prefaces his remarks by saying that it is not long since tribes could be found there whose members ate human flesh for what was, for them, a good and adequate reason: they liked it and it was readily available. But in almost every African instance that Hogg cites, details emerge that reveal beyond all doubt that this cannibalism was steeped in ritual and was an integral part of the local religion. If people were to eat, say, pork or beef, not as a ritual but just because they liked it, every member of the tribe would expect to get his share; equally, male and female animals and even their young would at times be eaten. But where man-eating was concerned, this was far from the fact. Complex rules prescribed who could partake of human flesh, whether man or woman, young or old, who was to be eaten, and what parts of their body should be kept as relics.

A colourful legend is told of a hawk that once flew over the hut of a chief. It held in its talons a piece of human flesh, which inadvertently it let fall into the cauldron in which the chief's soup was being prepared. The chief was so enchanted with this soup that he ordered his cooks to repeat the same taste every day. Nonplussed, since they had not seen what had fallen out of the sky, they tried every fish and fowl and even added reptiles and insects to the broth; all to no avail. In a rage, the chief slew his head cook and told the others to cut him in pieces and throw them into the soup he could not make. When the chief began to eat his soup that day, a broad grin of contentment spread over his face; he then told the surviving cooks to kill a slave each day and throw him into the cauldron. Unfortunately, the king eventually ate every member of the tribe who had not fled, until one day he found himself all alone, with no more subjects to devour. Such was his passion for human flesh that he at once began to tear pieces from his own body; at last nothing of him remained but the parts that he could not reach, and so he died.

This story has a clear moral. Far from extolling cannibalism, it serves to show that unless governed by stringent rules, it leads to self-destruction. If the eating of human flesh became the common daily fare and was not confined to special people on special occasions, such compulsive man-eaters would end up by devouring their own people and their neighbours to the point of total extinction. The anthropologist C. H. Meek wrote in the 1930s that tribesmen of the Niger Basin "who were willing to answer questions" made it clear that they ate human flesh purely as meat. And yet these same tribesmen themselves belied such statements by the details they gave to Meek of the rituals involved: normally only enemy captives were eaten; their skulls were carefully preserved and when young men went to war, they drank medicine out of these trophies. Women were strictly forbidden to touch human flesh.

Even Garry Hogg, who at times appears to take the more horrendous reports at their face value, adopts at others a cautious line and agrees that anthropologists—as opposed to amateurs—stress the wide range of tabus that attended the eating of human flesh. In this context, he tells how in New Guinea the slayer or captor might not eat of the slain, except for a small portion of the liver, after it had been ceremonially treated with symbolic herbs. The ban also applied to the captor's mother and father and nearest relatives; they were convinced that their genitals would swell if they broke the tabu. Exactly the same ban applied to the captor of a prisoner in Mexico, though his relatives were allowed to eat part of his body.

Among the Ganawuri and the Rukuba human flesh was the exclusive preserve of the tribes' old men. Young men were merely smeared with the oily soup left over in the pot in which the flesh had been boiled—a custom also followed by the Human Leopards of Sierra Leone. Zumperi warriors handed over captured heads to their fathers to eat and satisfied themselves by licking the blood off their weapons. In some places the head-winner had to hide in a neighbouring village to escape from the dead man's soul. The Yergum always boiled the head separately from the body and it would only be eaten by those who had killed an enemy in battle. The Jawara also separated the head, plastered it with dried mud and cooked it in a different manner to the body. Among the Suras, women were not even allowed to see human flesh.[15] The Hill Angas had a different custom; they sacrificed and devoured the old men of their tribe when still in full possession of their faculties, while young men captured in battle were not eaten but sold into slavery. The flesh was ceremonially eaten and again the head was carefully preserved in a pot, in front of which sacrifices were made and prayers spoken at regular intervals of time.

These reports confirm that the eating of human flesh was not a matter of pure zest or appetite but was bound by strict ritual and tabu. Almost without exception men, not women, were consumed. The participants were in some cases young, in others old, but seldom both. Ever-present is the cult of the head, that timeless practice known already to Neanderthal man. The principle behind man-eating was universal: to imbibe magic strength by the transference of soul-stuff—particularly identified with the head—from eaten to eater, whether it was the novice who ate the mature to absorb his wisdom, or the veteran who ate the youth to restore his vigour. To fill one's own belly was a secondary object, however enjoyable the feast. The killing and eating of old relatives, as will be explained in more detail below, far from being a tasty if scraggy meal, was basic to the deep-rooted African cult of the ancestors.

Ewald Volhard, the German scholar who in 1939 published much the most exhaustive study of cannibal customs, explains that in northern Nigeria the capture of an enemy head was a passport to manhood. A warrior who had not done so was still looked upon as no better than a girl, and was not a full member of the male community. Head-hunting rituals and tabus varied widely from tribe to tribe. For instance among the Basange, a feast of seven days' duration followed the first capture of a head by a young warrior. The head-winner was only allowed to sleep during the day-time. His temples were swathed in a white bandage, into which feathers were stuck.

In the other great centre of cannibalism, the Congo basin, mostly situated within the present-day Republic of Zaire, matters were rather different. Reports of man-eaters in that region mainly derive not from anthropologists but from missionaries. Writing at about the turn of the century, they poured forth harrowing tales that have since been faithfully copied from one book to another, not as the opinions of untrained observers, but as facts.

The Rev Holman Bentley in his two-volume work *Pioneering in the Congo*, published in 1900, painted a lurid picture. He says, perhaps correctly, that all tribes from the confluence of the Congo and the Mobangi rivers—some five hundred miles from the coast—to Stanley Falls, were enthusiastic man-eaters. He tells how eager natives begged to be allowed to restock their larder with the flesh of the river-steamer crews because their meat was "sweeter"—which meant that it had a saltier taste, since the sailors came from the sea coast. For Bentley, the typical attitude of local tribesmen is epitomized in the remarks: "You eat fowls and goats and we eat men. Why not?" and "You white men consider pork to be the tastiest of meat, but pork is not to be compared with human flesh". His prose is laced with astringent epithets such as "fiendish", accompanied with the inevitable but patronizing rider to the effect that these wild men were all the same very "lovable" and had splendid possibilities once the grace of God had got hold of them. He justifies conversion by saying that his reformed cannibals "are living earnest, gentle Christian lives, in striking contrast to some of the white men who go and live among them". Converts were offered the incentive of a special place in heaven, where cannibals would be banned, since they would eat the angels.[16]

Worse still, on the Mobangi river humans were reportedly sold in an emaciated condition and then fattened up for the table. A group of people would club together to buy all or part of a body "wholesale"—rather as in India in pre-refrigeration days British families would join forces to buy a whole sheep and eat it the same day. Children reportedly took part in the Mobangi river banquets: "Dear little bright-eyed boys and girls grew up accustomed to these scenes from day to day. They ate their own morsels from time to time . . . to this awful depth have these children of the Heavenly Father fallen".[17] Bentley quotes a colleague who had established a mission station at Mosembe in the territory of the dreaded Bangala tribes. As a postscript to horrendous accounts of processions of men carrying human arms and legs on poles, the story is told of some doughty warriors who burnt a poor sick old woman alive in her hut; they made a huge joke of the matter with a gleeful mock imitation of her agonies. The usual comment follows as to how the Bangalas were really such merry and manly fellows.

We are also indebted to Herbert Ward for a classic and oft-quoted account of the human flesh markets of the region. Ward was an artist but writes more like a missionary in describing "dark deeds of barbarism" and the natives' "delight" at sacrificing human beings. He tells how a number of slave depots existed along the tributaries of the Congo where hundreds of captives of all sexes and ages were to be seen lying in groups, waiting to be sold. The artist states that these unfortunates were sent to market for the sole purpose of being killed and eaten; however, we are not told how he was so sure that they were sold as meat and not as working slaves—a more usual custom in Africa. His assertion that the most succulent parts of their bodies were marked by coloured strips of paper is not very convincing.

Another writer on cannibalism, Christian Spiel, frequently mentions the German ethnologist, G. Schweinfurt, who lived among the Mangbetus of the Congo before they came under European influence. Schweinfurt made them famous as the "people who had no graves", not because they burnt their dead, but because they ate them up. Schweinfurt's account lacks at times the detachment expected of a scholar and scientist. Unlike the sentimental asides of the missionaries on the "jolly" nature of their cannibalistic flock, he portrays the Mangbetu chief Munsa as a fiend incarnate. He writes of the wild fire of animal sensuality that lit his eyes, and the greedy and cruel leer that besmirched his lips: "These features expressed no feelings of the heart".[18] Schweinfurt relates that the chief ate a young child daily, but admits that he never actually saw him thus breakfasting off a newborn babe and merely says that "the general rumour was current" that this occurred.[19] The Bagesu tribe are also described as eating their dead. The relatives would mourn for three or four days in the house in which the death had taken place and then cook and eat the flesh of the departed, destroying the bones and leaving no remains.

Whatever the scale of cannibalism in the Congo, it was slow to subside. The Belgian anthropologist and agronomist J. P. Hallett reports that as late as 1950 he found a case of cannibalism in Maniema. He was given a piece of meat and only learned afterwards that it was human. His indignation knew no bounds, but rather than denounce his hosts to the Belgian authorities, he treated them to a private lecture on the enormity of their deeds. The people of neighbouring Zandeland, living just over the present-day border between Zaire and the Sudan, went even further. When Zaire was still a Belgian colony, they are reported to have caught a Belgian officer on leave, whom they tore limb from limb and ate raw.

Many tales of the Congo are replete with horror but lacking in precision. In spite of Schweinfurt's eminence as an anthropologist, he seems to have been rather gullible. He was requested to produce specimens of skulls for the Berlin Anatomical Museum, but it later appeared that three of those to be put on display had been cooked before he received delivery. His reports abound with self-righteous judgments, more to be expected from the missionaries who actually witnessed the man-eating and wrote of slaves being fattened up like poultry and of markets that specialized in human flesh.

These missionaries, of course, were faced with the problem of promoting their cause to a public that even in those more god-fearing times was only half convinced of the wisdom of imposing on every heathen the white man's gods. Already in the seventeenth century, the great French moralist Michel de Montaigne had suggested that cannibals should be left in peace, since the customs of Europeans, although different, were just as cruel. Two centuries later Herman Melville questioned whether to enjoy human flesh was any more barbarous than having condemned traitors in England drawn and quartered, their entrails torn out of the living body and the head then placed on a pole to rot in a public square. To gain support for their cause, the missionaries were bound to paint darkest Africa in the darkest colours and depict ignoble savages fallen from grace and steeped in a sink of iniquity, not purposely to distort the truth but to justify their own actions. The tone of the missionary endeavour is typified by an appeal, dated 1836, on behalf of those champion cannibals of all time, the inhabitants of the Fiji Islands:

> It is on behalf of this cannibal race that we appeal to you. Let all the horrors of a CANNIBAL FEAST be present to your minds while you read . . . Pity CANNIBAL FEEJEE, and do so quickly. Come, then, ye Christians, and teach the poor, idolatrous, war-loving, man-devouring FEEGEEANS better things.

. . . We spare you the details of a cannibal feast: the previous murders, the mode of cooking human beings, the assembled crowd of all ranks, all ages, both sexes, Chiefs and people, men, women and *children*, anticipating the feast with horrid glee. The actual feast. The attendants bringing into the circle BAKED HUMAN BEINGS, not one, not two, nor ten, but twenty, thirty, forty, fifty at a single feast!

The appeal, after describing the happy-go-lucky Fijians as a deeply depraved people, then reports yet another banquet at which the numbers of those eaten is put at the gargantuan but implausible total of two hundred; it ends by mentioning, more credibly, a form of local suttee that involved the strangling of widows. Reay Tannahil, English author of another book on cannibalism and related topics, quotes the Rev John Watsford's report of a Fiji chief who, if he set eyes on anyone fatter than himself, even a friend, had him killed at once and roasted. As Tannahil remarks, all these appeals were splendidly emotive, just the thing to stir the imagination of the stay-at-home and to loose his purse strings. Their authors may have been extraordinary people, but they were separated from their flock by an unbridgable gap in human understanding; most were simply incapable of even attempting to enter the minds of their tribal converts.[20]

Many of these horror stories are prefaced by "it is said" or "we have heard". Doubtless these travelling zealots who related the stories were apt to be told simply what people thought they wanted to hear —a problem that confronts many visitors to third world countries even today. Moreover, it would have been pure grist to the mill of the missionaries' star converts to paint the most lurid picture of the bad old ways that they had so righteously cast off. Christian Spiel remarks that in Fiji they went out of their way to conceal the elaborate ritual that surrounded the eating of human flesh; for instance, no one could touch it with their fingers and it had to be eaten with special forks. Both these forks and the pots in which it was cooked were strictly tabu. Spiel rightly remarks that not only in Fiji but in Africa too most of these reports, smacking even of racism, derive from a single witness, who invariably tends to exaggerate.

Such subjective attitudes seem even at times to have affected other anthropologists than Schweinfurt. Meek, for instance, accepts at its face value the remark that people in the Niger basin ate human flesh purely as meat, although he then goes on to describe the precise rituals that accompanied such eating. Inseparable from Niger Delta cannibalism is the cult of the head and the notion of imbibing the strength of captive enemies. This principle is well illustrated by the case of the Ashantis who avoided eating most parts of the human body; the Ashanti witch doctor would merely cut out the heart of an enemy warrior and apportion it among those who had not yet slain an adversary in battle, in order to give them valour. On one occasion, however, the Ashantis overdid themselves, when they ate the heart of an English administrator, Sir Charles McCarthy. Among the Yorubas of West Nigeria cannibalism was also rich in symbolism; the king would solemnly eat the heart of his predecessor. Such strictly ritual cannibalism was found in a number of places in West Africa. On the Ivory Coast, for instance, to the west of the Ashanti region, when a new village was founded, a captive was tied to a tree and wounded with spears, while the women danced and sang round him. After he was decapitated, only his heart and liver were put in a frying pan, along with a hen and a fish—both symbols of fertility. The rest of his body was then thrown into the bush. All present had to partake of the meal.[21]

If victory was the main objective of these precise rituals, justice was another. In Angola in South-west Africa, even after several centuries of Portuguese administration, cannibal executions were still used as a punishment for a wide range of crimes. Though the missionaries paid scant attention to motives, the German traveller Peter Frassle reports that in the Congo, before the arrival of the Europeans, in cases of adultery both offenders would be condemned to be eaten unless the male culprit could produce a virgin to take the other woman's place. People complained that the fines imposed by the Belgians were a poor substitute as a means of stopping adultery.

Ancestor-worship—so common in Africa—was yet another motive for cannibalism. Some writers dwell on the consumption of the bodies of elderly relatives. Sometimes they were killed; at others they were left to die a natural death and so hardly rank as human offerings. Most comments on this form of man-eating display a wilful ignorance of African religions. Eating of parents was emphatically not just a cheap way of adding protein to the diet; it was a profoundly religious act on the part of people who preferred to absorb their old and infirm into their own bodies, rather than let them rot in the cold earth. For people so imbued with the cult of their forbears, to have treated them as a culinary titbit would have been a sacrilegious outrage. To say that people ate their relatives simply to satisfy their hunger is rather like saying that a Hindu widow mounted her husband's funeral pyre in order to warm herself in the flames.

E. G. Parrinder, in stressing the part played by ancestor-worship in African religion, tells of the Ashanti ceremonies in honour of the departed that lasted three weeks; they were called "rest" or "lying down". Each forbear was represented by the stool he had used in his lifetime, and with which his soul was linked. Water was poured on the ground for the ancestor to "wash his hands". "Soul food" of mashed yams and plantains was then put in little dishes before each stool. The dead are ever-present in Africa and receive gifts on many occasions. For instance, among people of the Kikuyu tribes of Kenya the elders, like so many other Africans, would put a little food on the ground for the departed spirits before eating.[22]

Cannibal execution crops up in different parts of the world and was in every sense a sacrifice in those many instances where no true distinction was made between the criminal and the sacrificial victim. Famous for their cannibal executions were the Bataks of Sumatra, where spies, traitors and even thieves were condemned to be eaten. The relatives of the criminal had not only to be present at the Batak executions, but also to provide salt and lemon, with which their loved one was then prepared for the charcoal fire.

The tendency to torture the candidate for the stewpot is another sign of the ritual nature of cannibalism, since intense suffering went hand-in-hand with many forms of human sacrifice. Hideous torments, for example, were suffered by Iroquois captives, who were sometimes forced to eat pieces of their own body; and in the Bismarck Archipelago, lying to the north-east of New Guinea, the living victim was boiled in a hot spring, like a lobster. In parts of New Guinea, a war captive would be kept alive for a whole week, while pieces of flesh were hacked off his body and eaten.

The most diverse African forms of sacrifice, whether the mass slaughter by Kings of Dahomey on behalf of the former ruler or the killing and eating of old people, are not only shocking but meaningless except as homage to the continued presence of the spirits of the dead among the living. The souls of one's forbears were part of the divine order, and the eating of their bodies often became a sacred duty. Similar practices were to be found in other continents; for instance, men of some Australian aboriginal tribes carried the remains of their dead in a little bag and, when they felt grief, ate a piece of the flesh. Christian Spiel rightly remarks that we ourselves are repelled by patrophagy, but that is our Western point of view. *Theirs* was different; they felt that their relatives were happier inside their stomachs than abandoned to the worms.

Cannibalism was fundamentally ritual and sacrificial, although this does not absolutely preclude men eating out of sheer greed. "L'appetit vient en mangeant." However solemn the feast at which a novice first tried human flesh (children seldom partook) a positive relish for this dish could develop, regardless of the occasion, especially in places where other meat was scarce or unpalatable. In Fiji, for instance, the only forms of meat were humans and rats. New Zealand was better provided with animal protein, but after the Maori chief Touai was brought to London in 1818 and had lived there for some years, he confessed that what he most missed was "the feast of human flesh, the feast of victory"; he was weary of English beef. Other cannibals often compared human flesh with pork, though they insisted that it was more tasty; in Polynesia it was known as "long pig". Though the Maoris mainly ate warriors to absorb their strength, Touai oddly maintained that he would rather eat women and children; if he ate a man, a black, preferably about fifty years old, was better than a white. The missionaries may have overstated their own risk of ending up in the tribal stewpot, since a kind of colour prejudice in reverse was quite common among man-eaters. It existed among the Australian aborigines, as well as in New Caledonia, to the north-east of Australia, where white men were considered too salty. In Australia, certain tribes developed a taste for Chinese flesh, as did the inhabitants of the Luisiade Archipelago, lying off New Guinea, who ate up all but four out of a Chinese crew of three hundred shipwrecked there in 1858.

In addition to the cannibal gourmandise of chiefs like Touai, which may properly be regarded as an offshoot of ritual man-eating, other cases from time to time have been dictated by sheer need, in places where cannibalism was completely tabu. Egypt has always been subject to famine if the Nile flood fails. In 1069 A.D., owing to several years of low flooding, food became so scarce that people began to eat each other. Passers-by would be caught in the street by hooks let down from windows, drawn up and killed; human flesh was even sold in public. Such stories do not come from jaundiced foreigners but from Egyptians, who lamented what they saw among their own people. Abd el Latif, an eye-witness during another famine in 1201, one day saw the body of a roasted child in a basket and two days later that of a youth, roasted and partly eaten.[23] The authorities tried to put a stop to such practices; in the course of their investigations, they found cooking pots containing the bodies of children in a number of houses.

Such instances in themselves have nothing to do with human sacrifice, but do serve to stress the difference between ritual cannibalism in, say, the Congo, and occasional man-eating of a purely non-ritual nature in Egypt and elsewhere. A more recent example of the latter variety gained so much publicity that its details need no repeating. In 1972 a chartered Uruguayan Air Force plane carrying fifteen young rugby football players and twenty-five friends was wrecked in the high Andes; the survivors were obliged to eat the bodies of those who had been killed in the crash, preserved in the sub zero temperatures of the Andean winter. After they had been rescued, a few of the team even sought to justify what they had done, not on grounds of plain commonsense, but in terms of the Last Supper, saying that they had gone "right back to the source of Christianity".

In some ways, however, this claim was less absurd than it sounded. After the official adoption of Christianity by the Roman Empire, the view of Jesus as a human sacrifice and of the bread of the Host as representing his body began to be interpreted in an absolutely literal sense. This sacrificial message was crudely expressed by arranging the particles of the Host in such a way as to imitate the shape of the human body, a practice that was forbidden by the Council of Tours in 567. But many Christians still believed in transubstantiation—the notion that in the Mass the wine and bread were physically changed into the body and blood of Christ—though for others the transformation was more symbolic than real. The disputation continued until 1215, when Pope Innocent III decreed that the bread of the Host was truly Christ's flesh. The sacrificial wafer did not *represent* his body; it *became* his body. Thereafter anyone foolish enough to so much as hint that the change was symbolic would himself have been sacrificed at the stake. Thus Christianity adopted as its most sacred rite an act of self-proclaimed cannibalism—a form of god-eating that goes back to those early cults of the deity who died a violent death and whose body was transformed into food and consumed by his worshippers.

No simple explanation can be found as to why, in Africa and elsewhere, cannibalism thrived in some regions and was abhorred in others. In certain parts of Polynesia it had apparently existed in former times and then died out before the arrival of the Europeans. For instance, in Tahiti the king would symbolically eat only the eye of the victim, rather as among the West African Yorubas, the king ate his predecessor's heart. Ostensibly both customs are a survival of the practice of eating the whole body. The uneven presence of cannibalism throughout the world undoubtedly defies logic but it must be remembered in any case that in a general appraisal of human sacrifice cannibalism is only a limited part of the whole story. Where it did occur, whether all the body was eaten or only certain portions, the repast was simply the end of a drama whose climax was marked by the killing of a man rather than by the eating. The sacrificial flesh, like the sacramental wafer, set the seal on an act of spiritual communion between the deity and his people, in which the victim became the god, slain and at times eaten for the safety and salvation of all.

When African sacrificial rites are taken as a whole, the resemblances to those of other lands are more striking than the differences. And if human sacrifice in Africa has unusual traits, these have little to do with cannibalism, which was rarer in that continent than, for instance, in Melanesia. The non-cannibal rituals of Dahomey, for their mammoth scale, have an originality not shared by Congo cannibalism. And yet the ancestor-worship that inspired the Dahoman offerings was present outside Africa, as was also the practice of making a medicine out of human bodies, developed to such a fine art by the people of Sierra Leone and Basutoland. Africa owes its place in the annals of human sacrifice less to the stories of cities of blood, related by untrained observers, than to those timeless vestiges of the king's own immolation when his potency began to wane. Such survivals take us back to the very roots of sacrifice, and to the primordial myth of the god-king, slain in his youth so that his people might thrive.

8

The
Other Side of Paradise

This chapter somewhat arbitrarily embraces an array of islands stretching from Borneo to Hawaii; some of them are huge, others mere specks of coral. It is obviously hard to generalize about a myriad of islands running from one end of the Pacific to the other. Nonetheless certain common traits emerge, and it is surely no coincidence that all these peoples spoke tongues belonging to the same linguistic family, known as Austronesian, and so must have shared a common, if remote, ancestry.

Throughout this vast area society revolved around the person of the king, or chief, as the god's elect. Human offerings marked births and deaths of princes, the tattooing of their children, the dedication of their temples, palaces or boats. Everywhere retainers were needed to serve the ruler in the hereafter, and in many places his wives strangled themselves by his graveside. Such rituals were universally connected with war, for fighting was inseparable from sacrifice since captives were the preferred class of offering; usually only tabu-breakers, criminals and sometimes slaves served as inadequate substitutes. War was therefore endemic, and even tiny Easter Island, with a population of barely six thousand, was racked with endless strife that claimed countless victims.

In Polynesia infanticide, though not unknown elsewhere, was another important form of sacrifice. Paradoxically, the killing of children was closely connected with ancestor-worship; babies would be promptly sent back to the nether world shortly after birth, because they were thought to be the best intermediaries between the living and the sacred dead, reborn on earth in the person of these infants. Particularly if a great man were ill, the little children were looked upon as the chosen advocates to plead his cause with his ancestors and beg them to make him well again. Ritual suicide was another special trait, though not as widespread as in India. The Polynesian practice of self-mutilation is more reminiscent of Mexico.

While their sacred rites had so much in common, the islanders differed in that some ate their victims, while others did not. Certain evidence, such as the pretended eating of the eye in Tahiti, while it was actually swallowed in New Zealand, suggests that cannibalism had once been universally practised in Polynesia, but had been abjured in some places. For even where it was not eaten, the human body was likened to a form of food: in Tahiti victims were hung up alongside fishes and were described as such in sacrificial verse.

The reasons why some were cannibals and others were not are obscure. It is an obvious temptation to fall back on material causes and to insist that religious customs were a mere by-product of the supply of animal protein. Admittedly the Marquesas, though normally well-watered, were subject to terrible droughts, and at such times people had little to eat but themselves; the Fijians had no form of animal food except rats, until the pig was introduced during the eighteenth century. By way of contrast, the diet of the non-cannibal Tahitians was richer. But this argument falls down if one recalls that the most voracious cannibals of all were the Maoris, who occupied a spacious and verdant land. The man-eating tribes of New Guinea hunted wild pigs and a rich variety of birds.

While, therefore, cannibalism was not a common factor, the cult of the human head was almost universal. Fervently practised among the Dyaks of Borneo and the New Guinean Papuans, it was far from absent in Polynesia, and the Marquesans also went on headhunting forays. Heads in Polynesia were a cherished trophy, often reserved for the priests and for the war god; they would be set on poles in serried rows, somewhat recalling the skullracks of Mexico. The cult of the head is both the most primitive and the most enduring form of sacrifice; it was practised in 20,000 B.C., if not before, and survived into the 1970s. However, while heads were everywhere sought, the benefits they bestowed differed widely from place to place. Among certain peoples they served to keep the cosmos in being, while others desired them merely as a tonic for their warriors. In Borneo the skull was a prerequisite of marriage; in New Guinea the novice needed it to become a true member of his tribe.

Human sacrifice went often hand in hand with torture, though here again methods varied from island to island. H. Schärer, the German anthropologist, wrote of the martyrdom suffered by Dyak slave victims; a similar form of death by a thousand cuts was practised by primitive tribes of Mindanao in the Philippines. He rejects the notion that torture sprang from a belief that the soul of a victim was apt to cling to his body and was encouraged to escape if death was inflicted by many separate wounds. He also insists that such cruelty did not spring from sadism or a mere delight in suffering, and sees it more as a need that arose because the slaves were killed as funeral offerings; every single relative had therefore to strike a blow against the victim, to seek release from the state of impurity brought about by the death. This theory, however, hardly accounts for other torments, such as the slow cooking of men by the Fijians. The distribution of torture, like cannibalism, was patchy, and therefore difficult to explain, even if the notion that only a victim's prolonged agonies could relieve man's load of guilt was widespread, if not universal. Simpler ends, such as the imbibing of strength through blood or by taking of heads, are easier to define, but these deeper motivations, such as the upholding of the cosmic order by the Dyaks, or the atonement of sin by the Tahitians, may involve concepts that have no equivalent in our scale of values.

Of all these sacrificial pursuits, headhunting was undoubtedly the most commonly practised throughout the islands as an integral part of the local religion. As champion headhunters, the Dyaks offer a convenient starting point; of all the cult's votaries none outdid the Dyaks of Borneo, for whom it was not a pastime but a passion. Sir Charles Brooke, British Rajah of Sarawak, wrote that his Dyak subjects were eternally begging for permission to go headhunting; their entreaties reminded him of children crying out for sugar plums. His father, Sir James Brooke, the first Rajah, in his journal, published in 1848, counted trophies on display within his kingdom. The Sintah tribe could put into the field about a thousand fighting men, and boasted of a store of a thousand skulls; the Bubaniks numbered only fifty warriors but had "heads plenty"; the Subatas had a mere twenty warriors, and a modest haul of twenty heads.[1] These trophies were taken from neighbouring tribes; those of Malay or Chinese immigrants were treated as a poor substitute.

Dyak is the generic term for a series of tribes living mainly in the eastern part of the great island of Borneo, most of which was a Dutch colony until World War II. Some also inhabit northern Borneo, in the ex-British Protectorate of Sarawak, now part of Malaysia. The Dyaks originally occupied inland valleys, but in Dutch colonial times some moved to the coast and came to be known as Sea Dyaks. Headhunting claimed even more victims among these Sea Dyaks, for Malay pirates would take them on marauding expeditions along the coast. The plunder was duly divided, with the heads going to the Dyaks and goods and female captives to the Malays.

Headhunting among the Dyaks was only stamped out by the Dutch after a bitter struggle. The custom probably reached an all-time peak in the early nineteenth century, when local requirements were boosted by, a brisk export market to meet the demands of European visitors to the South Pacific, who had become eager buyers. Headhunting was still in full swing in the interior of Borneo in the 1860s, but by the end of the century had been drastically curtailed. Henry Ling Roth, who made a close study of the Dyaks that was published in 1896, relates that at that time they still doggedly sought permits to hunt heads. The Dutch authorities by then invariably refused and would try to round up any group that set out on an expedition. If, however, as often happened, the Dyaks evaded pursuit and took some trophies, they had to surrender them and were punished with a heavy fine.[2] Since to do without heads was unthinkable, people would then resort to stealth to obtain them; they would even behead guests while they slept.

In earlier times expeditions were launched with great pomp and ceremony. The chief of a tribe would summon all the male members; after a period of devout fasting—often in isolation in the tabu house— the armed party set out to attack a nearby village; heads of the slain were carried off in triumph while live captives were kept as slaves and as victims for future sacrifice. The preparation of the treasured prize was so elaborate that Ling Roth covers ten pages in describing the details. Methods varied from tribe to tribe: some preserved heads complete with flesh and hair, while others retained the bare skull. In all cases heads were cooked, smoked and dried; often skulls were painted with red and white lines and certain tribes on the east coast carved intricate patterns on their trophies, some of which can still be seen in European museums.

Skulls were displayed in many different ways. The Land Dyaks of the interior built special houses for the purpose. The headhouse lay apart from the rest of the village and also served as a general council chamber and a sleeping place for unmarried youths. The building had a large fireplace in the middle, and in one account it is described as "a very pleasant and comfortable abode". Among the Sea Dyaks the skulls usually became the personal property of the captors and were used to adorn their private dwellings. If only one head was taken on a raid, it was sometimes divided into pieces, and a fragment given to each warrior. At times the Land Dyaks too would split a head in two, and the elaborate ceremonies were repeated for both halves, as if they were whole trophies. Unlike the people of Fiji and New Guinea, the Dyaks were not cannibals; only among the Bahou Tring group were the bodies of trophy heads occasionally eaten.[3]

The Dyak passion for headhunting had therefore nothing to do with cannibal feasts; as a basic feature of their religion, it was prompted by deeper motives which are well explained by Schärer. Any major event might upset the cosmic order in fearful ways; to restore its balance, to ward off evil, and to purify the tribe, human blood was essential, whether from a ritual sacrifice or a captured head.[4] Skulls, therefore, did not merely confer physical strength as in some other lands; they were vital for the ordering of the universe, shaken by any evil done; such evil was washed away by the taking of a head. The sacrifice of slaves, which survived for some time after headhunting had been curtailed, served the same ends. Slaves were offered on the tomb of an important man, particularly on the death of a chief, to restore the cosmic order that had been profoundly upset by the event. Accordingly the very existence of the universe required these two forms of sacrifice; the tribute paid to a dead ruler was a necessary part of this process and even the use of heads as wedding gifts made sure that brides would be fertile and the race survive.

The world of each Dyak group, which had to be maintained at such cost in human life, was a very small one; it embraced only the village itself, whose population might amount to a few hundred, the neighbouring fields, the forest in which they hunted, and a section of the nearest river. At the edge of the village, the dead had a territory of their own; they were not looked upon as beings apart, but as people who still saw and heard all that went on among the living.

The tribe was thus a tight entity, bound together by common ancestors; all who dwelt beyond the confines of the village, and who did not share these forbears, were looked on as not merely alien, but barely human. They were, therefore, worthy objects of raids for heads, needed both to comfort the dead and to succour the living.

Headhunting was sanctified by colourful myth. At their head festivals the Sea Dyaks would invoke the exalted presence of Singalang Burong, God of War. This was because, according to legend, their tribal hero, Kling, had made a great feast and begged Singalang Burong to attend in person. The moth and the swallow were first sent to seek the god; with one bound they cleared the space between the earth and the clouds, beyond which he lived. Eventually Singalang appeared upon the scene, dressed in full regalia, complete with war charms tied round his waist, but he then declared that, before the feast could begin, he must call from the jungle his daughters and sons-in-law. One daughter, however, wife of the bird Katupong, at first flatly refused to come, saying that she would remain at home unless she was given a particular precious ornament. This ornament, the cause of such toil and trouble, turned out to be nothing less than a human head, whether in the form of a mass of putrefying flesh or a black and charred skull. The legend underlines the role of the Dyak women as prime movers in the taking of heads; and it was they who most fiercely resisted its suppression.

Out of the myth of the divine headhuntress sprang the notion of the head trophy as the ideal homage to a lady and the idea that no woman could be wooed with any other gift. It became essential for a warrior to possess at least one skull before he could even contemplate marriage. Often if a man sought to obtain a bride, he would accompany a party of some fifty to a hundred men on a raid into the interior, and would then attack anyone he chanced to meet for the sake of getting his precious dowry. As a native explained to Rajah James Brooke: "No aristocratic youth dares venture to pay his addresses to a Dyak demoiselle, unless he throws at the blushing maiden's feet a net full of skulls. In some districts it is customary for the young lady to desire her lover to cut a thick bamboo from the neighbouring jungle, and when in possession of this instrument, she carefully arranges the cadeau d'amour on the floor, and by repeated blows beats the heads into fragments, which, when thus pounded, are scraped up and cast in the river; at the same time she throws herself into the arms of the enraptured youth, and so commences the honeymoon. The usual practice, however, is to guard the skulls, pickling them with care, as from the extreme heat of the climate, constant attention is required to preserve them".[5]

A sad story is told of an eighteen-year-old youth called Achang which illustrates the problems posed by the implacable demands of Dyak ladies in the 1880s when heads were becoming a luxury. He had fallen in love with a girl even younger than himself, but had been turned down because he had never caught and cooked a head. Achang, aided by a companion, faced his fiancée's challenge by seeking lodging for the night in the house of a Chinese trader; they planned to decapitate him at midnight, since after his head was duly boiled, no one would guess that it had not belonged to a warrior from a rival tribe. The plot failed, since the whole village was roused by the piteous howls of the victim, who was then rescued by a crowd of fifty people with his face gashed all down one side. Achang got off rather lightly; he was left in irons for over a month, but was then released.[6]

Apart from their special use as a dowry, severed heads served many ends. As part of the process of keeping the cosmos stable, they were required for any major event, particularly if it concerned the royal family of a tribe. Whenever a rajah died—as already mentioned—heads had to be secured to mark the event and to serve him in the hereafter. If a child were born to a chief, fresh heads were needed before it could be named; heads were also the best form of guarantee that the women would be fertile. More trivial motives at times sufficed; when an important man had a bad dream, in which he was threatened by sickness or death, he could only free himself from such dire prospects by taking a head or, in later times, by offering a slave.

The atonement for sin and the healing of sickness were in practice linked, since illness was held to be a punishment for some evil deed. The story is told of Rohan, a famous headhunter who had won himself many a skull and, as a result, was rich, powerful and respected. Suddenly he fell ill, suffering from headaches so excruciating that they nearly drove him mad. Since he was not fit to go headhunting, his father-in-law devised a less chivalrous way for Rohan to obtain another trophy in order to get well again. He told his slave-girl to go down to the river to fetch water; he then gave

Rohan his sword and let him out of the house by another door; Rohan crept down to the river and at one blow decapitated the unsuspecting wench. The father-in-law soaked a bundle of leaves in the girl's blood and rubbed it all over Rohan's body, saying: "I wash away your disease; I wash away evil". The remedy, though drastic, was of no avail, and the patient died.[7]

The Dyaks were obsessed with the notion that severed heads continued to exist as living beings. Among the Sea Dyaks, after a head had been brought to shore with elaborate ceremonies and wrapped in leaves of the nipah palm, it was for months the object of deep reverence and flattering speech. Choice morsels from the table would be thrust into its mouth, and at the end of the meal a cigar would be placed between its lips. Having shaken off all former loyalties, heads were treated as adopted sons of the tribe that had taken them. Accordingly, when Rajah Brooke recovered some skulls and offered them to the relatives of their original owners, they refused to take them back.

After headhunting had been largely suppressed, less ostentatious forms of ritual killing survived into the twentieth century. Schärer, writing in the 1940s, uses the present tense to describe in detail the sacrificing of slaves, although the Dutch had officially banned slavery in 1894. He insists that since headhunting and slave sacrifice served the same purposes, the latter "must" have been a modern substitute, brought into use when the supply of heads began to dry up. But while Schärer is probably right to suggest that the two forms are mere variants in Dyak ritual, he cites no clear evidence that slave sacrifice was at all new; one suspects that, like so many "new" practices, discovered by the white man, it really had a long history as an alternative to headhunting. Slaves' heads only differed in that they enjoyed lower status than captured enemy heads and, far from being adopted, remained aliens. As Schärer stresses, a slave was always obtained from a rival group and was not merely without rights, but without sanctity as a human being, since he was unconnected with the spirits and ancestors of the group. His death did not alter his standing and he remained the slave of the dead man for whom he was sacrificed. He was, in modern terms, a non-person among his masters.

The standard method of obtaining slaves was by purchase, and the current price at the end of the century was about four hundred guilders. To spare the man's feelings, negotiations for his purchase were not conducted in his presence. Sacrificial slaves could also be robbed from another village by means of a raid—a surreptitious version of the headhunting forays of earlier times. Occasionally condemned criminals from within the tribe were also used for sacrifice. Slaves could be killed in one of two ways. The first was by a sudden blow, which had the advantage that the victim expired quickly, before he had had time to utter a curse on his slayers—an omen that aroused the deepest dread. More often, however, they died a slow death towards the end of a feast for the departed, just before the moment when the latter's soul was thought to enter the village of the dead. When the victim was about to be sacrificed at the grave the presiding chief would address the dead man: "Soul of my father, accept the soul of this man. He will be charged to accompany you and to obey your command. He will fish for you and cut bamboo staves, he will row you and will arrange your abode in the City of the Dead, where you can live in peace and comfort. Cease therefore to press upon your children and grandchildren, and to make our life burdensome". To the victim the chief would say: "Be no longer sorry for yourself. You will have to accompany my father. Do not be obstinate, when he orders and commands you, but heed his words in the rich city".[8]

The slave was first bathed, richly adorned and given food. After this, he was tied to the sacrificial pole, called a Sapendoe, standing about ten feet high and usually carved in the form of a human figure, in recent times often a white man, missionary or explorer. At nightfall the victim had to suffer a cruel and slow death, described by Schärer as a true martyrdom. During a long and elaborate ritual dance, those present would jab his body with long needles, sharp bamboo sticks and other instruments, until he eventually expired. The corpse was then placed on the ground, the head facing towards the rising sun and covered by a cloth. A curious ceremony followed, during which the relatives of the dead man walked over the body. After this the priest, facing first east and then west would say: "I lift you up in the direction of the sunset. All is now extinguished: all evil, all ritual tabus, all fevers, sicknesses and pain; all is now extinguished." Then, turning, he would continue: "I lift you up in the direction of the rising sun. Now can we, the living, once more full of peace and holiness, seek our living in agreeable fashion, feed ourselves and care for ourselves, as long as we are separated from you . . . we are freed from all evil and all ritual tabus . . . we can once more work and tend our fields."

Thus, like headhunting, slave sacrifice served as a kind of purification or atonement—that basic ritual whereby the one was chosen to lift the load of guilt from the many. In addition, Dyak slave offering is a good example of how practices can change under outside pressure; for even if slaves were killed for certain ends in much earlier times, as I suspect, they also served in the twentieth century as a convenient substitute for severed heads, when these could no longer be found. Change in this case was hardly for the better; unlike a slave a decapitated head at least could not be tortured.

Second only to the Dyaks in the headhunting league were certain Papuan tribes of New Guinea, living mostly in the swampy areas in the western half of the island, which was formerly Dutch New Guinea and is now part of Indonesia. Headhunting and cannibalism were by no means confined to the Dutch half, and in Australian New Guinea to the east, some peoples, isolated and unobserved, such as the Baktamans, hunted heads into the 1960s. Unlike the Dyaks, the Papuans were enthusiastic cannibals. In Australian New Guinea, headhunting raids from the western half of the island were a constant menace and the cause of many Australian protests to the Dutch. Gerard Zegwaard, who during the 1950s lived among the Asmats, a tribe numbering about twenty thousand, wrote in 1959 that they were still hunting heads then, though the neighbouring Jaquai had already been forced to give up the custom. Zegwaard was the first white man to live among the Asmats and no official was present to enforce the Dutch edict against headhunting.[9]

The dark-skinned Papuans are of Melanesian stock and, therefore, more closely related to many Pacific Islanders, such as the Fijians, than to the Dyaks of Borneo, which lay some thousand miles to the north-west of New Guinea. Nonetheless, there is so much in common between Dyak and Papuan headhunting that it is hard to describe the latter in any detail without risk of repetition. But if the heads, so eagerly sought in the two great islands, served spiritual purposes in both, the emphasis was often different. In Borneo they mainly restored the balance of the universe, while in Papua they gave added strength to the individual.

Heads (and bodies) in Papua were also formerly hunted by full-

scale warlike expeditions, launched after the most elaborate ceremonies. Here too, when such tactics were banned by the colonial
authorities, raiders came to rely on stealth in place of valour. Tribesmen would then simply go out and snatch the first people they came
upon, such as a party of women found fishing or a single individual
unwise enough to walk alone in the jungle. A rigid rule decreed
that the prisoner was never killed by his captor. Anyone close at
hand might be called upon, and this second person, besides slaying
the captive, had the singular privilege of biting off his nose. He was
therefore known as the Poke Vake, or "nose man". The Papuan
captor was subject to strange and strict tabus: he could not drink
pure water from a river, but only that which had been stirred up
and made muddy; he had to enter his house by the back door and
was restricted to food roasted in the fire that he had cooked himself;
he also abstained from sexual intercourse. After three days' seclusion
in his house, he bathed in the sea and was freed from his tabus.

Prisoners taken on a full-scale headhunting raid—when these were
still possible—were not usually killed on the spot, but taken home
alive, to be tortured as part of their sacrifice. Sometimes, however,
victims would be beheaded one after the other, every time the party
reached the confluence of a river. A few captives were never killed,
but, as among certain American Indians, adopted as members of
their captors' tribe. Among the Kaimaris and certain other groups,
heads were first offered to a strange image known as a "Kaiemunu",
a large wickerwork figure standing up to twelve feet high. On occasion, the head or even the whole body was thrust into its mouth as
an offering. Each Kaiemunu, as the trophy was placed in its mouth,
was made to rear and dance, as if in jubilation; finally it spewed out
the offering onto the floor.

Papuan headhunting rites, like those in Borneo, were basic to the
ancestor cult, and the Asmats had a colourful myth to account for
their origin. There were two brothers, the elder called Desoipitsj,
and the younger Biwiripitsj. One day the younger of the two brought
home a pig, which he proceeded to decapitate. When he apologised
for not having produced a human head, Desoipitsj answered: "Well,
you can have mine". Biwiripitsj took his brother at his word, killed
him with a spear, and beheaded him with a bamboo knife. The loose
head, however, became very loquacious and began to give orders
to Biwiripitsj, which he dutifully obeyed. It first taught him the ideal

techniques for decapitation and laid down the rites for headhunting raiders when they returned in triumph to their village. It then decreed the key role to be played by heads in the initiation of youths. Finally, it taught Biwiripitsj, and hence future generations, how to prepare the already severed head. In the evening it had to be roasted; during the night it was to be kept in a loft and then scalped the following morning. After the brains had been removed and eaten, the skull was to be painted with ash, ochre and chalk, and decorated with tassels of cassowary feathers and beads. Thus adorned, it was ready to be used in an initiation ceremony.

Torture was applied if the tribe sought vengeance for wrongs done by neighbours. In such cases, care was naturally taken to bring the prisoner back alive to the village. The widow of any man whose death was to be avenged would have him dressed in her mourning garments and at times had the added privilege of blinding him. The victim was then led to the special stone circle reserved for such ceremonies, enveloped in coconut leaves and lashed to a tree. The leaves were lighted and as a rule he soon expired, being thereby spared the more prolonged agonies inflicted by Dyaks or Fijians on captives. Beheading in these cases was performed after death.

Heads were required for a whole variety of purposes, such as the dedication of a bachelor's house or the death of a chief. A severed head was above all an indispensable item of equipment in the complicated ritual initiation rites for adolescents, as decreed in detail by the decapitated Desoipitsj, the original victim. The decorated skull would be placed at the beginning of the ceremony between the spread legs of the initiate, who sat on the floor of the bachelor's house in this pose of shame. The head was placed against the groin of the youth, and remained there for two or three days; during this time he had to gaze intently into its countenance and could only take food secretly, when no one was looking. After this long vigil, the villagers dressed up in their best finery, and their canoes were freshly painted. The initiate would stand in his relatives' canoe, the skull placed before him in the vessel. First he had to behave as a worn-out old man, growing progressively weaker and weaker, until he finally collapsed and lay down on the bottom of the canoe. At that stage he was lifted up by one of his mother's brothers and, together with his skull, was immersed for a while in the sea. After this act of purification, he was "reborn" and played out the opposite role of a baby and then a child who did not know how to handle the paddle (such notions of being purified and then born again as a tiny infant are a common feature of initiation rites in many lands). These ceremonies were followed by elaborate dances, in which the novice bore aloft the severed head. In the myth of the first initiation, the head of Desoipitsj had at this point been roasted and scalped (though this apparently did not stem its flow of words). And just as the first legendary initiate had taken Desoipitsj's name, so it was usual for initiates to adopt the name of the skull used in their rites. Hence, when a head was taken, it was vital to discover the name of its owner. Zegwaard relates that in 1954 three Asmats had been received in a certain village as guests but were then marked down for decapitation. Accordingly, a song was intoned in their honour and they were asked to give their names so that they could be mentioned in the song. Once the names were known, they could be duly beheaded.

Unlike the Dyaks, the people of New Guinea did not regard a head as indispensable for marriage. Instead, the young men required his head at an earlier stage in his career, to develop his body and help him reach sexual maturity. When the head was laid between the spread legs of the boy, it was placed so that it touched his genitals. Villagers insisted that after this, the boys grew very fast. The role of the head was thus in effect reversed: the young Dyak had to take a head, as proof of martial vigour already attained, while for the Papuan it was not the proof of manliness, but the means of gaining it.

Cannibalism in New Guinea was less an end in itself than a sequel to headhunting, even if in certain instances, strangers may have been killed and eaten as a convenient form of food. Such cases were, however, an exception to the rule that eating of human flesh came as the finale to an elaborate ceremony, in which all leading villagers partook, except the slayer himself. Certain scholars, such as C. G. Seligman, who writes copiously on New Guinea, stress the role of "revenge" cannibalism; Seligman goes so far as to state that in most cases in the south-eastern district of Papua, cannibalism was a "solemn act of revenge". Garry Hogg, taking his cue from Seligman, whom he quotes freely, even heads his chapter on New Guinea "revenge cannibalism". In certain cases an element of revenge was certainly present, as when a widow had the right to blind the victim. But Seligman begins his long account by admitting that "lack of time" prevented full enquiries and his conclusions seem open to question. In contrast, Zegwaard spent several years among a single group. His account of the Asmats shows in detail that headhunting was basic to tribal myth and religion; hence both the taking of a head and the cannibalistic aftermath were unquestionably a human sacrifice. War, an integral part of headhunting, was itself a religious ritual, even if tinged by motives of revenge. Invariably, warfare among village societies is highly ceremonial, and New Guinea was no exception in this respect. Warriors painted and decorated themselves, strengthened their arms with magic incantations, danced ceremonial dances to invoke their ancestors, submitted to tabus and performed acts of purification before setting out. Therefore suggestions that headhunting in New Guinea was more often to be viewed as a secular act of revenge have missed the point. The ends to be achieved were sacred and universal: the burial of the dead, the initiation of the novice, and the safeguarding of the tribal world.

Even a particularly ghoulish form of man-eating that only slowly came to the knowledge of the authorities—the exhumation and eating of corpses—probably had a supernatural basis. The motives behind the act have never come to light; nonetheless it recalls the eating of the dead by certain African tribes as part of their cult of ancestor worship. For instance, the reason why two women dug up a child in New Guinea (the daughter of one of them) and ate her was not explained to the court that tried them and punished them with a short term of imprisonment.[10]

We have mentioned that the Asmats were not the only people of New Guinea still to be practising ritual cannibalism in the 1950s; indeed, some others went on doing so for considerably longer. The Swedish anthropologist Fredrik Barth in 1975 published a book on the Baktamans, who numbered 183 persons and occupied a tract of mountain rain forest near the centre of the island. In 1950 the Baktamans made war on a neighbouring group; in the first attack, they killed and ate five of their enemies. The struggle continued for some time, but in 1964 Australian patrol officers entered the Murray Valley and since then warfare has more or less ceased. Nonetheless, when in 1968 the Baktamans held an initiation ceremony and invited some neighbours, the latter refused for fear that their hosts might resort to the favourite local ruse of turning a banquet into a cannibal feast by killing and eating all the guests. Barth stresses the sacrificial nature of cannibalism among the Baktamans, who regarded human victims as a gift from their ancestors, granted in answer to prayers. In the war temple, known as the Yolam, until recently a ritual took place in which only the élite among the initiates, the seventh grade, could take part. The ancestors were thought to participate in the ensuing feast, in which a leg of pig and a human leg were steam-cooked over the sacred cooking-stones; during the eating, prayers of thanks were recited and scraps of flesh were offered to the Holy Fire.

The American anthropologist Robert Glasse writes in 1967 of the strange phenomenon of kuru in the eastern highlands of New Guinea. Kuru, a nervous disease completely unknown outside this isolated mountainous centre, affected about 35,000 people. Doctors and geneticists, after decades of intensive study, concluded that it was most probably caused by eating human brain material. The disease still takes an annual toll of a hundred lives. Patients gradually become paralyzed and in the terminal stage often roll over and suffocate; women and children are especially vulnerable. Between 1957 and 1964, 1416 people are known to have died of kuru, and the victims were themselves mostly eaten; sometimes the bodies would be buried for several days to give them more flavour and because maggots were treated as an extra delicacy. The high proportion of female sufferers may be due to the special rights of women over the brain of the deceased. In one part of the region a man's brain was eaten by his sister, and in another by his son's wife, his sister and his maternal aunts. Since 1960, when cannibalism more or less ceased, there has been a remarkable decline in the incidence of kuru. Experiments are now being made with chimpanzees, who are injected with the brain tissue of people who died of kuru; the more direct method of feeding them with brain material from a diseased animal is of no use, since, unlike humans, chimpanzees refuse to eat the brains of their fellow creatures.

In the south-western part of the island headhunting and cannibalism seem to have ceased at a slightly earlier date, though memories lingered on. The Swedish naturalist Sten Bergman revisited the village of Atsj in 1957–8, where he met Ojepietsj, the head of the largest bachelor house, who had enjoyed great fame as a headhunter. Ojepietsj still had eighteen human skulls hanging on a rotten rope in his house, the spoils of past triumphs, since by 1957 the village was under Dutch Government control and headhunting was punishable by three years in prison. Another great headhunter, called Pinim, conceded that life was better now that headhunting was a thing of the past: everyone, including the headhunters themselves, could sleep more soundly at night.

New Guinea is still not fully explored and it cannot, therefore, be stated as a fact that ritual cannibalism—however circumscribed—does not still exist. British anthropologist Paul Sillitoe of Cambridge uses the present tense when he writes, in 1978, of endemic warfare among the tribes of the interior, in a study based on the findings of a computer programmed with data on war among twenty-seven of these tribes. Most of the latter, according to Sillitoe's map, live in eastern New Guinea, now an independent state. He mentions the high incidence of cannibalism as part of the warlike tradition, but does not say how far, if at all, the practice continues.

Certainly the notion of headhunting seems to command a certain respect in New Guinea, even in places where the practice has ceased. On 24 March 1977, as reported in the London *Times*, Queen Elizabeth II was presented with a headhunter's trophy, complete with heads, when she attended a "people's welcome" in the Port Moresby sports stadium. This Ariba, or skullrack, now in the British Museum, probably dates from the early years of this century and came from Goaribari Island, the only place in New Guinea where missionaries are known to have been eaten by cannibals. The Rev James Chalmers, his assistant and eleven young Papuan converts were clubbed to death there in 1901. The Queen's skullrack, standing about three feet high, takes the shape of a crouching human figure; tied to its. arms are two yellowed human skulls, as well as the stuffed head of a hornbill and several hornbeam beaks.

The 1970s have been hard on headhunters, both in New Guinea and elsewhere. The anthropologist Michelle Zimbalist Rosaldo writes that among the Ingolots, a group of some 3,500 farmers in the hills of northern Luzon, headhunting was a declining but still lively practice in 1969. However, to the best of her knowledge, the last beheadings took place shortly before the declaration of martial law in the Philippines in 1972. She insists that the killing was strictly ritual and was not affected by politics: "Ingolots explain headhunting by reference not to politics or property, but the desires of men who, because of insult, grief, or a sense of youthful inadequacy have felt a 'weight' which they would cast off from their 'hearts'. Severing a human head—regardless of the social provenance or status of one's victim—and tossing it directly to the ground, is said to 'lighten' what were 'cloudy and distracted' thoughts, provide killers (and, through celebration, the community at large) with new energy and vitality and (by inciting envy) encourage other men to kill."

Killings of a rather different kind seem still to occur in the Philippines. If ritual is lacking, religion of a sort is present, since the killings are attributed to "cultist" groups. According to the *Manila Bulletin Today* of 16 August 1979, Edgar Arguelles, aged twenty, was one of four witnesses to the slaughter of four persons in South Cotabato in the island of Mindanao. He was forced to eat of their flesh before he escaped from the group. He said that the cult members usually cooked human flesh with noodles, but one time he vomited because "he could not take it".

Though they were not headhunters, the head of one victim, Antonio Dayin, was brought to police headquarters in nearby Santos City. A further victim, Pepito Guymon, was a preacher of the Christian Missionary Alliance. Another witness said that he saw a man named Saguil butchered in order to celebrate the birthday of the wife of the cult leader. The parish priest of Santos City even managed to bring the matter to the notice of the Deputy Minister of Defense of the Philippines when he visited the area.

Melanesians in countless other islands were not to be outdone by the Papuans of New Guinea in their cult of sacrifice and cannibalism. East of New Guinea and north-east of Australia lie the Solomon Islands; their inhabitants had the distinction of being the first of this dark-skinned race to be seen by a European, centuries before anyone had heard of Australia or New Zealand, let alone of Tahiti or Hawaii. For over seventy years after Columbus had discovered America, the Spaniards enjoyed a virtual monopoly over the Pacific Ocean, but knew none of its islands except for the Philippines. However, in 1568 Don Alvaro de Mendaña first sighted the Solomon Islands, so named because the isles of the Pacific were the fabled repository of the treasure of King Solomon. Mendaña soon discovered to his horror that the Solomon Islanders ate baked human flesh. Since he felt that cannibals deserved to be "punished", he ordered their villages to be set on fire. Not unnaturally the news spread, and the natives of the next island where he landed gave him such a hot reception that he sailed away, still convinced that the land he had discovered must be filled with gold. For two centuries the Solomon Islanders were left to their own devices, and no Europeans came to visit them again before the eighteenth century.

Of all the Melanesians, none were more fervent than the Fijians in their cult of cannibal sacrifice. Fairly ample reports from laymen supplement the lurid accounts of Christian missionaries and inform us about what went on in Fiji and the beliefs that prompted their acts. We are here more concerned with the sacrifice than with the cannibalistic aftermath that so shocked Christian susceptibilities. It has, nonetheless, to be borne in mind that flesh-eating—symbolic or real—is itself an integral part of certain acts of sacrifice. Fijians claimed that the best way to cook a man was to bake him whole. This method was, in any case, prescribed by ritual, since elaborate ceremonies had to be performed round the whole cooked body before carving and eating could begin. At the time of the European discovery, Fijians used for the purpose iron pots in which South Pacific traders cured sea-slugs—a valued article in the Chinese market. These pots were large enough to take two entire men at a time; bodies were normally boiled in a sitting position. The noted traveller, Alfred St Johnston, describes how, before a man was cooked, they would paint his face as if he were a live warrior, and one of the chiefs would stand by the corpse, which was already arranged as if seated, and talk to it for some time in mocking tones, after which it would be handed over to the cooks.

Some of the most famous Fijian cannibals are reputed to have eaten hundreds of human beings; sometimes a gourmet chief would reserve for himself the whole body—or bakolo, as human flesh was called— for his own consumption, having the flesh partly baked and salted in order to prevent its going putrid. The effects of such gluttony were not always salutary. When Berthold Seemann went to Fiji in the 1850s, the half-brother of King Kuruduadua had just died and the court was still in mourning for him. His head wife took Seemann to the prince's grave, lamenting all the way that if only he had abstained from eating so much bakolo, he might still be alive; his friends had done all in their power to convince him that he was ruining his constitution by such overindulgence. Fijians regarded bakolo as hard to digest, even for the strongest and fittest among them, and stated that after a cannibal feast people tended to become constipated. To ease such ailments, human flesh was always served with green vegetables, sometimes also garnished with yams and taros.

Professional flesh guzzlers, however, were an exception to the rule and, as already stressed, if all cannibal tales were to be taken at their face value, many peoples would simply have eaten themselves out of existence—an unknown phenomenon. Seemann points out that it would be a complete mistake in the first place to suppose that all Fijians ate human flesh. For instance, among the Nekelo tribes, the common people, as well as women of all classes, were forbidden to touch it; cannibalism was reserved for chiefs and nobles. At the time when Seemann was writing, in 1862, what might be called a "liberal" or enlightened party had come into being in Fiji, consisting of people who refused to take part in cannibal banquets; it was the "conservative" chiefs and gentry who looked upon the eating of bakolo as a solemn duty which they owed to society.

Accounts of Fijian beliefs lack many details. Enough is known, however, to show that cannibalism was essentially sacrificial. One observer, the American anthropologist A. P. Rice, states that it was the gods who demanded man-eating as a form of offering; parts of the bodies were often given to the war god, and the heads turned over to the priests. Seemann tells of a ceremony in which some limbs were eaten, while one leg was taken and deposited at the grave of the deceased king. St Johnston, notwithstanding the ceremonial rites that he describes, became convinced that the Fijians ate human flesh more out of greed but Seemann is almost certainly right to deny this and insist that they lied to foreigners about these practices, which cannot be divorced from their religious content. The use of torture—so often a part of sacrifice—is significant. Sometimes the victim was not killed beforehand but placed bound in the pot and then boiled. One hideous form had a special name, Vakatoga; a man's limbs would be cut off while he was still alive and then baked and eaten before his very eyes. Garry Hogg quotes missionary reports of people who had their tongues torn out by a fish-hook and eaten in their presence.

Certain other kinds of sacrifice existed in Fiji that did not involve cannibalism at all. Retainers' bodies were buried with a dead monarch to serve him in the next world. Relatives were expected to make sure that a great man had plenty of "grass" to line his grave. "Grass" signified the corpses of male and female slaves, strewn at the bottom of the tomb for the dead man to rest upon. Often his wives were strangled just as their master was dying. Other universally practised forms of non-cannibal sacrifice were in use, such as the live burial of men in a standing position in the post-holes of a chief's house or of a temple. A few observers offer us statistics for Fiji. A report of two hundred and sixty people being roasted and eaten at one time is almost certainly an exaggeration, and most accounts tell of two or three victims at a time. Seemann counted in a village over four hundred stones, one of which had been set up each time that a victim had been slain; these stones, however, could have been the work of decades, if not centuries.

Beyond Melanesia lies Polynesia, inhabited by people of much lighter skin. The Polynesian Islands occupy a triangle, at whose apex lies the Hawaiian group and whose base stretches for nearly five thousand miles from New Zealand north-eastwards towards the tiny outpost of Easter Island. Both the peoples' religion and their language have much in common throughout this vast stretch of ocean. Where human sacrifice is concerned, however, the panorama is more varied; many common features are to be found, as well as certain differences. Not all Polynesians were cannibals; in all the islands, however, the slaying of men and women was centred upon the king, particularly to honour his death, and in most his widows committed their peculiar form of suttee. Universally, in these sea-girt isles, the human victim was likened to a big fish. The gods of Polynesia shared a special fondness for child offerings.

To describe the sacrificial rites of each of the countless archipelagoes would require a volume to itself and I will therefore concentrate upon the three principal island groups, the Hawaiian Islands, the Society Islands (centred upon Tahiti) and New Zealand. In addition, Tonga and Samoa, situated at the western end of Polynesia, deserve mention, since archaeology has proved that these were the first islands to be reached by man. To judge by a primitive form of pottery unearthed in recent years, Tonga, the most westerly group, was already settled by about 1100 B.C., and Samoa, to the north-east, by 800 B.C. Tonga is also nearest to Fiji, and though racially distinct, its inhabitants, as a result of travel between the two groups, adopted many Fijian customs, including cannibalism.

An important Tongan feast was the coming-of-age of the chief's heir, when it was usual to sacrifice about ten people; a chief's death also claimed many victims, often including the wives of the departed, who strangled themselves. Auto-sacrifice was a common sign of mourning; when an important man died, people would cut off their fingers, slash their arms with knives, and burn their skins. The amputation of children's fingers was thought to be an excellent means of moving the gods to cure the ailments of a nobleman. In addition, petty wars between the islands yielded a rich haul of captives, who were sacrificed and at times eaten. The Tongans claimed that these customs were introduced after a few enterprising mariners had gone to Fiji and become versed in local tactics and rituals.

From Tonga and Samoa, some of the Polynesians eventually sailed eastwards in about 300 A.D. and settled in the Marquesas. This group of islands acted as a springboard from which other archipelagoes were later peopled. Tahiti was settled first, and other canoes landed in Hawaii in about 600 A.D.; New Zealand was finally reached in about 1000 A.D. by people coming from Tahiti. This sequence has to be borne in mind as a background to methods of human sacrifice in the different island groups.

The Marquesans, like the people of Tonga and Samoa, whence they had come, were avid cannibals. No major event was allowed to pass without at least a few human offerings. People would be harpooned through the mouth with a huge hook made of human bone and dragged by a line, like fishes, to the scene of sacrifice, accompanied by solemn chanting and singing; epidemics and even the chief's nightmares were also a pretext for such rituals. Like the Dyaks, the Marquesans went on expeditions to take heads, whether openly or by stealth. In cases where stealth was used, mainly women and children were the victims; the children would be secured by a kind of wooden clamp fixed to chin and mouth, and then slung over the side of the canoe for the return journey. Suttee was widely practised by wives on the ruler's death. In addition, great prestige attached to other forms of ritual self-slaughter and it was commonly believed that suicides went to a special paradise shared only by nobles, fallen warriors, and women who died in childbirth. The rest of the departed were doomed to the dark abode known as Hawaiki.[11]

The fairy-tale scenery of Tahiti (or Otahiti as it used to be called) surpasses every dream of Pacific Island beauty. On his first visit to this earthly paradise, Captain James Cook was surprised to find not only abundant signs of human sacrifice, but warlike operations on a mammoth scale; when he arrived, three hundred vessels had been fitted out for the invasion of the nearby island of Moorea, manned by eight thousand resplendent warriors. But if the Society Islands were plagued by warfare, their customs were perhaps a trifle less savage than those of their neighbours. Cannibalism was unknown and torture less in evidence. Cruelty, however, there was in plenty, and the German anthropologist Alfred Schoch, in his invaluable study of human sacrifice in Polynesia, vividly sums up the situation in fun-loving, happy-go-lucky Tahiti. The romantic euphoria that surrounded this island, based on accounts of a life of uninterrupted song, dance and sex, is contrasted with the cruelty and lust for war that presented the Islanders in a double light. This darker side to their nature was probably intensified by the shock of European contact.[12]

Tahiti is of special note because Captain Cook—on his last voyage in 1777—attended in person a human sacrifice of which he provides an excellent eye-witness account. Formerly his Tahitian friends had been reticent on the subject of sacrifice, but they now cast aside all reserve and pressed him to attend a ceremony. The English visitor was told by Chief Touha that he had ordered a man to be killed and that he was to be sacrificed to seek the aid of the great god in the war against Moorea. This act of worship was to take place at the Morae, or temple, at Attahooroo. Cook went, accompanied by the artist John Webber, who painted the scene. According to Cook's written account, two priests made high-flown speeches to the body of the victim; as they spoke, both held aloft tufts of red feathers. One of them then plucked out the corpse's left eye and offered it to the presiding chief on a leaf; four pigs were also sacrificed. As an explorer and a man with few religious prejudices, Cook makes no effort to hide his interest in what went on. His account of the long drawn-out proceedings conveys the tension in the air and the ecstasy of communion with the sublime, achieved by the sacrifice. He fully sensed the celebrants' conviction that these rites alone could bring the unseen powers to their side in the coming war.

Webber's picture soon became celebrated and was endlessly reproduced. As the picture shows (see the illustration), he was a clever draughtsman, with a special flair for painting tropical vegetation as well as native ornament and costume, though his Tahitian priests have a very Italianate look. Cook stands to one side with Touha and other nobles. He has removed his hat, but dressed in breeches, stockings, long waistcoat and top-coat he must have been suffocating with heat, as he stands close to a blazing fire, on which two boys are roasting a pig as part of the sacrifice. In contrast, the priests depicted on the other side of the scene, two of whom beat drums, are stripped to the waist. The body of the victim in the middle is trussed to a pole like an animal, and two men are digging the grave in the background. Webber's "Sacrifice" was later used by the London Missionary Society to serve its own ends; new engravings were made and his rather graceful Tahitians were touched up to give them a more brutish look and the skulls in the background redrawn in sharper outline.

On this occasion Cook counted in all forty-nine skulls of former victims lying before the Morae; most seemed fairly fresh. He was convinced that the Tahitians were reformed cannibals and that the custom of plucking out the left eye and offering it to the king, who *pretended* to eat it, was a survival of this. Our astute observer was probably right since in cannibal New Zealand the victim's left eye was also plucked out and actually eaten before the rest of the body was consigned to the stewpot.[13] In the Marquesas, the chief priest also had a right to eat the victim's eye.

When I first saw Webber's illustration of the sacrifice that he and Cook had attended, in which the victim had already been killed, I could not help feeling that the gruesomeness of the performance had been deliberately muted for Cook's benefit, and that the victim, supposedly dead, was in fact still alive, ready to be slain as soon as Cook had left the scene. For almost invariably in sacrificial rites, the awesome climax is marked by the actual death of the victim on the god's altar in the presence of the god, whom he personifies. By comparison, a ceremony performed over a mere corpse seems tame, amounting to little more than an ordinary funeral. Cook and Webber, however, were evidently correct in their description and Schoch confirms that the victim was normally killed outside the temple, since to slay any man within its precincts was treated as sacrilege. The Hawaiians shared this view, and no blood could be shed inside their temples.

By Cook's time, the war god, Oro, greedy for human victims, reigned supreme in the Tahitian pantheon. His cult had started in another of the Society Islands, Raiatea, where the hallowed shrine of Opoa stood, and he later became the patron god of the whole island group.

The right to offer human victims on Tahiti was the strict preserve of the king, who exercised it on a generous scale. Pretexts for sacrifice were many: the investiture of a chief, the burial of the dead, the start of a military campaign or the making of peace, the dedication of a temple to Oro, the launching of a holy boat sacred to Oro, which acted as a kind of flagship. Such events required one or more human offerings. In addition to war captives, victims were taken from the lowest class of society, people without property and without rights of any sort, as well as those who had committed a crime or offended a chief or a priest. If one member of a family became a victim, then the whole family was liable for eventual sacrifice.

All such offerings were a tribute to Oro. Douglas Oliver in his book *Ancient Tahitian Society* describes the great sacrificial feast of the god that according to tradition had been established at Opoa in 1350 A.D. and continued till the end of the pagan era.

> The time of such a gathering was one of awful solemnity to those on land and sea. The old and infirm, and women and children, with their domestic animals, retired to places far inland prepared for them; all was still along the shore, even the sea and elements, which, tradition states, were hushed in unison for the festivity of the gods.

Just as the day broke the canoes in double file approached the sacred passage of Te-ava-moa, filled with countless dignitaries of high rank, in grand array, unarmed and unaccompanied by women and children.

> Across the bows connecting each double canoe was a floor, covering the chamber containing idols, drums, trumpet shells and other treasures for the gods and people of Raiatea; and upon the floor were placed in a row sacrifices from abroad, which consisted of human victims brought for that purpose and just slain, and great fishes newly caught. . . . They were placed upon the floor . . . alternately a man and a cavalli fish, a man and a shark, a man and a turtle, and finally a man closed the line. Behind this grim spectacle stood two or three priests in sacerdotal attire, which consisted of a plain loin girdle, a shoulder cape reaching down to the waist . . . and a circular cap fitting closely to the head—all made of finely braided purau bark bleached white.[14]

The canoes were quickly drawn up on shore and were greeted by the king of Raiatea, together with his priests and nobles. Then everyone set about disposing of the newly arrived sacrificial victims. They strung them through the heads with braided cord (a procedure known by the special term *tu'i-aha*), and then hung them on the boughs of trees, the fish alternating with human bodies. When this was done, the priests of Oro chanted the magic words: "Now eat of thy long-legged fish, Oro-mata-'oa! O my king. Eat of thy fish of the sea, my king". Other slain victims were then laid on the road that led up to the inner marae, and over their corpses were drawn the canoes containing the idols of the gods. Mystic rites were performed in the inner temple, where no fire was kindled and no food eaten during the day. At nightfall, the clergy entered the court of the marae, invoked all the gods to partake of Oro's hospitality, and ate a sacred repast in the shadow of the suspended and prostrate bodies, arranged in the manner ordained by the deity. Early the next day the human "long-legged" fish were taken down and buried, along with the mutilated bodies that had served as rollers for the canoes; they were placed in a sitting posture in their graves. This ceremony also had its special name, *ha'apou* (setting down).

In these sacrifices to Oro, atonement was a major theme; ever-present was the need to be freed from sin and to make amends for wrongs both intended and unintended. At another Oro ceremony involving sacrifice, after the great "dismissal" of sin, the priest would chant: "The evil of the sovereign and of the clans is ended; the inner service has wiped out sin, the closing prayer is finished, and all is clean. Here are the ura feathers, here is the peace token of coconut flowers, here is thy man, from his head down to his feet, his feet to his head, to arrest thine anger of great growth, O god; for great crimes, for family discord, for hasty words, for irreverence to the gods, for imperfectly scraping off the moss of the marae, for rankling rage concealed, for mutual estrangement of friends, for cursing, for annihilating by sorcery, for sending evil spirits into others. They are the sins which displease thee, O god".[15]

The much larger group, named by Cook the Sandwich Islands, but now called Hawaii, was forcibly unified with the aid of firearms. By 1810 A.D. all the islands had come under the sway of the Kamehameha dynasty of Oahu, where Honolulu is situated; whereas each had possessed its warring kings, a single monarch now reigned supreme. As lords of, by Polynesian standards, such a vast domain, the kings of Hawaii were held in peculiar awe by their subjects. Even in the times of Kamehameha I's forbears, the king's tabu was so strict that if the shadow of a common man fell across the monarch, he had forthwith to be sacrificed. Any subject who saw him by day had to die and for that reason the king went out only at night.

Like the rulers of Tahiti, the Hawaiian dynasty had its own special god, Kukailimoku, to whom human sacrifice was frequent. The king was the god's high priest, and in a land where the monarch was semi-divine, human offering was the preserve of his dynasty and its household god; since he was also god of war, many offerings took place before and after battle, in the days before hostilities between the islands had ended. Such rites aimed to secure the wellbeing of the royal family in a multiplicity of ways. If the king was sick, men had to be killed to assure his recovery; twenty people might be sacrificed at a time, and many were slain before the final illness and death of Kamehameha I: when he died in 1819 the toll was even greater, and many of his household were dispatched to provide him with a retinue in the next world. On other occasions, if war captives were not available, people of the lowest class, as in Tahiti, or sometimes condemned criminals would be chosen. The building of royal canoes claimed many lives; a man had to be slain at the foot of the tree from which the wood was to be cut; another was killed when the vessel was completed and further deaths marked its launching ceremony.

In Hawaii the flesh of the victim was not normally eaten. Here too the left eye was ceremonially offered to the ruler or presiding chief; a harsh custom also survived whereby the god might suddenly demand the eye of someone present; the priest would point to the unfortunate individual and his eye would immediately be scooped out and offered to the god. Certain missionaries maintained that the Hawaiians were part-time cannibals, and suspicions are aroused by the fate of the body of Captain Cook, after he had been killed in a skirmish on the great island of Hawaii in 1779. His head and extremities were distributed to the chiefs, while the rest of his body was cut into small pieces and given to lesser nobles, who supposedly burned them. However, when some bones and ten pounds of flesh were handed back to his countrymen at the instance of the high priest, it was noticed that these returned morsels bore traces of an attempt at salting.[16] Cook had incidentally been hailed by the islanders as a reincarnation of the god Lono.

But if cannibalism was at least rare, cruelty to victims was not. Great sacrificial ceremonies were held for the dedication of a new temple. The climax of the elaborate rites came with the offering of a large and rare fish known as Ulua. In the frequent event that no such fish could be caught, several men were made to take its place. They were treated just as if they were fishes and were swung aloft by a great hook driven through chin and mouth; their skulls were placed on the fence that surrounded the temple.

Infanticide was common in Hawaii, whether for sacrificial purposes or for mere convenience. The status of children was anomalous; due to the Hawaiian belief that the newborn babe was the reincarnation of a revered forbear, grandfather or great-grandfather, from the very day of his birth he took precedence over his father and was treated as the rightful owner of his property. On the other hand, parents had a perfect right to kill their own offspring, and often exercised this right after two or three children had been born. If for no other reason, they did this simply to rid themselves of the nuisance of rearing a large family—hardly in itself an act of sacrifice. In Hawaii infanticide served an additional role as a means of preserving status; if women of high rank became pregnant through a commoner, her relatives would watch for an opportunity to take the newborn child and put it to death. Hawaiians told William Ellis, one of the first Englishmen to write about them, that children, as at the mouth of the Ganges, had once been thrown to the sharks.[17] Ellis doubted that a single mother was to be found who had not killed at least one infant. A hole would be dug in the floor of the dwelling; sometimes the infant was buried alive, but more often it was stifled by placing a piece of cloth over its mouth and it would then be trodden down into the earth.

Child-killing, far from being confined to Hawaii, was widespread throughout Polynesia. In Tahiti, the people spoke to foreigners with utter complacency about how they had killed their infants and would calmly visit missionaries' houses almost before their hands were cleansed of their infants' blood. King Pomare I had killed some of his own offspring. In the cannibal Marquesas, in times of food shortage, children were sometimes killed and eaten, a practice not unknown among Australian aboriginals. On a superficial level, therefore, infanticide might be viewed as an easy way of relieving the irritation of parents and the overcrowding of the nursery. But on closer examination, the practice appears in a very different light, as basic to religion and essential for the survival of society. The death of a child was believed to give added strength to the living; in the Tonga Islands for instance, it became a positive duty for parents to strangle infants, in order to strengthen and preserve their rulers. In Tahiti child-killing not merely pleased the gods; for some of their chief votaries, it was a duty. The Arioi formed a tightly-knit élite among Oro-worshippers; they are pledged to kill all infants born to them and were relegated to secondary rank if they failed to do so. Douglas Oliver, who wrote extensively on Polynesia in the 1950s, records that the childless chief Tupaya thought himself much greater than King George III of England on the grounds that the latter was said to have a large family. Oliver quotes an eighteenth-century account that stresses the sharp distinction between those Arioi who bore children and those who were childless: "If an Areeuoy [sic] preserves any of His Children (which they seldom do till they advance in Years and the Fire of their Youthful Passions is a little quenched) they are not treated with so much respect as when Batchelors . . . and are not entertained at the feasts until after the Batchelors are served." [18]

Schoch also insists that in its origins, Tahitian infanticide was far from being murder, but was a sacred institution that served to honour their ancestors and to preserve the purity of the noble families. If it came into more general practice in Polynesia in the early period of European contact, this serves as another reminder of how in times of stress ancient rituals may serve as an excuse for acts of violence. In the case of infant-killing, the spread of such abuses may have been exaggerated since the more harrowing tales come from missionaries, who as usual went out of their way to discredit those religious beliefs which it was their purpose to uproot.

In any case, infant sacrifice in one form or another is so universal that its absence in Polynesia would have been more surprising than its presence. Not only were children immolated in their hundreds in Mexico, but even in the Old Testament, the fiery Tophet—as we have seen—claimed countless such victims. Cannibalism often went hand in hand with infanticide and burning in Israel merely symbolized the eating of the victim by the god; among the Ancient Greeks, mythology is rich in tales of infants who were slain and often eaten.

Outstanding among Polynesians, both for the creativity of their art and for the savagery of their customs, were the Maoris of New Zealand. They were a people dedicated to war; because of the size of their territory, they could launch campaigns on a scale unknown in other islands. New Zealand was first occupied, probably from Tahiti, in about 1000 A.D. But unlike the Tahitians, the Maoris were fierce cannibals, a trait that lends substance to Cook's belief that the Tahitians had also formerly been man-eaters. Cook, who first sighted the North Island in 1770, on his first voyage, was not slow to find out about their eating habits:

> Soon after we landed, we met with two or three natives who not long before must have been regailing themselves upon human flesh, for I got from one of them the bone of the fore arm of a Man or Woman which was quite fresh and the flesh had been but lately pick'd off which they told us they had eat, they gave us to understand that but a few days ago they had Kill'd and eat a Boat's crew of their enemies or strangers . . . Mr. Banks [a noted botanist of his time who sailed with Cook] got from one of them a bone of the fore arm much in the same state as the one before mention'd and to shew us that they had eat the flesh, they bit and naw'd the bone and draw'd it through their mouth and this in such a manner as plainly shews that the flesh was to them a dainty bit.[19]

A few days later some natives brought alongside Cook's vessels four of the heads of the men that they had lately killed, still with hairy scalps and skin on their faces. Joseph Banks bought one of these skulls, whose owner had been killed by a blow on the temple.

An even odder scene took place on Cook's last visit to New Zealand. Some of his officers went ashore and stumbled on the remnants of a cannibal feast. The broken head and bowels of a victim were strewn on the ground, while the heart had been stuck on a forked stick, fixed to the head of a canoe. Pickersgill, one of Cook's officers, gave two nails (then greatly prized in Polynesia) for the head and took it on board; he was also given a piece of the victim's flesh. This was solemnly boiled in the ship's galley and given to a Maori present on board, who ate it ravenously; another piece was boiled and consumed in like manner before the ship's company. Cook, however, understood very well that the Maoris normally ate only the flesh of slain enemies, and that this custom had been handed down from earliest times; in this he was perfectly right and later visitors fully confirmed that New Zealand cannibalism was inseparable from ritual warfare.

Other forms of human offering existed, not usually cannibalistic, and not directly linked with war, although also centred upon the person of the tribal chief. Sacrifice was required for the building of his house and the tattooing of his sons and daughters; after-life attendants had to be provided at his funeral and widows often strangled themselves at the graveside. Nonetheless war remained the principal motive for Maori sacrifice and for the flesh-eating that followed. The head of the first captain taken in a campaign would be offered to the god of war, and the heart, as the source of life, was consumed by leading warriors to give them added strength. In the last Maori war against the British invaders in the mid-nineteenth century, the chief Keriope made his braves drink the blood of a white missionary to stiffen their resolve, while he smeared his own face with the same blood.

Warfare was a sacred institution, whose origins sprang from a mythical struggle between the children of Rangi, the Heaven, and Papa, the Earth. A special feature in New Zealand was the use of a large palisade, known as a pa. Both attackers and defenders of such fortresses resorted to human sacrifice to further their ends; it was firmly believed that to obtain results, the victim had to be someone very precious to his sacrificers. Like King Agamemnon, prepared to slay his daughter, Iphigenia, in return for a favourable wind, the Maori chief Kaharau, anxious for help in defending his fort, killed his own son, cut him open and offered his heart to the gods. In another recorded instance, a chief who was attacking a palisade burnt his son's heart in a fire kindled outside.[20]

Suggestions have often been made that human flesh was used primarily to enrich an otherwise meagre diet—a theory that has provoked controversy among students of Ancient Mexico. But it was usual for only war captives and fallen warriors of other tribes to be eaten by the Maoris. The supply of flesh was therefore limited and those eaten were known as "the fishes of Tu"—that is to say, victims of the war god. As among the Fijians, the flesh was forbidden to women, with the exception of a few priestesses. The victims' heads were kept as trophies and often set upon posts. Like other religious practices, those of New Zealand were open to abuse at the time of

European contact, when the Maoris found that they could trade heads for firearms and other European goods, a commerce initiated by Cook's crew when they made their first purchase. By 1820 tattooed Maori heads were quite a common article of trade in Sydney and for a while some chiefs even killed their slaves to satisfy this new demand. The traffic provided an added incentive to war, since heads taken on campaigns could be traded for muskets, which could then be used to acquire yet more heads. This state of affairs lasted until 1831, when the government of New South Wales made the possession of human heads a penal offence in the colony.

The trained anthropologist today is often baffled when he tries to attune himself to tribal ways of thinking and to bridge the spiritual gulf that yawns between himself and his informants. In recent years much attention has been devoted to this problem of how best to grasp and then to express in terms of modern science native notions that are both complex and alien to the Western mind. It is, moreover, easy to forget that so many accounts of these customs come from travellers quite unable to fathom the thought processes of people whose speech they could barely understand, even when informants *tried* to tell them the truth—at the best of times, a dubious assumption. New Guinea still boasts of seven hundred languages and dialects, each spoken in a tiny valley of its own. A story told by J. H. P. Murray, Lieutenant Governor and Chief Judicial Officer of Papua in the early years of this century, illustrates the problem that has arisen in other parts of the world where a babel of tongues is also spoken.

A man in Cape Nelson had been charged with having killed and eaten a baby, but could not be brought to trial as no one spoke his language. Eventually a cook was produced who was able to talk to the culprit in Port Moresby jail, but the problem was still unsolved because no one else could talk to the cook. Finally, with the aid of three different interpreters, translating from one language into the other, communication was established with the cook. The trial could then be held but the prisoner could not speak to the judge, nor the judge to the prisoner until every phrase had been translated and re-translated four times through a string of interpreters.

When a series of translations is needed, the final version often bears only a vague resemblance to the original. Murray cites another case in which two natives had cut the throat of another with a tomahawk and gouged out his eyes with a knife. "Why", Murray asked the first interpreter, "did they put out his eyes? To cut his throat was surely enough?" After double translation this question was put to the prisoner as follows: "The governor says it was quite right to cut his throat, but you ought not to have put out his eyes".[21] Murray knew enough of the language in question to realize the error.

Without fluency in the informants' tongues, the facts are at best garbled, and often erroneous. It was much easier for a native to smack his lips and by this gesture of delight imply that he *liked* human flesh than to explain in more abstract terms the complex notion that when he ate the flesh, he was taking part in a communal act of atonement for sin. Moreover in many cases, even if abstract concepts were present in the speaker's mind, the language had no terms in which to express them. The reverse is also true and European concepts are often untranslatable into native tongues; for instance, no word for resurrection existed in Lower California when the Spanish friars arrived in the eighteenth century. The only way to convey the notion was to plunge flies into water and to bring them out when they seemed dead but just managed to struggle to life again. Surviving texts in the Aztec Nahuatl, used to instruct the people in the Catholic religion, are laced with Spanish expressions that had no true Nahuatl equivalent.

Relying on information distorted by barriers of language and mentality, we are tempted to over-simplify and to define one type of killing as a religious sacrifice, while another is dismissed as the product of greed, or sadism. But in most ancient societies, such attempts to separate the sacred from the profane are vain. All activities were centred upon religion and all happenings ordered by the supernatural, not only birth and death, but eating and drinking, lovemaking, fighting, the tilling of the soil, the mixing of medicine, and even the dreaming of dreams. The life and death cycle, whether of man himself or of his animals and crops, was governed less by his own actions than by the caprice of the gods. Therefore while a European may look on the taking of heads and the killing of slaves as straightforward slaughter, for those who took part the meaning was different. A Maori skull might become an amusing souvenir in Sydney but at home it was a holy relic, in whose presence whole families would sob, in memory of their beloved dead.

9

The
Pot and the Kettle

To most people the name "Aztec" is synonymous with sacrifice and brings automatically to mind visions of palpitating human hearts proffered to the sun's orb and then piled high in the vessel of the eagle, the sun's symbol. No sane critic would deny that human offering was basic to the religion of the Aztecs—that is to say, the people who conquered most of Ancient Mexico in the century before the Spanish Conquest. However, if they enjoy a special fame as the super-sacrificers of all time, this is as much due to the circumstances of that conquest as to the nature of their rites. For on closer examination, the worldwide aspects of Aztec practices are as evident as any unique quality they may have possessed. And while the scale was stupendous, the ends were orthodox: to honour the dead and give sustenance to the living. Even the methods of killing find many parallels, and the choice of victims follows a familiar pattern.

Yet, when we first approach sacrifice in a purely American setting, the perspective is somehow altered, just as it changed when we moved from Europe to Asia. If actions were comparable, attitudes were different; all reticence is cast aside, and sacrificial scenes are freely painted in Mexican codices and even set in clay by Peruvian potters. Accordingly, plenty of other evidence helps to fill the gaps and correct the errors of the Spanish Conquistadors' story. For in their emotional approach to native religion, the Spaniards offer a stark contrast to the detached attitudes of the Age of Enlightenment, typified by Captain James Cook and his urbane botanist, Joseph Banks, or to the worldly-wise comments of nineteenth-century travellers like Sir Richard Burton. Unlike these latter-day explorers, the

Spaniards were men with a mission, intent upon saving Indian souls from hell by forced conversion, while extracting from their converts their every ounce of gold. No quarter was offered to the old idols, usually termed devils: such demons, with whom compromise was unthinkable, had to be swept from the face of the earth. Their images were smashed, their scriptures burned, and their temples razed; on their sites rose Christian churches and cloisters, built by the same hands out of the same stones.

Hence, while Spanish accounts of the conquest are vivid, they are not those of actual eye-witnesses of Mexican sacrifice. A Conquistador would have faced a thousand years in purgatory had he acted as guest of honour at such a ceremony or calmly inspected the rows of victims-to-be as Sir Richard Burton did in the victim-shed of the King of Dahomey. Where proceedings against Indians survive, they concern subtler forms of heresy, rather than human sacrifice, something to which few native Indians would have dared to confess in a Spanish court. Apologists of Spanish rule in the Indies often complain of the "Black Legend", supposedly invented by defamatory Protestants. But if, under their sway, noble intent went hand in hand with cruel deed, that other Black Legend, pinned by the Spaniards on to the Aztecs, is equally motivated.

The vogue may have passed of treating the Conquest as a knightly enterprise in which the forces of Christ crushed those of Antichrist, as told in the studied and stately prose of William H. Prescott, who wrote the first modern account in 1843. And yet the argument goes on between those who esteem and those who disparage the Aztecs. While both Spaniards and Mexicans had their virtues and their vices, such arguments amount to nothing but a case of pot calling the kettle black since, in terms of sheer cruelty to fellow-humans, the Aztecs lacked many of the refinements of their contemporaries, the Inquisitors. We may justly be shocked by Aztec rites but certain horrors devised by other peoples of both the Old World and the New were notably absent. There were no mass suicides, as in India; no prolonged torments, as in Oceania, North America and Europe; no tribes were doomed to extinction, eaten down to the last woman and child, as in Fiji; no one is known to have been buried alive, as in Ancient Ur and in South America; the dead were not exhumed and devoured, as in New Guinea.

The Conquistadors were genuinely revolted by Aztec religion and burned their sacred books. Nonetheless, rich data have survived, mainly because the good friars who followed in the wake of the invaders were less bigoted and delved deeply into Indian rites, if only as a means to combat them. These clerics were better placed to unravel ancient beliefs than many a nineteenth-century missionary in Africa or Oceania. Loved by the Indians as beings cast in a different mould from the haughty Conquistadors or from their own blood-drenched priests, the friars went out of their way to study native tongues and become fluent in the language of their converts, even preaching their sermons not in Spanish but in the Aztec Nahuatl language, which became the main medium of conversion.

The greatest scholar among them was Fray Bernardino de Sahagún, whose work on prehispanic America has no rival among European accounts of newly discovered peoples. In the twelve volumes of his magnum opus, he recorded all that his native informants told him of every conceivable aspect of Mexican life, whether ecology, fauna, flora, industry, trade, medicine, social structure, government or, in particular, religion. One of these precious tomes, Book II, deals with the various festivals to honour the gods, each demanding its special forms of human sacrifice, described in minute detail. And in addition to the post-Conquest works of Sahagún and of other Spanish clerics, the ancient codices faithfully depict each form of sacrifice, whether children borne off to the mountains festooned in paper ornaments, men pinioned with arrows to honour the God of Hunting, or the more usual excision of the heart of outstretched victims.

For the Conquest period, evidence comes mainly from documents, both Spanish and Aztec, but for earlier times we rely on archaeological finds that bear ample witness to the long history of sacrifice throughout the length and breadth of Mexico. More recent excavations have brought to light countless sacrificial instruments, as well as parts of bodies of what were obviously victims. These belong to every age, derive from every part of Mexico and Central America, and show that the awful Aztecs merely gave added impetus to timeless customs. Some of the earliest evidence comes from the Valley of Tehuacán, 120 miles southeast of Mexico City. Dating from about 5000 B.C., skeletons wrapped in nets have been found that bear witness to the use of ceremonial, including sacrifice. Among the finds were children's remains that had been ritually burned; the head of one had been separated from its body and toasted, after the brain had been sucked out. In another burial, a man, a woman and a child lay together; the man had been burned, while the woman and child had had their heads flattened, apparently deliberately.

The Olmecs, starting in about 1500 B.C., created the first great civilization and its vestiges survive in many parts of Ancient Mexico. In their capital of La Venta, on the coast of the Caribbean, the first pyramids and palaces of Mexico tower over broad plazas, tiled with fine mosaics. These genial Olmecs have much in common with the first great cultures of the Old World; ruled by resplendent priest-kings, whose images remain graven on many reliefs, they were pioneers in architecture, stone sculpture, jade carving and even the art of writing. All these achievements were the outward reflection of beliefs that for all time set the pattern of Mexican religion and that were grounded in the need to offer men to the gods.

C. E. Moser, in his valuable study of human decapitation in Middle America, gives many examples of Olmec sacrifice and of their cult of the human head. Far from being an Aztec invention, such acts are set in stone on stelae carved over two thousand years before their time.[1] On some of these reliefs, gaudily dressed beings complete their regalia with a head worn on the girdle or simply carried in one hand. A stela from El Jobo in Guatemala, also of early date, shows a warrior with a severed enemy head in his hand, while a decapitated foe kneels in front of him; another in Izapa, on the Pacific coast, from the end of the Olmec era, depicts a richly robed chief with a head in one hand and a sacrificial knife in the other; he tramples on the headless trunk of his enemy, from which serpents sprout. The identical theme of snakes emerging from the beheaded victim reappears in every age of Ancient Mexico, whether in the ball court scenes of Mayan Chichen Itzá from about 1000 A.D. or in cyclopean Aztec statues of their Mother Goddess sculpted just before the Conquest.

The first eight centuries of the Christian era are usually known as the "Classic" period; it is so rich in evidence of human sacrifice that only a few instances can be cited. In Coxcatlan, in the Tehuacán Valley, a thousand urns were found, each containing the charred remains of children who had not died natural deaths. In this creative age, the prevailing power was Teotihuacan, whose great pyramids lie adjacent to Mexico City. In that grandiose site sacrificial knives abound, recalling those shown in the painted codices from the last period before the Conquest. A few of the finest specimens, with turquoise handles, are to be seen in the Museum of Mankind in London, together with the famous Aztec crystal skull. These sacrificial blades were not just the inanimate tools of sacrifice, but were thought of as its living symbol. Certain gods wear a knife as part of their headdress or hold one in their hand. In the codices, these symbols proliferate, usually painted as ovaloid flints without handles, pointed at each end; endowed with eyes and teeth, they take on human form and themselves "devour" victims, as in the famous scene of the Codex Borgia known as the "Nocturnal Underworld". (see the illustration) In Kaminaljuyu, a site intimately linked with Teotihuacan and now submerged beneath a new suburb of Guatemala city, many skulls were placed on the floor with the lower jaw in position, suggesting that they were severed heads rather than mere reburials.

In the corresponding Maya period, also called "Classic", many decapitated burials have been found—the heads of adults and children being buried separately in bowls. In the important Maya site of Palenque, a low relief panel from the seventh century shows the installation of a priest-ruler; on his left sits a man who presents him with a quetzal feather headdress, while on the other side is another who gives him a trophy or stuffed head—perhaps that of his predecessor on the throne. A contrast has often been made between the refined Mayas and their sanguinary neighbours. Their art is generally devoted to serene and peaceful subjects but the great portraits in stone relief of their rulers often include a trophy head or two among the intricate symbols of their attire; even in the famous mural of war scenes from Bonampak, priests who blow long horns have one or more small heads hanging upside down from their collars.

In Uaxactun, another Mayan ruin in Guatemala, adult male skeletons were found whose skulls were placed between the knees. In one case the skull had been sawn laterally and the facial part removed; this exactly recalls an eye-witness account of how the Aztecs sacrificed some Spaniards, flayed their faces and then cured them with mud.[2] In Aztec times, moreover, facial skins were often fixed to the outside of mortuary bundles. The most arresting of all sacrificial scenes from the Classic age in Middle America are graven on the stelae from Santa Lucia Cozamaluapan in Guatemala, decorously displayed in the

Ethnographical Museum of West Berlin (see the illustration). One of these, unique in ancient Mexican art, shows a ball-game player in an act of adoration to the resplendent Sun God, to whom from below he offers the severed head of his opponent. Another stela depicts a ball-game player and four messengers, each bearing large heads.

Human sacrifice, then, was as old as civilization and thrived in every corner of Central America. Far to the south-east, in Costa Rica, statuettes have been discovered that are known as Huetar figures, named after a chief who lived at the time of the Spanish Conquest; however, the figures themselves are older, since they were found in association with much earlier objects. The typical Huetar statuette shows a priest bearing in his left hand (as so often in Mexico) a victim's skull and in his right hand a sacrificial knife.[3] Costa Rica forms a link between the cultures of North and South America; and these Costa Rican statues also recall those of Northern Peru, in which a priest decapitates the victim with a knife.

The next period, running from 900 A.D. until the rise of the Aztecs in about 1400 A.D., witnessed a mounting scale of human offering, as the earlier and more benign cultures yielded to others dedicated to war and hence to sacrifice. Central Mexico then came under the sway of Tula, lying to the north-west of Mexico City. Here the cult of sacrificial death is omnipresent. The "Serpent Wall" behind the Great Temple displays a frieze of serpents from whose fangs skeletal humans emerge. In other friezes a procession of coyote dogs, jaguars and eagles, symbolic of sacrifice, grasp human hearts dripping with gore. Mayan Chichen Itzá rose to power at about the same time as Tula and there is an uncanny likeness between the art and architecture of the two places, situated at opposite poles of Ancient Mexico. In Chichen the same grisly art forms abound, and here one of the first known skull racks was unearthed. In the great ball court reliefs, scenes are depicted in which the team that lost the game also lost their heads. And in Chichen and neighbouring cities the priests would throw maidens into wells, known as cenotes, to act as messengers to the gods, a cult that survived at the time of the Conquest. An expedition led by Mexican archaeologist Ramon Piña Chan in 1967–8 partly drained the Chichen cenote with the aid of elaborate equipment. Many skeletons of adults and children of both sexes were dredged up; the platform was also found from which people were cast into the well. Piña Chan thinks that a small steam bath located nearby was used to purify victims, as in Aztec times, when slaves were always bathed before sacrifice.[4]

If most of what we know of Aztec sacrifice comes from Spanish and native documents, their data are supported by several archeological finds. One hundred and seventy skulls, for instance, duly perforated for stringing on the poles of the skull rack, were unearthed in Tlatelolco, twin city of the Aztec capital of Tenochtitlan, and much material evidence of a more monumental kind is on public view, such as the stone model of a skull rack in the Museum of Anthropology in Mexico City, together with the huge headless figure of the great Mother Goddess Coatlicue, from whose torso emerge two serpents.

Unique, however, in the annals of sacrifice is the rich contemporary literature on the theme, and Mexican codices abound in sacrificial scenes of every kind. These codices consisted of a single long sheet of paper, made of the inner bark of a native fig tree, folded in screen or accordion fashion. Both front and back are painted with series upon series of convoluted figures that seem weird, if not sinister, to the untrained eye; the Spanish thought they were the work of the devil himself. Colour was all-important and certain gods can be identified by this alone. Aztec codices are post-Conquest copies of the original, destroyed by the Spaniards; however, pre-Conquest writings from other areas survive that bear ample witness to the widespread use of human sacrifice in the centuries before the Spanish invasion. For instance, human offerings feature in the Dresden Codex, the best known Maya document, thought to have been painted in about 1200 A.D. The five codices known as the Borgia Group (from the Borgia Codex in the Vatican) predate the Conquest; scholars believe that they derive from the Puebla area, which lies to the east of the snow-capped volcanoes and was never conquered by the Aztecs. Frequent in this group of codices are warriors' heads in bowls, apparently being cooked so that the flesh can be removed. Other illustrations show whole bodies boiling in pots. Heads also appear as temple offerings; in the Borgia Codex, for instance, no less than thirty-three severed heads can be counted. The most complex sacrificial sequence occurs in the Ferjervary Mayer Codex, another of the Borgia Group, now in the Joseph Mayer collection in the Free Public Museum of Liverpool. The first scene depicts a battle between an axe-wielding warrior, or god, dressed as an opossum and a naked opponent, armed with a javelin thrower, complete with darts and shield. The next shows the victorious opossum dancing headless; after this, he performs a ceremony over the head of his victim, which rests face up on a slab-legged pot; he is pouring hot stones and bone ash into the head, a process not unlike that of the modern Jivaro headshrinkers of Ecuador.

In several codices of this series, gods and goddesses themselves perform sacrifice or are sacrificed. In the Borgia, for instance, a leading goddess Xochiquetzal, known as the Flower Quetzal, beheads a warrior; in both the Borgia and the Ferjervary Mayer, the God of Maize pierces a severed head with a bone awl. In another scene from the Borgia, the Merchant God is himself being boiled in a pot. In the Codex Aubin, an Aztec document, the goddess known as Obsidian Butterfly (Itzpapalotl) is seen with a decapitated figure out of whose headless trunk emerge two serpents, a recurrent theme in sacrificial scenes. In these codices many of the victims are distinguished not only by their very special paper ornaments but by their naked bodies, painted vertically with red stripes; often the sacrificer holds diminutive nude victims by the hair. The codices are also rich in illustrations showing auto-sacrifice which did not lead to death, though the ends it served were similar; moreover, people who practised such self-inflicted torture often suffered agonies more acute than those who were killed. Not only codices but earlier Maya reliefs abound in such scenes of self-sacrifice; many depict individuals drawing entwined cords through their tongues, while others, even more numerous, show exalted persons drawing blood from their penis. So hallowed was this fertility rite that the penis perforator became a kind of deity in its own right. Yale Mayan scholar, David Joralemon, gives copious illustrations of the instrument: its point was fixed to an effigy handle in the shape of a god, who wears a special headdress made of knots and feathers.[5]

Notwithstanding such ample pictorial signs of sacrifice, the rites are described in more arresting form in the writings of Fray Bernardino de Sahagún, confirmed by those of Padre Durán and other friars. If Spanish eye-witness reports of sacrifice are lacking, the accounts of Sahagún's native informers survive, unique in their dramatic detail of just what people saw who once took part in them. Their words are immortalized in the sonorous, if repetitive, imagery of classic Nahuatl, as spoken by the noblest Aztecs. Ideal for describing the symbols of their gods and intoning their litanies, it is at times harder to transcribe into our more prosaic idioms. To produce this compendium of information on Ancient Mexico was a prodigious feat. Sahagún toiled away in Tlatelolco until his powers failed him, checking and comparing all that his informants told him. Like so many semi-literate peoples (their codices were merely pictorial), they had fabulous memories; most stemmed from the old élite and more than one of them may, as a young man, have himself put the finishing touches to a victim's rich attire, adjusting his quetzal plumes, fixing his jade bracelets, attaching his paper wings, and even buoying his spirits with a soothing draught before he mounted the pyramid. This inside view of events, not by bystanders but by believers, is without parallel in the story of sacrifice.

The survival of Sahagún's work is another miracle. His twelve books, in Nahuatl and Spanish, were sent to Spain in 1577, but such a detailed study of idolatry was judged unfit for publication and was buried deep in the archives. A Spanish version first saw the light of day in 1829, and the Nahuatl text only began to appear, with an English translation, in 1950. To do full justice to every ceremony recorded in Sahagún's second book would require a separate volume. Most were part of the eighteen monthly feasts of twenty days of the Aztec calendar (to complete the year they added five extra days, regarded as ill-fated). Each feast was marked by elaborate rituals and devoted to a leading member of the pantheon, to whom men and women were offered in appropriate form. Sahagún describes the dresses worn, the dances performed, the food consumed, the numbers slain, the method of killing and the disposal of the victim's relics, including in some cases his own body. From such a rich store of fact, one can only make a minute selection and focus upon a few salient features of human sacrifice in Mexico and—by inference—elsewhere, since its implications are universal.

A convenient start may be made by taking the first of the eighteen monthly feasts, held in honour of the rain gods. (The translation is that made by two American scholars, Dr Arthur Anderson and Dr Charles Dibble, of the twelve volumes in Nahuatl of the Florentine Codex.) The text states that at this feast blood offerings were made and sacrificial banners were hung on all the mountain tops (sacred to the rain gods), as well as in a town on the shores of the lagoon, called Pantitlan: "And there they took children, known as 'human banners'

—those who had two cowlicks of hair and whose day signs were favourable. They were sought everywhere and bought. It was said: 'These are precious blood-offerings. [The rain gods] receive them with rejoicing; they are thus satisfied and given contentment.' "

As part of the ritual, green poles were erected at all the local temples throughout the capital as symbols of fertility and rain; white paper flags were placed on top of them, dotted with large and small drops of liquid rubber—also symbolic of rain. In all, seven different places are named where child sacrifices then took place; in each their paper finery was different; in one instance the child, referred to as the "human banner" was arrayed in black and red striped paper, in two cases the colour was brown and in another blue. One was adorned with stripes of liquid rubber while another wore strange vestments covered with mussel shells. Wearing headbands with sprays and sprigs of quetzal feathers, greenstone necklaces and bracelets, in all their glorious array they were carried along in litters covered with quetzal feathers. At first men wept for them but "if the children went crying, their tears coursing down and bathing their faces, it was said and understood that indeed it would rain . . . Therefore men were joyful; thus were their hearts at rest".[6]

At the close of the account of the solemn rain feast, preparations are mentioned for that of the second month, when prisoners of war were to be sacrificed to the Flayed God:

> This last time they anointed [the prisoners] and gave them presents; for this last time they wore their red array—so that in it their fate would come, they would be slain, they would breathe their last, they would be the sacrificial striped ones [i.e. sacrificial captives as painted with red stripes in the codices]. . . . And those who had taken prisoners, who had captives whom they had taken, also anointed themselves with red; they covered themselves with feather down; their hands and feet were covered with white turkey feathers.

Other rituals followed, during which the captors smoked tobacco, danced with their victims, took mementos of hair from the top of their heads and made offerings of blood from their ears. Then the final scene is described:

> Those who slew the captives were the priests. Those who had

taken them captive did not kill them; they only brought them as tribute. . . . They thus went leading them up to the top of the temple. And when some captive faltered, fainted, or went throwing himself upon the ground, they dragged him. And when one showed himself strong, not acting like a woman, he went with a man's fortitude . . . he went strong of heart and shouting, not without courage nor stumbling, but honouring and praising his city . . . speaking as he went: "Already here I come! you will speak of me there in my home land!"

The captives mounted one at a time the steps of the War God's temple; six priests stretched them upon the sacrificial stone, cut open their breasts and tore out their hearts, using a wide-bladed flint knife. The hearts, named "precious cactus fruit" were held aloft towards the sun, called in this context the "turquoise prince, the soaring eagle". The hearts were cast into the eagle vessel and those who died were called "eagle men". After being killed, the bodies were rolled down the steps and carried off by the old men to the temples of the different districts of the city. There they were cut in pieces, a thigh of each being set aside for the Emperor Moctezuma. "And as for the captor, they there applied the down of birds to his head and gave him gifts. And he summoned his blood relations . . . that they might go and eat at the house of him who had taken the captive. And here they cooked each one a bowl of a stew of dried maize, called tlacatlaolli, which they set before each, and in each was a piece of the flesh of the captive". (Tlacatlaolli literally means "dried maize with human flesh".)

Finally, as a climax to the feast of the second month came the strangest rite of all, the gladiatorial sacrifice. After a solemn procession, the celebrants gathered round a special circular sacrificial stone, seating themselves in strict order of rank. The start of the ceremony was marked by the sounding of trumpets and the blowing of large conch shells. The first of the captives who were to take part was then seized; he was first given four drafts of the sacred pulque, which he drank from a long hollow gourd; a priest then offered up a quail in his honour.

Having done this, then they made the captive climb upon the round sacrificial stone . . . Then the wolf-priest took the rope holding the captive, which reached and was attached to the centre of the stone; then he tied it about the waist of the captive.

And he gave him a war club, decked with feathers and not set with obsidian blades. And he placed before him four pine cudgels, his missiles, with which to lay about him, with which to defend himself.

The first gladiator, a member of the order of eagle and ocelot warriors, then performed a dance, all the while carefully surveying his victim. He sought the spot where he could most easily inflict a fatal wound. In the most improbable event of the captive, armed with a club set with soft feathers, defeating this foe, equipped with weapons of flint, three more opponents were pitted against him. Finally, if the incredible occurred and he survived this unequal contest, he was offered no escape, for a fifth opponent, who was left-handed, was sent to deliver a thrust that could only be parried backhand. The blood of the victim was first offered to the sun and then used to anoint the images of many gods.

> And the captor thereupon took the blood of his captive in a green bowl with a feathered rim. The sacrificing priests came to pour it there. In it went the hollow cane, which also had feathers. And then the captor departed, that he might also nourish the demons. He went into and came out of all the shrines . . . On the lips of the stone images he placed the blood of his captive, giving them nourishment with the hollow cane. He went in festive attire.

Each body was taken to its captor's house and flayed. The flesh was cut up and consumed but the captor ate none, saying, "Shall I eat my own flesh?" For when he first won the prisoner on the battlefield, he uttered the traditional words, "He is as my beloved son". And the captive had then said, "He is as my beloved father". The skins of the victims were carefully preserved and worn by different people for twenty days. To complete the gladiatorial sacrifice a dance was held round the sacrificial stone, at which the dancers held the heads of the various victims. This was called "the dance of the severed heads".

The principal sacrifice of the fifth month was very different, for it claimed a single being, in honour of one of the two principal members of the Aztec pantheon, the Smoking Mirror God. The youth, chosen to embody the person of the deity, had to be physically without blemish. The description of his perfection, covering a whole page of print, begins as follows: "He was like something smoothed, like a tomato, or like a pebble, as if hewn of wood. He did not have curly hair, but straight, long hair; he had no scabs, pustules or boils on his forehead nor was he large-headed." At the end comes a stipulation that his buttocks were to be neither hatchet-shaped nor flabby. This rare victim was dressed and fêted like a monarch: "He was acknowledged as our lord, treated like a lord; one begged favours, with sighs; before him the common people bowed in reverence and kissed the earth." He even had to watch his figure; if he was seen, after such luxurious living, to be getting fat, they made him drink brine, which helped to make his flesh firm. He even received special honours from the Emperor Moctezuma: "Thus Moctezuma adorned the impersonator well and arrayed him in varied garb . . . for verily he took him to be his beloved god."

For a whole year he went garlanded with sweet-smelling flowers, and adorned with the finest jewels, with golden bracelets on his arms, and gold bells on his legs. For the last twenty days before he was to die in the name of the god, he was given four brides, arrayed as leading goddesses. The last four days of his life were spent dancing and feasting at four prescribed spots on the shore of the lagoon (the number four was for the Aztecs especially sacred).

After they had sung and danced, then he embarked in a canoe. The women went travelling with him; they went consoling him and keeping him merry. Then the canoe arrived; then it touched the shore; then it was beached at a place called Acaquilapan, or Caualtepec. For here he was abandoned . . . When he arrived where he was to die, where a small temple stood, called Tlacochcalco, he ascended by himself, of his free will, to the place where he was to die. When he climbed the first step, as he passed one step, he there broke, shattered his flute and his whistle. And when he had mounted all the steps, when he had reached the summit, then all the priests fell upon him; they threw him on his back upon the sacrificial stone. Then one cut open his breast, seized his heart, and raised it as an offering to the sun.

Sahagún sums up the Aztec attitude to the prisoner's fate: "And this betokeneth our life on earth. For he who rejoices, who possesseth riches, who seeketh and coveteth our lord's sweetness, his gentleness —riches and prosperity—thus endeth in great misery. For it is said:

'None come to an end here upon earth with happiness, riches and wealth.' "

In the tenth month, in honour of the Fire God, prisoners were thrown onto a huge fire and pulled out before they were dead; their hearts were then cut out in the usual manner. In this case the Spanish version of Sahagún's text is more lurid than the Nahuatl (the two vary in many details):

> Then they took them, tied their hands behind their backs, and also bound their feet. The priests then lifted them on their shoulders and took them up to the top of the temple, where a great fire had been lit, with a great pile of timber. Having reached the top, they put them into the fire; and as they threw them in, a great cloud of ashes arose, and each one made a great hollow in the fire, where he fell, because it was all embers and fragments of timber, and there in the fire the wretched captives began to belch and vomit; their bodies began to crackle, as when some animal is roasted, and blisters rose in all parts of their bodies.

After this, they were pulled out and sacrificed in the ordinary way; their bodies were thrown down at the foot of the statue of the Fire God.[7] Padre Durán accompanies his parallel account with an illustration of the scene. The feast of the eleventh month was in honour of the Goddess Toci. On this occasion, one woman slave was chosen to die as the goddess. They did not officially tell her beforehand that she was going to be slain but after elaborate ceremonies and dances, they surrounded her as she danced and suddenly cut off her head.

These few instances may give the reader an inkling of Sahagún's text. Some rites were so prolonged that they went on for the entire twenty-day month. And in all these ceremonies, not a garment was worn, not a headdress donned, not a dance performed, not a meal eaten nor scarcely a gesture made that did not exactly reflect the symbolism of a particular deity, whether the god of rain, sunshine, maize, fertility or fire. Each god had his special colour, such as green for maize gods, or turquoise for those of water and rain. The rain god was very particular about colour; he decreed that his victims, old or young, be dressed from head to foot in blue or, if naked, should be painted blue. Some were drowned; the hearts of others were even put into blue vessels and then cast into the waters of the lagoon, where they were taken in a canoe with oars coloured in the same hue.

Paper adornments—with special designs for each feast—were a major item of attire for the victims; in modern Mexico paper decorations of all kinds are still widely used to decorate streets and churches for the name-day of a patron saint. Sahagún meticulously describes how the prisoners were garlanded with such emblems before death; for instance, in the fourteenth month, paper banners were carried before them as they mounted the steps of the pyramid where they were to meet their end; victims slain to honour the god of the sacred drink, pulque, wore a kind of tail or train of paper, several yards long. Children borne off to the mountains as offerings to the rain god are also shown in codices festooned with paper finery. These paper ornaments worn by victims were jealously preserved as relics.

While almost all monthly ceremonies involved human sacrifice, none occurs in Sahagún's account of the fourth and ninth months. In the latter, turkeys and dogs were offered instead of men. The omission may be a lapse of memory on the part of his informants, since in the feast to correspond to Sahagún's fourth month Padre Durán describes the sacrifice of children under twelve years of age, suitably prepared by lengthy fasting on bread and water. Only on the last day of this vigil, just before death, were the infants gorged with all the food they could swallow.[8]

Sahagún gives the impression that, as a general rule, the numbers slain on each occasion were not large. The chosen victims were those favoured all the world over—war captives, children and slaves; the children were mostly bought from their parents for the purpose. A few ceremonies claimed a single victim, who was first fêted and then suffered alone as the incarnation of a god or goddess. The concept was deep-rooted that the prisoners, whether one or many, themselves became the god for whom they died. We have already mentioned the ceremony of the fifth month when the Smoking Mirror God was honoured in this way. Sahagún also tells of one slain as the Aztec tribal god, The Humming Bird of the South (Huitzilopochtli), while Padre Durán describes the death of a similar victim to honour the Plumed Serpent (Quetzalcoatl). For forty days the chosen youth became the Plumed Serpent, though to guard against any unseemly escape from his lot, he was kept in a cage at night. He was dressed exactly as the god, including the duckbill mask, worn by the god in countless codex illustrations. The old men of the temple revered him and addressed him as "your majesty"; when about to be sacrificed, he was cheered with a lavish potion of pulque since it would be a fearful omen if he appeared downcast.

The Aztecs also used to fashion statues in the god's likeness out of a paste prepared from seeds or out of wood. Sometimes these idols were symbolically "killed" or destroyed at the same time as the human offering; both human carcase and paste image were then eaten by the celebrants. Alternatively, food sacred to the deity in question would be consumed after the sacrifice. For instance, in the eighth month, one woman, her face painted in red and yellow, symbolic colours of the corn goddess Xilonen, was decapitated. Those present then ate the first ears of green maize, which until that date had been forbidden food. In the seventeenth month, a wooden statue was made of the God of Fire. A beautiful mosaic mask covered the upper part of its face and a second mask of black stone was made to represent the god's beard (old gods, such as the god of fire, were always portrayed with beards). On the statue's head was placed a crown of red feathers, surmounted by a great quetzal plume; thus arrayed, it was set upon a throne and offered food in the form of maize flour. After these rituals, human beings were sacrificed to the god before his wooden likeness; they were also treated as "images" of the Fire God, dressed alike but made of flesh instead of wood. On another occasion, a great statue was made of the God of War, using a paste made of edible seeds. First quails and men were slain, and then finally they "killed" the idol itself, striking it in the chest as if to tear out the heart; the pieces of paste were distributed to all the people to eat. Fray Juan de Torquemada, from whom this report derives, omits to say what was done with the bodies of the men and quails.[9]

Spanish accounts of Aztec sacrifice—based on the Conquistadors—stress the offering of human hearts to the sun. But this was in many cases an oversimplification since native versions devote more space to fertility rites. The monthly offerings are more concerned to seek good harvests than to keep the sun on its course; sun-worship and rain-god rites are, however, related themes, since both elements combine to make the corn ripen, and it is surely no accident that the sun and rain gods jointly occupied the top of the Great Temple. Of the eighteen feasts, three are dedicated to rain gods (or to the mountains where they were thought to abide), one to water in general, and two

to maize or to maize deities. As many as six are dedicated to goddesses and concern fertility in one form or another. In contrast, each
of the two supreme gods of the pantheon, the Lord of the Night,
known as Smoking Mirror, and the War or Sun God, the Humming
Bird of the South, has to make do with a single feast in his honour.
This rather selective pattern reflects not only the compelling need
for such things as rain and maize; it also suggests that the ceremonies
were very ancient and were fashioned to honour old and traditional
gods of pre-Aztec times—a further reminder that it is sheer fantasy
to suggest that these latecomers invented such rites.

The standard way of killing was to cut out the heart of the victim,
splayed on the sacrificial stone; four priests held his arms and legs,
while the fifth slashed his ribs and tore out his heart—a process once
euphemistically described as "cardiectomy" in a tourist brochure,
whose author preferred to play down the seamier side of past glories.
Some victims, such as those of the sixth feast, were drowned; those
chosen for the ninth month were burned, while the main offering of
the eleventh month was suddenly decapitated. Prolonged torture was
conspicuous by its absence; a specially cruel fate, however, awaited
those prisoners cast into the fire and snatched out alive for their
hearts to be cut out. Sahagún twice mentions victims who fainted;
and in the seventh month some were gagged, lest they cry out.
These, however, were exceptions to the rule and if the god was to be
duly honoured, his living image had to die with dignity.

As an integral part of such offerings, people cherished as holy
relics the victim's remains, such as his hair and bones, and all his finery. The skin of the gladiatorial victim was lent by the captor to his
friends, who would wear it for a time as a special mark of distinction;
the captor himself kept the bones. A male priest would don the hide
of the woman killed as the goddess Toci. Above all, the heads were
hallowed trophies and invariably ended on the skull rack. This cult
strengthens the impression that these Aztec sacrifices derived from
those earlier peoples who wore human heads on their persons. No
skull racks have been found dating from before 1000 A.D. but it seems
clear that the Aztecs were merely making modifications to a ritual
whose principle was age-old—the veneration of the human head, a
cult duly observed by those captors of the gladiatorial victims, who
danced round the sacrificial stone, holding aloft their prisoners heads
before these were impaled on the skull rack. Sahagún lists four of

these stones in his description of the Aztec capital; one occupied part of the site of the present-day cathedral.

War in ancient Mexico was sanctified by the hunger of the gods for captives to be slain at their altars; no female prisoners were offered and therefore goddesses had to content themselves with slaves. Tactics were devised so as to secure the maximum haul of prisoners, both to honour the gods who presided over the eighteen monthly festivals and to provide for other rites. These future victims were kept in readiness in the various districts of the city, although not necessarily "fattened up", as Spanish reports suggest.

Unlike Sahagún, Padre Durán devotes one of his two volumes to a history of the Aztecs from earliest times, which closely follows the work of another sixteenth-century chronicler, Alvarado Tezozómoc, a prince of the royal blood. Their style is repetitive and rambling but the narratives give a lively version of the events of each reign. These histories tell of endless warring campaigns and of the cohorts of captives taken. Not all of them were killed at the monthly ceremonies, described by Sahagún, although the numbers slain at these obviously depended on how many happened to be available. For instance, Sahagún is rather vague as to how many died at the second monthly feast in honour of the Flayed God; nonetheless Durán states that on one occasion hordes of captives from the Caribbean coast arrived at the capital just in time to be used for this ceremony. Accounts also vary for other monthly feasts. Sahagún writes that in the eleventh month, four captives were normally sacrificed to the goddess Toci, but Padre Durán insists that in the reign of the luckless Moctezuma II, which began in 1501, countless Tlaxcalan prisoners were burned in honour of Toci at this same ceremony. Probably the formal quota for the event was far exceeded on this occasion simply because so many favoured victims were at hand (the gods were thought to prefer people of nearby places, rather than those from distant lands, who spoke alien tongues).

While these Aztec historians write constantly of the taking of captives, they do not always say what happened to them. Tezozómoc, for instance, speaks of large numbers captured in campaigns on the Gulf Coast in 1451 A.D.; they were led away, marching in rows with their hands bound and their necks clamped together by wooden collars. On arrival at the capital, they were welcomed in the different parts of the city and treated with great honour. But we are left to speculate how their story ended. Possibly more victims were slain in the course of the eighteen monthly feasts than Sahagún implies, and huge numbers were also claimed by once-and-for-all events. It was probably more for these than for regular feasts that captives were kept in cold storage. The supply was at times increased by presents made to appease the Emperor; Durán tells how Moctezuma II received gifts of prisoners from the neighbouring city of Tlatelolco and how he kept a reserve quota for occasions when they might be needed, such as the death of a great nobleman or for an important feast in a nearby place. In other words, the Aztecs took their prisoners from others but were also ready to return the favour for immediate neighbours and vassals.

In addition to the eternal plea for good crops, important people could not be sent to the next world without an appropriate retinue. The histories describe in dramatic terms the exequies of Ahuitzotl, the greatest conqueror and sacrificer of all. Two hundred slaves of his household were named to accompany him to the hereafter; they were dressed in fine robes and little hampers were put into their hands as provisions for the journey. The emperor's body, richly adorned, was carried in a litter amidst solemn chanting; the corpse was burned on a funeral pyre and the slaves were then sacrificed one by one. Their hearts were first torn out in the orthodox manner and they were then thrown onto the blaze, already dead. Ahuitzotl's ashes were buried beside the famous Aztec Stone of the Sun, now displayed in the National Museum of Anthropology in Mexico and originally carved as a recipient for human hearts.[10] Significantly, no reports survive of widows being slain with the Aztec ruler. The beginning of a reign was no less bloodthirsty an affair than its end, and an imperial coronation also claimed many victims; when the last emperor, Moctezuma II, was crowned, countless prisoners were sacrificed during the four-day celebrations. In order to provide these, custom ruled that each monarch before his enthronement should wage a special war for the purpose. Ahuitzotl in particular campaigned far and wide to collect a vast haul for the holocaust that was to inaugurate his reign.

Aztec chroniclers frequently refer to a ritual combat called the "War of Flowers" (xochiyaotl), which was not a war of conquest, but a kind of tourney, arranged through diplomatic channels with independent neighbours, such as Tlaxcala. On these occasions, the rival armies supposedly marched to an appointed rendezvous and, after a mock battle, returned home with a good stock of prisoners to sate the appetites of their gods. Such stories of mock battles make good reading but may be rather exaggerated where the Aztecs are concerned. They were inveterate conquerors, and to win captives was not their only goal in waging war. They set out to vanquish vast domains, which yielded gargantuan supplies of tribute. Stories abound, for example, of the bitter tears shed by Moctezuma when his armies failed to conquer such a tiny adversary as Tlaxcala. Yet the Aztec war machine was geared more to the capture than to the slaughter of the enemy. In the military hierarchy, rank and honour depended upon the number of captives taken; a man who took no prisoners carried no esteem, even if he were a prince. This obsession partly accounts for their dismal performance in the open field against the small band of Spaniards, who sought to kill with their swords, while Aztec weapons were more suited to wound.

The greatest recorded sacrifice of all time took place in 1487, in the reign of Ahuitzotl, to inaugurate the Great Temple. The Emperor, together with two allied rulers and his leading official, led the way, accompanied by throngs of priests; both they and the victims were dressed as gods. The captives, duly painted and feathered, had been formed into interminable lines that stretched along the main causeways into the city. The performance was watched by a huge crowd, since the people of neighbouring towns were ordered to come to the capital on pain of death; no one was exempt and not a man, woman or child was to be seen in their streets. The sacrifice lasted four whole days. When Ahuitzotl and his royal colleagues wearied of gashing open the victims' breasts, the priests took up the knives in their place.

Tradition relates that the victims numbered 80,400, a figure repeated by several sources. But in the space of four days to slay such myriads in a city of some 200,000 people and to dispose of the bodies is impossible. Let us suppose that one captive was slain every minute (i.e. each of the four sacrificers on duty killed one every four minutes), and that the operation went on night and day without pause; even accepting these unlikely assumptions, it would take not four but about fifty-six days to complete the slaughter. Even the killing of 20,000 prisoners, a figure given in other accounts, would take nearly fourteen days to complete. In any case, the figure of 80,400 is in itself strange. The Aztecs counted in units of twenty; in codices, a flag (pantli) indicates twenty, repeated again and again for quantities up to the next unit of 400 (20 x 20), called a tzontli and denoted by a sign like a fir-tree. The largest unit, the xiquipilli or 8000 (20 x 20 x 20), was illustrated by a little bag of cacao beans, which were often used as a form of currency. Now 80,400 would be ten xiquipillis and one single tzontli, in itself an incongruous number for what is clearly more an estimate than a head-count, and it seems probable that some scribe misread the original text, perhaps deliberately.

Spanish estimates are notoriously unreliable and they most certainly exaggerated the size of the native armies they fought. Cortés, for instance, in his letter to the Emperor Charles V gave the absurd number of 140,000 men for the Tlaxcalan force that he met before he became their ally, but for the actual town of Tlaxcala he makes a more sober estimate and puts the total population at 45,000. As fervent Catholics, the Spaniards maximized the horrors of Aztec religion, and tended to over-emphasize the numbers sacrificed. Bernal Díaz, when over seventy years old, wrote the story of his experiences as one of Cortés' soldiers. His work, rich in detail and vivid in imagery, enthralls the general reader and enlightens the specialist, but some of his data should be treated with the greatest caution, particularly on native religion, and his statement that 100,000 heads were displayed on the skull rack of Xocotlan, a fairly small place on the way to the capital, is surely open to question. Andrés de Tapia, another of that select band of Conquistadors who left personal memoirs, writes of the great skull rack of Tenochtitlan:

> The poles were separated from each other by a little less than a vara [about a metre] and were crowded with cross sticks from top to bottom, and on each cross stick there were five skulls impaled through the temples: and the writer and a certain Gonzalo de Umbría, counted the cross sticks and multiplying five heads per cross stick from pole to pole, as I said, we found that there were 136,000 heads.

But taking the figure of slightly less than five skulls per yard, this means that if all the cross poles and their skulls were stretched out end to end, they would have reached for about eighteen miles. Skulls, moreover, are durable items, and even supposing this figure to be accurate, it could have been accumulated at the rate of about 1500 trophies per annum since 1428, the year in which the Aztec Empire began; only in one instance are we told that old skulls were burned to make way for new ones. It is worth recalling—as already mentioned—that in Tlatelolco, Tenochtitlan's sister city, archaeologists unearthed 170 skulls perforated for stringing on poles, not 136,000.

Cortés also wrote to Charles V that among the Mayas of the Yucatan peninsula where he first set foot in Mexico, there was scarcely a temple where fifty people were not offered every year. For the main shrine of an average township, this figure would be acceptable. Bernal Díaz, however, states that in Cempoala, north of the modern Veracruz, where the Spaniards became guests and allies of the famous "Fat Chief", four to five victims were sacrificed daily, or, say, 1500 per annum. This number makes little sense for a place whose population could not have exceeded 15 to 20,000. At that time, Cempoala was not a power in its own right but a tributary of King Moctezuma, who had purloined the Fat Chief's jewels, a loss which the latter bewailed bitterly to Cortés. As a subject of the Aztec Empire, he had no scope for making war on his neighbours or for drawing on them for captives for his altars. But had he sacrificed his own slaves on that scale, he would soon have exhausted the supply; and had he, in desperation, offered freeborn citizens, he would in a matter of years have found himself in the awkward predicament of that legendary African chief we mentioned earlier, who ate all his subjects and then had no one to eat but himself.

Bernal Díaz alos reports that Moctezuma II sacrificed "many boys" each day to find out from the gods what to do about the Spanish invasion. The statement implies the use of sacrifice for divination, as practised in Ancient Rome as part of the cult of Mithraism but not mentioned by other writers in Mexico. The very apparition of Europeans, first spied as houses floating on the sea, and then as centaurs coursing along the shore (horse and rider were thought to be one), was a most hideous portent. Just as in Africa the mere arrival of a white missionary might be celebrated by a human offering, so in Mexico the terror struck by a whole cohort of white Spaniards, who belched thunder like the God of War from his Fire Serpent, gave an added motive for sacrifice; it was wiser to offer every available man, woman and child once and for all upon their altars, than to be abandoned for ever by the gods.

Where Conquistadors' accounts are concerned, problems of communication must always be borne in mind, since they did not, unlike the friars, speak the tongues of the people whom they met. In Cempoala, for instance, the words of Cortés and his men had first to be translated from Spanish into Maya by Jerónimo de Aguilar, who had been a captive in Yucatan, and then translated again by the famous Doña Marina from Maya into Nahuatl, and finally by the Fat Chief's interpreter into his own native Totonac. The Spaniards' reports differ from native accounts in other respects; they harp on the ill-treatment of Aztec prisoners while the latter insist that, once they had reached the capital, they were fêted and feasted. Known as the "Sons of the Sun", captives were beings already sanctified as the gods' property. Alvarado Tezozómoc tells how the first Moctezuma (1440–1468) himself greeted and consoled Sons of the Sun from the Gulf Coast and commanded that they should be treated with affection and plied with food.[11]

This sentimental kinship between captor and captive is a strange feature, though not confined to Mexico. The act of capture was the decisive factor. From that moment on the die was cast; even the prisoner accepted his role and saw himself as a being apart, the god's elect. His sacrifice then became merely the climax to an implacable chain of events, already set in motion when he was first seized.

Such abnegation on the victim's part is a difficult concept for the modern mind to appreciate but rewards offered in the hereafter went a long way towards tempering the dread of violent death on the altar. For among the Aztecs warriors killed in battle and those sacrificed shared the same privileged after-life, and went to the House of the Sun, where they joined the Sun God on the first part of his daily journey from east to west. Half way through his course, the sun was greeted by that other favoured group, women who had died in childbirth, in the act of producing future warriors. The victims of the rain god were also assigned to a special paradise, which they shared with those who died by drowning or of dropsy or venereal disease. In contrast, people who met their death neither on the battlefield nor on the altar, faced a dismal future: they were delivered to the Ninth Underworld and to the grim custody of the skeletal god of the nether world.

Spanish and native accounts concur that in many forms of sacrifice parts of the victim's body were eaten. Bernal Díaz saw near the Great Temple of Tlatelolco many pots filled with water, in which

A platform sacrifice in Agbomey, Dahomey. Prisoners in dunce caps, together with a cat and a crocodile, are about to be hurled over the precipice. (From *A Mission to Gelele*, Sir Richard Burton)

A human sacrifice in Tahiti witnessed by Captain Cook and painted by
John Webber (*British Museum*)

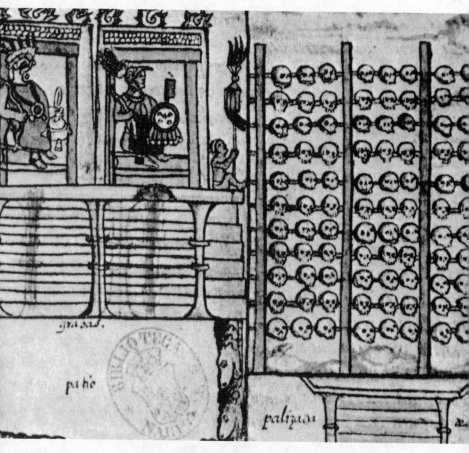

An Aztec skullrack and bloodstained temple (Illustration from *Historia de Las Indias de Nueva España e Islas de la Tierra Firme*, Padre Durán)

A scene from the Codex Borgia in which stylized sacrificial knives swallow victims (*Codex Borgia, Vatican Museum*)

The god Quetzalcoatl pierces a victim's eye. (*Codex Borgia, Vatican Museum*)

Nomad Chichimecs perform an arrow sacrifice. (*Historia Tolteca-Chichimeca*)

A prisoner is sacrificed over fire to the Aztec fire god. (Illustration from *Historia de Las Indias de Nueva España e Islas de la Tierra Firme*, Padre Durán)

A modern representation of an Inquisition burning in Mexico City (After a seventeenth-century colonial painting)

The decapitation of a human victim by an owl demon (Moche pot, Peruvian, c. 500 A.D.; *Museum für Völkerkunde, West Berlin*)

Sacrificial scene on a Cozamaluapa stela from Guatemala (*Museum für Völkerkunde, West Berlin*)

A clay figure from Colima, Mexico, adorned with skulls (*Museum für Völkerkunde, West Berlin*)

The suicide by burning of Elizabeth Weniger of the Ananda Marga sect in Manila on 14 June 1978 (Courtesy of Ruther D. Batiguas)

were cooked human bodies, just like those in codex illustrations. But while Sahagún's account of the second monthly feast mentions the eating of the victim, in most other cases he does not relate what happened to their remains. Sometimes he *implies* that they were eaten; for instance, in the third feast celebrants donned the victims' skins and it seems unlikely that the flayed bodies were merely buried or burned. More light on the flesh-eating aspect of Mexican sacrifice is shed by Sahagún in another context in his Ninth Book, devoted to the merchants, who played a leading role in Aztec society. Their feasts, according to the Spanish friar, ended with the eating of human bodies.

The merchants were often an object of envy to the Aztec establishment on account of their riches. As a kind of insurance policy, they would spend part of this wealth on financing lavish ceremonies to honour the ruler and the warrior caste. Like other Aztec festivities, they were highly ritualized and their central theme was the sacrifice of slaves. These had to be bought in the slave market of Azcapotzalco, then a separate town but now a drab suburb of Mexico City. The slave dealers did all they could to attract customers; their human merchandise, richly arrayed, was made to dance, sniff posies and even smoke tobacco. Candidates for the offering were meticulously picked as fine physical specimens. The usual number involved was either one woman and one man, two men and one woman, or two men and two women. Before the feast, the host prepared his slaves. The prescribed attire was elaborate and expensive:

> First [the merchant] arrayed his bathed slaves. He gave them what pertained to them: capes, the breech clouts, the skirts, the shifts along whose border they had placed the trimming. He added leather ear plugs with their pendants, or long, curved labrets. He added crushed paper which they had sewn with fine, pointed quetzal feathers, bound with red cord to place them in their ears. And on their ankles he placed rattles; on the edges of a band of ocelot skin he laid shells. On each ankle he bound them on. And he tied shining hair strands about their temples, which were decorated in this way: alternating strips of turquoise and gold, reddish coral shells and black mirror stones. From the tips of the strips they hung bits of hair. Hence

it was called "shining hair strands". Then he assembled them. He did nothing but make them continue dancing. Now they nevermore abandoned flower necklaces, the garlands of flowers, the shields of flowers, the tubes of tobacco. Every day he decked them with flowers. They did nothing but continue to smell the flowers, and to smoke the tobacco tubes.[12]

This was by no means all. Before the assembled guests the slaves were crowned with a device made of turquoise and feathers. Over their sumptuous robes, they were bedecked with feather jackets, decorated with a design of skulls on a field of human bones. Brightly coloured paper wings were fixed to their shoulders. The slaves are constantly referred to as "the bathed ones", stressing the fact that they had been purified by ritual bathing; in Mexico too this was an act of atonement through the washing away of sins. War captives at times were also bathed before their death.

The ceremonies were immensely long, and the sacrifice only took place on the fourth day. The slaves, plied with an intoxicating draft, were taken to the temple of the great Aztec Sun and War God, where further lengthy rites awaited them, and it is hardly surprising that by this time they positively longed to die. "And the ceremonially bathed slaves, all during the night they slept not. And when the dawn broke, they thereupon gave them food. No more could they eat, although strongly did they urge them; it was as if they were anguished in spirit; they looked forward only to their death." After yet another whole day of ceremonial, the slaves were dispatched at the top of the temple by a priest dressed as the god. Many of the common people came to watch, and a special seat, covered with ocelot and wolf skins, was reserved for the Emperor Moctezuma.

For the finale came a repast at which the victims' bodies were eaten. As in the feast of the second month, the recipe was plain, and the flesh was served with maize, boiled separately: "They cooked [the slave] in a jar. Separately, in a jar, they cooked the grains of maize. They served his flesh on it. They placed only a little on it. No chilli did they add to it; they only sprinkled salt. Indeed all [the host's] kinsmen ate of it." The elaborate relics of the victims were kept as heirlooms until the merchant's death, when they were burned.

The question of which parts of the human body were consumed on this and other occasions remains a mystery. It is commonly held that only the arms and legs were eaten, a belief that derives from a statement of Bernal Díaz, repeated on four occasions. But Bernal Díaz could only rely on hearsay since he never attended ritual banquets. He further insists that the torsos were not eaten, but were thrown to the wild beasts of Moctezuma's zoo. This explanation, seldom if ever questioned, is most implausible. Accounts agree that the victims *became* the god to whom they were sacrificed. To throw these deified remains, that were the god's own flesh, to impure beasts would have been no less an outrage than if a Catholic priest were to throw the consecrated remains of the Host to the neighbourhood cats. Moreover, if victims were really so numerous, the zoo's inhabitants would have been gorged to bursting point. And, quite apart from the religious objections to the notion, it does not explain what happened to the torsos in thousands of provincial centres where the ruler had no menagerie. If the custom of other lands is anything to go by, ritual eating would not have been confined to the extremities of the body. It was always the vital organs, the liver, entrails, heart and brain that were the most sacred since they contained the victim's soul matter. In Mexico the hearts were reserved for the sun, but it is hardly likely that the other vital organs were treated as offal and fed to animals.

Regardless of which morsels were involved, the eating of human flesh was part of an elaborate ritual. No native text suggests that people were simply filling their bellies with a form of food that they found palatable. And yet Marvin Harris in *Cannibals and Kings* implies precisely this. A chapter devoted to the Aztecs is entitled "The cannibal kingdom"; he quite rightly points to the lavish scale of Aztec sacrifice and quotes generously from Spanish writers, citing such items as Tapia's dubious description of the mammoth skull rack. In asking what was the underlying basis of such offerings, Harris writes of the "genial discovery" of Michael Harner, who with the greatest intelligence and courage pursued the subject and who "alone deserves the credit for solving the riddle of Aztec sacrifice".

Michael Harner, an anthropologist whose work on the headhunting Jivaros and other South American tribes commands wide respect, has adopted a more sensationalist approach to sacrifice in Ancient Mexico. His views on the subject, published in February 1977 in the *American Ethnologist*, caused such a stir that on 19th February of that year *The New York Times* published an article under the heading "Aztec Sacrifices Laid to Hunger, not Just Religion". Roused to fury, a number of scholars sent a telegram to *The New York Times* that was printed under the caption "Aztec Experts Deny as Ridiculous Professor's Charge that they Withheld Data on Extent of Cannibalism". Harner's views pleased Harris, but they solved no riddles whatsoever and were nothing but his personal opinions on a difficult problem, supported by rather hackneyed excerpts from the writings of the Conquistadors, cited in dozens of commentaries on sixteenth-century Mexico. The scope for withholding data is non-existent; Sahagún, among others, is explicit on Aztec practices and archaeological evidence for these is simply not available, where bones were burned on the captor's or slave-owner's death. Pre-Aztec signs of sacrifice, but not of cannibalism, are graven on many stelae. To complete his case, Harner gives evidence—of a kind that is obvious though unproven—of an inadequate supply of animal protein to form a balanced diet in the absence of human flesh. Hence this became, according to Harner, a basic foodstuff and a vital supplement to a rather meatless and fatless fare.

Notwithstanding his other arguments, Harner goes out of his way to admit that human flesh-eating was the normal preserve of the nobles and even quotes Sahagún and others to that effect. But he oddly insists that the very foundations of the Aztec state—dependent upon the utter submission of the masses—reposed upon the slender hopes tendered to the protein-starved plebeians of a meagre share of the human flesh that was mainly guzzled by the élite: "By encouraging the lower class to engage in war through the reward of human flesh—distributing rights and elevation in status, the Aztec rulers were able to motivate the bulk of their population, the poor, to contribute to state and upper-class maintenance by participating in offensive military operations. It was in the interests of the ruling class and the state to prohibit the eating of human flesh by the commoners, precisely because they were the group most in need of it. By so doing and also by providing a path, through war service, of obtaining meat, the Aztecs were assured of an aggressive war machine." [13]

Henry Nicholson, leading authority on Aztec religion, wrote an effective reply to Harner in an article in *Natural History*, published in April 1977. He first makes the major point that Harner is much too ready to accept at face value the accounts of the Conquistadors, who were not unbiased witnesses and knew next to nothing about Aztec religion. Nicholson rightly insists that Harner's admission that commoners were normally prohibited from eating human flesh cuts the ground from under his thesis. The article treats as unconvincing the idea that this rule was happily waived as a goad to induce the commoners to fight harder for their masters; moreover, it shows that Ancient Mexico was not as bereft of animal protein as Harner would have us believe.

What Harner and others also overlook is that if their view is taken at its face value, Aztec motivation becomes self-defeating. It is claimed that their people were goaded into fighting wars of conquest with the bait of a few mouthfuls of captives' flesh. But such wars could in the end only serve to exhaust the supply of this very bait that was their mainspring. Once conquered, a domain would provide no further captives unless it rebelled, as sometimes occurred. A submissive province yielded not a single victim but instead provided a cornucopia of tribute. The amounts taken from each region are set out in detail in the Codex Mendoza; while distant lands paid tribute in the form of exotic but portable finery, such as the eight hundred handfuls of yellow parrot feathers sent by the remote province of Soconusco on the Guatemalan border, those near at hand produced large quantities of maize and beans. Accordingly, their conquest provided the protein-starved plebeians with increased supplies of starchy staple foods and reduced the chances of eating human flesh, no longer to be had from subjugated peoples. Thirty years before the Conquest, the Aztec armies had swept all before them and were then subduing Soconusco. A sharper incentive is surely needed to spur men to march 1250 kilometres over mountain tracks than a mere hunk of human haunch.

To dismiss the Aztec realm as a "cannibal kingdom" displays a woeful ignorance of their sacrificial rites which served more complex ends. If the main object was merely to slaughter human livestock brought on the hoof to the capital, cheaper and less time-consuming methods could surely have been found than all this lavish and interminable ceremonial. As anthropologist Marshall Sahlins puts it in the *New York Review of Books* of 23rd November 1978, Sahagún's account of the merchants' feast makes it clear that the Aztecs were not in the sacrifice business for their health and it takes a heroic act of utilitarian faith to conclude that the whole system was their way of getting some meat.

Neither Harner nor Harris strengthens his case by inaccurate or dubious statements. Harris, for instance, commits a mammoth howler when he describes the Dresden Codex as "a sixteenth-century document written in Nahuatl, the language of the Aztecs". The Dresden Codex is thought to date from about 1200 A.D. and is written in Maya hieroglyphs; any student of pre-Columbian Mexico learns in the first month of schooling that the Dresden is much the most important of three surviving Maya codices. Harner, while avoiding such gross errors, writes in support of his theories that "Some [captives] might be sacrificed and eaten on the field of battle". This statement is totally at variance not only with *all* surviving accounts but also with the very essence of Aztec sacrifice, inseparable as it was from lengthy ritual. He even repeats Bernal Díaz's implausible statement that the torsos went to the royal zoos—and if the object was to appease protein-hungry plebeians, why throw part of their protein supply to the king's beasts? Harner's remarks about eating captives on the spot are better applied to New Zealand, where the Maoris indeed used human flesh to supplement field rations.

Mexican gods, as we have seen, hardly differed in their choice of victims from those of other peoples: slaves, male and female, children and above all war captives—the people who had no rights of their own. In few parts of the world do we find other kinds of victims, except perhaps for widows, who did have rights and possessions of a kind often coveted by others. Also less in evidence in Mexico are those other candidates for sacrifice, criminals; when adulterers, for instance, were stoned to death, that was not a true religious rite. And while sacrifice in Mexico has so many worldwide features, the idea that the victim had to be in some sense a "sinner" or to be "made sin" in order to lighten the general load of guilt is notably absent. More current is the Old Testament insistence that the victim be without blemish.

Moreover, as already explained, the ends to be served by sacrifice differed little from those sought elsewhere, such as supplying retainers for the next world or human supports beneath buildings. The urge is particularly strong in Mexico to kill humans to procure good crops. A parallel to Old World rites involving corn kings are the many offerings to the gods of the sacred plant, maize, and to the gods of rain and water. Another basic theme is the upholding of the cosmos, with an almost desperate stress on the preservation of the Fifth Sun by giving him human hearts, piled in the Eagle Vessel. The Mexicans were ever mindful of the legend that the Fifth Sun, which was to be the last, was the resurrected form of a god burned in the fire at the Great Pyramids of Teotihuacan. The present world was born of sacrifice and the process could not cease if it were to be kept in being.

Over the centuries since the Spanish Conquest, human sacrifice in Mexico has accumulated a mythology all of its own, as something unique in the annals of human cruelty, but stripped of all flights of fancy, little is left of such uniqueness. With its emphasis on skull racks in the last phase and on trophy heads in pre-Aztec sculpture, Mexican sacrifice can be traced back to the worldwide cult of the human head. Whether in India, Africa, Hawaii or Borneo, skulls were at times worn as trophies and at others placed on racks and poles or used to decorate the walls of temple compounds; sometimes they were merely piled high in front of sacred buildings. And just as the general objectives recur with monotonous regularity in all parts of the globe, so also the details repeat themselves: the Mexicans, like the Dyaks, paid great attention to the bathing of slaves before sacrifice; even the strange gladiatorial sacrifice finds parallels among the Tsimshians of Alaska or the Tupinambas of Brazil; just as in Mexico special honours in the after-life were reserved for two select groups, sacrificed captives and women who died in childbirth, so also in the Polynesian Marquesas Islands precisely the same two categories went to a heaven set apart for them.

In terms of sheer numbers slain, the Mexicans were in the top league, but shared the distinction with others. For Dahomey, Europeans gave close estimates; it will be recalled that in Agbomey, an *average* year claimed five hundred lives, rising to a thousand when a king died, in a town whose population was barely 20,000, or less than one tenth of the Aztec capital. To compete with the Dahomans in terms of sacrificial victims per capita, the Aztecs had to slay some five thousand people in a normal year, rising to ten thousand under special circumstances, such as the dedication of a major temple or the death of a monarch. Sahagún mentions no such numbers, but the figures are at least plausible. The possibility of even greater numbers depends upon the accounts of single monster holocausts for once-and-for-all events. I personally doubt their accuracy but the truth can never be known. Fijians and Maoris could also claim a place in the top league, if there is any substance in reports of cannibal banquets involving two hundred or three hundred people—a relatively easy number to estimate. The ratio of victims per capita would rival the statistics for Mexico and Dahomey since we are dealing with mere villages.

Uniqueness in motivation or even in quantity, therefore, hardly applies to the Aztecs. What did distinguish them from others is the way they recorded their deeds. Aztec sacrificial literature *is* unique, whether expressed in codices, in oral native traditions, in informers' post-Conquest narratives or Conquistadors' reports. In most parts of the Old World, following partial but not total abandonment of human sacrifice by Egyptians, Greeks and others, the feeling perhaps spread to other regions that, however hallowed, the practice was not something to be openly praised in sacred writings. In ancient Sumer, the texts are silent on the subject. An exception to this reticence can to some extent be found in India. In two episodes in the Rig Veda, written in about 1500 B.C., a god is either the subject or the object of an act of human sacrifice. As we have seen, the Puranas, dating from the early centuries of the Christian era, often refer to sacrifice, and popular ballads of the eleventh and twelfth centuries, such as the Gopi Chandra, also extol human offering. Viking literature mentions the subject, as we have seen in the already quoted lines of the Verse Edda, ending with the words "gashed with a blade, blooded for Odin". The Dyak muses entoned the virtues of headhunting:

> *When I have gone on the war-path*
> *Never did I return unsuccessful*
> *Bringing a basketful of heads.*

These lines are taken from the Mengap, the song of the Sea Dyaks' Head Feast, written in a special poetic form of their language. The priests who made offerings to Oro in Tahiti sang ritual chants beginning, "Now eat of thy long-legged fish, Oro-mata-oa, O my King". Even in these literatures, however, treatment of the theme is muted in comparison with Aztec texts that go out of their way to extol the role of human sacrifice. Scarcely a folio of the religious codices is without its decapitated heads, skulls, skeletal figures and sacrificial knives, if not actual bodies, from which spurts the "beautiful blood" (chalchiuheztli) of the gods' victims or even of the gods themselves.

This sacrifice of the Mexican gods recalls Mircea Eliade's notion of the primaeval act of communion, whereby after the first deed of violence, the god had to die so that the world might be saved and the vegetation cycle preserved. The Aztecs drew inspiration from the legend of that great ancestor of their own dynasty, the priest-ruler of Tula, Topiltzin Quetzalcoatl, named after the Plumed Serpent God. He first learned that his face had become lined and withered when he was shown a mirror by a rival magician. Distraught, he drank five draughts of pulque. Later, ashamed at his own intoxication, he fled the city; dressed as the god of the Morning Star, he was consumed by fire and rose to the sky as the planet Venus. In other words, the king of Tula, as surrogate of his god, is himself made the victim. Significantly, the God of the Morning Star, who is simply the Plumed Serpent God in another guise, is invariably depicted in codices with body painted in vertical red stripes, after the manner of sacrificial victims.

Certainly at the time of the Conquest, and probably in the great age of Tula, some four hundred years earlier, war captives in fact took the place of the ruler; the legend may really refer to former times when the death of the god-king in person may have formed the basis of sacrifice in Mexico, as also practised not only in Africa but at the very birth of Egyptian civilization, when Osiris, the god-king, was killed and dismembered.

10

Love-Hate
Relationships

On the eve of 11th April 1649 the city of Mexico was in a ferment as its citizens eagerly awaited the Auto da Fé that was to take place in the Plaza del Volador, not far from where the Great Pyramid had stood. This was to be the most lavish ceremony of its kind ever held in New Spain; ten thousand persons had been brought in to the capital to swell the throng, totalling fifty thousand souls. The condemned were to occupy a special structure, with a broad base on which reposed ten tiers, each narrower than the one below, and reached by steps eighteen inches high. The procession set forth at dawn, led by the sacrificial victims, who had been regaled with extra food to give them strength to bear their long ordeal. Effigies were carried of other offenders, who were to suffer lesser punishments. Strict usage governed the dress of both priests and participants.

All this might suggest that under the Spaniards sacrificial rites had hardly changed. The huge crowd brought in from all sides, the effigies, the procession of offenders, the colourful ritual, the symbolic attire and the pyramidal dais would have been a fit tribute to any Aztec god. Even the sermons recalled the speeches which the Aztecs had been apt to make to their victims. Certain differences, however, may be noted. Spanish ceremonies were duller, the music more doleful, and sermons took the place of dancing. To make up for this added tedium, the prisoner's agony at the stake intensified the drama. Moreover, the priests of the old gods, for all their finery, could hardly compete with the panoply of the Apostolic Inquisitors, who brought up the rear of the procession, accompanied in person by Don Juan de Mañozca, member of the Council of His Catholic Majesty King

Philip IV and Visitor General of the Holy Office of the Inquisition of New Spain. And, finally, the victims were no longer dedicated to the God of War, but to the "Prince of Peace".

Accordingly, before writing of human sacrifice among the many Stone-Age Indians who inhabited the rest of America, the rites of the Aztecs' steel-armed European conquerors must first be taken into account. In so doing, it soon becomes clear that the latter, whilst more self-righteous, were at times no kinder to their fellow men than the Aztecs, not to speak of the North American Iroquois or the Tupinambas of Brazil.

History has been rather unfair to the Spaniards since people tend to think that the cruel forms of retributive sacrifice that prevailed in Europe were invented by them. The Holy Office has become so inseparably linked with Spain that we are apt to speak of the *Spanish* Inquisition, as if no other existed. But in reality the Inquisition came into being centuries before Spain became a nation.

During the early Middle Ages in Europe, whilst many forms of cruelty still thrived, there was scant evidence of human sacrifice. At that time Christians and Jews lived peaceably side by side. But by about 1100 A.D. this tolerance began to evaporate and all heretics came to be regarded by the Church as the servants of Satan; the Jews, who were to be systematically persecuted by the Inquisition from the twelfth to the eighteenth century, were accused of such imaginary crimes as the ritual murder of Christian children, the torturing of the consecrated wafers of the Mass, and even the poisoning of city wells.

The human urge to seek sacrificial victims and martyrs, which had risen once again to the surface in Roman times, before the Empire became Christian, had been muted but not stilled by the teachings of Jesus. The challenge which gave renewed impetus to such urges in the twelfth century first came not from the Jews but from heretics known as Catharists. They presented a far greater threat to established religion than previous sects, since they not only exalted celibacy, but even opposed marriage and childbearing. Their doctrines, brought from the Near East by the Crusaders, had much in common with Persian Zoroastrianism since they viewed life as an unending struggle between the forces of good and evil.

Mainly to deal with this threat, the Holy Inquisition was set up in Germany in 1231, and its powers were extended to other countries a year later; by then the Catharists had become well established on the Rhine, as well as in northern Italy and throughout France. For the Catholic Church it was a positive duty to claim the lives of such dissenters. Faith was a gift of God and the key to the gates of heaven; a single heretic unpursued could imperil the whole fabric of the Church and affect not only the lives but the eternal after-lives of all its members. The burning of heretics can therefore fall within our study of human sacrifice just as much as does the offering of victims in other parts of the world to restore or preserve the cosmic balance or to ward off the anger of the gods. The notion that burning was a punishment does not alter the principle; for example, as we have seen, the Romans, among others, often made no distinction between sacrificial victims and criminals.

As a climax to the anti-Catharist campaign, a great army was sent against them. The dissenting forces were crushed at Sermione, near Verona, where a Catharist bishop had ruled. Following this disaster, no less than two hundred heretics were burned before a huge crowd in the Roman arena at Verona on 13th February 1278, probably a more bestial ceremony than any that took place after the rise of the Spanish Inquisition.[1] This was not the end of the fight against these heretics. At Albi, a leading centre of the sect (who were also known as Albigensians), six leading citizens had died unsentenced after periods of confinement, often in chains and in dark, grim cells, ranging from one to eleven years. As a result Pope Clement V in 1310 ordered the immediate trial of all other imprisoned suspects, but though the Pope twice repeated his command, it was ignored by the Inquisition, so powerful had it become. Finally, in 1319 Guillem Calverie and Issarn Colli were brought out from the dungeon in which they had by then been immured for almost twenty years; they promptly retracted the confessions that had been dragged from them by torture. This paved the way for the final scene in their horrendous drama—death at the flaming stake.[2]

Except for the Visigoths, torture had been unknown among the barbarians who fathered the modern nations of Europe after the collapse of Rome. But in 1252 the bull Ad Extirpar of Pope Innocent II authorized its use by the Inquisition to extract confessions, if necessary by torments prolonged over a period of years. First offenders against the canons of the Church more often faced prison sentences or penances, whilst burning at the stake was normally reserved for those who had relapsed into their former erroneous ways. The Inquisitors even pursued heretics beyond the grave and often dug up the remains of the dead and heaped indignities upon their bones. Of the 636 trials conducted by the distinguished French Inquisitioner, Bernard Gui, 88 were posthumous.

The Spanish Inquisition, established in 1480 by King Ferdinand and Queen Isabella, soon progressed to being a state within the state. The Inquisitors were named by the Crown, not by the Pope as elsewhere, and the property of condemned heretics went to the state, not to the Church as, for instance, in Italy. No Spaniard, however distinguished, was safe from the prying eye of the Holy Office, particularly if he had some association with Jewry. For instance, Archbishop Hernando de Talavera of Granada, like many other high officials of the time, had a strain of Jewish blood. He was accused by the Inquisitor Lucero, who coveted his property, of being involved in a vast plot aimed at replacing Christianity with Judaism; the conspirators were pictured as riding by night on demon goats. Not only was Talavera himself condemned, but Lucero also had burned at a single ceremony one hundred and seven other victims, charged merely with attending Talavera's sermons.[3]

Since its basic purpose was to extract a confession, torture had a deeper meaning for the Inquisition than, say, for the Iroquois, and the agony of its victims was infinitely more prolonged. The proceedings could take many years and charges were often made on the most trivial grounds. For example, in 1568, the Inquisition of Toledo tortured a woman accused of secret leanings towards Judaism, solely on the grounds that she would not eat pork. The American scholar Henry Charles Lea fills many pages of fine print with quotations from the original record of this case; despite her frantic cries for mercy, her screams of pain and her pleas for death—all minutely recorded by the attendant scribe—the Inquisitor simply repeated the demand: "Tell the truth".

In his study of the Inquisition John A. O'Brien gives gruesome details of its techniques: "When the Inquisitors wanted to get faster action, they made the imprisonment incredibly harsh. Chains and starvation in a stifling hole quickly brought confessions from reluctant lips. So widespread were the rumours of these and worse tortures that an official investigation of the prison at Carcassonne was conducted. It disclosed not only a woeful lack of beds and a deficiency of food, but also the implements of the torture-chamber: the rack, burning coals and the *strappado*. The rack was a triangular frame, on which the prisoner was stretched and bound so that he could not move. Attached to his arms and legs were cords connected with a windlass, which when turned dislocated the joints of the wrists and ankles." [4]

Fire was also used to extract confessions of guilt. After a good blaze was started, the prisoner was stretched out on the ground, his feet manacled and turned towards the flame. Fat or grease was rubbed upon them so that they would be severely burned. From time to time the torturer would place a screen between the victim's feet and the brazier, so that the Inquisitor might be able to resume his questioning. In a letter dated 28th July 1319, Pope John XXII refers to this type of torture being inflicted upon a woman by the Inquisition of Toulouse. The *strappado* or vertical rack inspired equal terror. The hands of the prisoner were tied behind his back and he was raised by a pulley or windlass to the top of the gallows, or to the ceiling of the torture chamber, and then dropped, with a jerk, to within a few inches of the floor. This torment was repeated several times. Sometimes weights were tied to the victim's feet to increase the shock and the piercing agony of his fall. To these well-tried methods the Spaniards merely added a few refinements, such as the Toca, or water torture. The offender was tied on a rack, his mouth held forcibly open; a linen cloth called the *toca* was forced down his throat to conduct water poured slowly from a jar. The sharpness of the pain depended on the number of jars used.

As a climax to such torments came the Auto da Fe. Unlike the Aztec monthly feasts, they were held not at fixed intervals, but only when enough victims were at hand to do justice to the event. As shown in many paintings and engravings, they drew immense crowds, comparable only to the throng that would spend all night at London's Tyburn in order to get a good view of the next day's public hangings. When the supply of prisoners was large enough, a date for the Auto would be fixed. One calendar month beforehand, familiars and notaries of the Inquisition marched through the streets proclaiming the great day, while orders went out to carpenters and masons to set up the scaffolding and fix the decorations. The evening before the event, a "procession of the Green Cross" took place, in which familiars carried the special cross of the Holy Office to the appointed site. Some culprits were "reconciled" to the Church and given suitable penances or other less drastic penalties, such as a lifelong ban on the wearing of silken garments, sewn pearls and other jewels. However, the more spectacular ceremonies included their quota of relapsed heretics, to be burned in the grand finale.

If the Spaniards never matched in sheer numbers the burning of two hundred Catharists at Verona, in their sense of the theatrical they outdid all others. We have an eye-witness account of the great Auto da Fe held on 30th June 1680 in the Plaza Mayor of Madrid in the presence of the King and his court; even the vast painted canvas of the scene that also survives does scant justice to the splendour of the proceedings, which took place amid the ruins of Spanish power. The ceremony opened with a procession, headed by a hundred coal merchants, accorded pride of place because they had supplied the wood with which the criminals were to be burnt. These were followed by the Dominicans, before whom a white cross was carried, and in its wake came the Green Cross of the Inquisition covered with black crêpe, accompanied by various grandees who were familiars of the Inquisition. When the procession reached the square, the Green Cross was placed on the scaffold. During the night the friars sang psalms and several masses were celebrated.

At seven o'clock the King and Queen, the Queen Mother and all the ladies of quality and the gentry appeared on the specially erected balconies and prepared to watch the long procession. As on the previous day, this was headed by the coal merchants.

Afterwards came thirty Men, carrying Images made in Pasteboard, as big as Life. Some of these represented those who were dead in Prison, whose Bones were also brought in Trunks, with Flames painted round them; and the rest of the Figures represented those who having escaped the Hands of the Inquisition, were outlawed. These Figures were placed at one End of the Amphitheatre. After these there came twelve Men and Women, with Ropes about their Necks and Torches in their Hands, with Pasteboard Caps three Feet high, on which their Crimes were written, or represented, in different Manners. These were followed by fifty others, having Torches also in their Hands and cloathed with a yellow Sanbenito or Great Coat without Sleeves, with a large St Andrew's Cross, of a red Colour, before and behind. These were Criminals who (this being the first Time of their Imprisonment) had repented of their Crimes; these are usually condemned either to some Years Imprisonment or to wear the Sanbenito, which is looked upon to be the greatest Disgrace that can happen to a Family. Each of the Criminals were led by two Familiars of the Inquisition.

Next came twenty more Criminals, of both Sexes, who had relapsed thrice into their former Errors and were condemn'd to the Flames. Those who had given some Tokens of Repentance were to be strangled before they were burnt; but the rest, for having persisted obstinately in their Errors, were to be burnt alive. These wore Linen Sanbenitos, having Devils and Flames painted on them, and Caps after the same Manner. Five or six among them, who were more obstinate than the rest, were gagged to prevent their uttering any blasphemous Tenets. Such as were condemned to die were surrounded, besides the two Familiars, with four or five Monks, who were preparing them for Death as they went along.

The victims, or criminals as they are called in the account, next walked under the King's balcony before taking their place on an amphitheatre that stood to the right of the scaffold, surrounded by a host of distinguished officers of the Inquisition. The last to take his place was the Grand Inquisitor, dressed in purple habit and accompanied by the President of the Council of Castille. Another Mass was then celebrated.

About Twelve O'clock they began to read the Sentence of the condemned Criminals. That of the Criminals who died in Prison, or were outlawed, was first read. Their Figures in Pasteboard were carried up into a little Scaffold and put into small Cages made for that Purpose. They then went on to read the Sentences to each Criminal, who thereupon were put into the said Cages one by one in order for all Men to know them. The whole Ceremony lasted till Nine at Night; and when they had finished the Celebration of the Mass the King withdrew and the Criminals who had been condemn'd to be burnt were delivered over to the Secular Arm, and being mounted upon Asses were carried through the Gate called Foncaral, and at Midnight near this Place were all executed.[5]

Statistics of numbers slain are almost as elusive as for the Aztecs. The figure was unquestionably high—even excluding the hundreds of thousands of victims of the great witch-hunt, that reached its climax in the sixteenth and seventeenth centuries. Henry Charles Lea studied the records of eight towns and provinces in Spain for the years following the establishment of the Inquisition in 1480. He arrived at an annual average of one hundred and thirty burnings, or a total of about a hundred and fifty, if the whole of Spain were to be included. In later years, however, at the time when the Spaniards were undisputed masters of the New World, the figure was much higher, even if the number slain in Mexico and in South 'America was not in itself very great. The King of Spain, who admittedly ruled a vastly larger domain, could probably boast an annual victim count equal to that of the King of Dahomey, amounting to about five hundred.

In the New World, odd variations from the Spanish formula were adopted: the Mexican Inquisition in 1664 had a penitent smeared with honey, then covered with feathers, and made to stand in the sun for four hours during an Auto da Fe. The tortures used in Peru, including all the more standard methods, are shown in lifelike form in the Inquisition Museum in Lima. In one group appears the outstretched victim of the *toca*, together with the torturer who pours water through the cloth and down the victim's throat, the overbearing Inquisitor, and the scribe who leans over the sufferer, intent upon recording every strangled word the victim utters. The diminutive cells or cages carved out of the rock, in which the victims were kept for years on end, have been excavated and restored to their original condition; to heighten the effect, each contains an emaciated waxwork figure. Also displayed are the public notices used to announce an Auto da Fe. At that which took place on 15th November 1573, only the last of the six offenders listed, Mateo Salada, was to be burned alive. The remainder, however, did not get off lightly: the first on the list, Juan Bautista, in addition to receiving two hundred lashes in the public street, was condemned to life imprisonment and to row in a galley in perpetuity (the notice adds "without receiving any pay"); he was also to wear a *sanbenito* for the rest of his days.

Cruelty, however, to fellow-humans was not a Catholic, let alone a Spanish, monopoly, and it would be an error to assume that the Protestants of the time were any better. Martin Luther was in favour of burning all witches at the stake; John Calvin felt no scruples at having his theological opponent, Michael Servetus, burnt to death. England hardly lagged behind in the persecution of heretics and others. Henry VIII displayed a genius for getting the best of both worlds; he burned extreme Protestants at the same time as hanging and beheading Catholic opponents of his religious reform, thus punishing both sides in the religious conflict. His daughter, "Bloody Mary", reversed the trend and burned three hundred Protestants in four years. In the reign of Queen Elizabeth, an average of four Catholics died annually for their beliefs; they were not burned, but hanged as traitors and conspirators.

In North America, certain of the Indian tribes vied with their Christian invaders, whether Catholic or Protestant, in terms of sheer cruelty to victims. Their sacrificial rites, and also those of many South American peoples, often bear a striking resemblance to those of the Old World. If the ritual executioner's weapons varied, this merely reflected the current level of technology; thus while a sword was available for use in eighteenth-century Africa, an obsidian blade served the purpose in Mexico, and a wooden club in the jungles of South America. Moreover, the ends to be achieved varied little, and, as in the Old World, cannibalism was rife but not universal. The very name *cannibal* derives from the Caribs, first encountered by Columbus, who, like Cook in New Zealand, was shocked to find in deserted villages the remains of the islanders' banquets of human flesh.

Evidence is lacking of the arrival of Old World voyagers in America before Columbus, except for the Vikings, who left scant remains. Such parallels between the two hemispheres are better explained by the broad Bering land bridge, joining north-east Asia to north-west America, which only sank beneath the waves in about 12,000 B.C.[6] The cult of the human head had existed long before America was thus severed from Asia; this and other primitive forms of religion were the common heritage of the bands of hunters who crossed over into the New World and of those others who stayed behind in Asia. Hence customs that were to develop along the same lines in Eurasia and America shared the same roots.

It is pointless to repeat a catalogue of ritual killings in the Americas that finds close parallels in places already described. Hence, in this chapter, I prefer to confine my remarks to those New World peoples whose rites have some special or unusual characteristics. For differences, at least in emphasis, do exist. For instance, if the idea was implicit in other regions that a victim had to be both friend and foe, both good and bad, it was more openly expressed in the Americas. In South America, and to some extent also in North America, some tribes followed the strange custom of first adopting future victims. An odd form of love-hate relationship was thus created between sacrificer and scapegoat. The victim ceased to be an alien and became a member of his captors' tribe before he was sacrificed, sometimes years later.

As we have already observed among the Aztecs, added stress was laid in the New World on active participation by the victim in those rites that were to culminate in his death; he was expected to dance and sing in frenzied fashion as part of the show. Another salient feature of sacrifice among North American Indians was the use of torture. The agonies were as intense and the methods as varied as those of the Inquisition and it has often been suggested that some of these techniques were inspired by the European invaders. Not only do certain rites in the Mississippi region of the United States recall those of Ancient Mexico; in addition, after Mexico was conquered and Spanish missionaries penetrated further north, the natives proved eager pupils both of Christ's gospel and of Christian techniques for tormenting enemies. When the Indians of Huale, Georgia, rose against these Spanish missions in 1597, a priest was taken prisoner and kept as a slave; on one occasion, as a disciplinary measure, they tied him to a post and put a pile of wood under him in imitation of an Auto da Fe. However, unlike the unbending Inquisitors, they then released him again. Early Spanish travellers to the southern United States seldom mention Indian forms of torture, and reports derive more from English and French accounts of later date. Therefore, even if Indian ritual torture existed before any contact with Europeans, one suspects that such contacts inspired new methods, and that live burning was part of an imported technology.

In the early eighteenth century, both the English coming from the north and the Spaniards from the south were involved in hostilities with the Yamassees, who lived to the north of the Savannah River; they would raid the Spanish-occupied lands on the opposite bank and take Spanish prisoners to their settlements, where they were made to suffer barbarous torments, including ones that were unknown to other North American Indians. Some they cut to pieces slowly, joint by joint, with knives and tomahawks; others they buried up to the neck, then stood away at a little distance, and aimed arrows at their heads. As a further variant, they bound prisoners to a tree and pierced the tenderest parts of their naked bodies with sharp-pointed stakes of burning wood; this, the most excruciating of all, was their most common form of torture.[7] Undeterred by such atrocities, in 1715 the Spaniards allied themselves with the Yamassees to drive out the English. Some English captives were also then tortured; among those who met a gruesome end was John Cochran, his wife and four children, together with a number of other women and children.

For details of ritual torture and killing by North American Indians, one is supremely indebted to anthropologist Nathaniel Knowles, whose account of this rather unfamiliar topic is both lucid and lurid. Knowles cites an eye-witness account dating from 1721 of the frame torture used by the Natchez on the lower Mississippi. The natives first construct a frame out of two poles planted upright in the ground and joined crossways by two other poles. The victim is then tied to the foot of the frame and left to bewail his fate whilst the warriors sit down to a meal.

> When the warriors have finished their meal, they come to the place where the frame is planted to which the victim is tied. They make him advance a little and turn his entire body around in order that the people may see him. The one who has taken him gives him a blow of his wooden war club below the back part of his head, making the death cry while removing the scalp in the best manner he is able without tearing it. . . . From the time they begin to take the scalp from the victim the young people go in search of dry canes, crush them, and make packages or bundles of the entire length of the canes which they bind in many places. The one who took him is the first one to take a single crushed cane, light it and burn the place he may choose. But he devotes himself especially to burn the arm with which he [the prisoner] had best defended himself. Another comes and burns another place. These, with their pipes filled with dry and burning tobacco, burn him about the foot. Those heat a nail red hot, with which they pierce his foot. All, in fact, one after the other, revenge themselves as best they are able on this victim, who, so long as strength remains to him, employs it in singing the death song, which, when closely examined, is

found to consist of grievous cries, tears, and groans. Some have been seen to sing and suffer continually during three days and three nights without anyone giving them a glass of water to quench their thirst, and it is not permitted to anyone to give it to them, even should they ask for it, which they never do, without doubt, because they know that the hearts of their enemies are inflexible.[8]

Sometimes this torture was inflicted on Europeans, and two Frenchmen were treated in this way in 1729 and 1730. The French returned the compliment and Governor Perier reported that after the Natchez rebellion he had four men and two women burned. The Chicasaws of Mississippi went even further; when the French made war on them in 1736, they tied twenty-six French soldiers and seven officers to stakes and burned them by slow fires.[9]

Harrowing accounts also survive of Cherokee rituals, but the most accomplished torturers of all were the Iroquois, Hurons and other neighbouring tribes of the north. An intriguing eye-witness was Mary Jemison, who became an adopted Iroquois and who tells of how the Shawnee of Kentucky tortured a white captive in 1759 by means of numerous small cuts, followed by whipping with tiny rods. Mary Jemison even lists the different techniques. Included among them were "applying brands, embers, and hot metal to various parts of body; putting hot sand and embers on scalped head; hanging hot hatchets about neck; tearing out hair and beard; firing cords bound around body; mutilating ears, nose, lips, eyes, tongue, and various parts of the body; searing mutilated parts of the body; biting or tearing out nails; twisting fingers off; driving skewers in finger stumps; pulling sinews out of arms". In 1782 the Shawnee slowly roasted a British officer named Crawford, while the squaws heaped embers upon his body.

Unlike the southern tribes who employed the frame, further north the standard method was to build a scaffold or platform on which the prisoners met their gruesome end. Reports on ritual torture among these tribes cover a period of over two centuries. French explorers and missionaries first met with the Algonkians and Iroquois of the St Lawrence River region in the opening years of the seventeenth century. The Jesuit Relations give a vivid account of their cruelties and make it clear that every contact with them carried the risk of death by torture. The details varied from group to group, but Father Le Jeune's factual report, cited by Knowles, of how the Hurons treated an Iroquois in 1637 is typical, if harrowing. Such practices went on unabated long after that date, until the time when the power of the Five Nation Federation declined. As late as 1838, the Pawnees of Nebraska roasted a fifteen-year-old girl over a slow fire and then killed her with arrows.

Father Le Jeune's description of the proceedings begins at dusk, with the lighting of eleven fires. With cries of joy young and old alike armed themselves with a piece of burning bark or a firebrand. The victim was then made to run around the fires, while each man attempted to burn him and torture him as he passed, reviving him whenever he fainted.

> There was no strife as to who should burn him—each one took his turn; thus they gave themselves leisure to meditate some new device to make him feel the fire more keenly. They hardly burned him anywhere except in the legs, but these, to be sure, they reduced to a wretched state, the flesh being all in shreds. Some applied burning brands to them and did not withdraw them until he uttered loud cries; and, as soon as he ceased shrieking, they again began to burn him, repeating it seven or eight times—often reviving the fire, which they held close against the flesh, by blowing upon it. Others bound cords around him and then set them on fire, thus burning him slowly and causing him the keenest agony. No one spared himself, and each one strove to surpass his companion in cruelty.
>
> As soon as day began to dawn, they lighted fires outside the village, to display there the excess of their cruelty to the sight of the Sun. The victim was led thither. . . . Meanwhile, two of them took hold of him and made him mount a scaffold six or seven feet high; three or four of these barbarians followed him. They tied him to a tree which passed across it, but in such a way as he was free to turn around. There they began to burn him more cruelly than ever, leaving no part of his body to which fire was not applied at intervals. When one of these butchers began to burn him and to crowd him closely, in trying to escape him, he fell into the hands of another who gave him no better reception.

From time to time they were supplied with new brands, which they thrust, all aflame, down his throat, even forcing them into his fundament. They burned his eyes; they applied red-hot hatchets to his shoulders; they hung some around his neck, which they turned now upon his back, now upon his breast, according to the position he took in order to avoid the weight of this burden. If he attempted to sit or crouch down, someone thrust a brand from under the scaffolding which soon caused him to arise. . . . They so harassed him upon all sides that they finally put him out of breath; they poured water into his mouth to strengthen his heart, and the Captains called out to him that he should take a little breath. But he remained still, his mouth open, and almost motionless. Therefore, fearing that he would die otherwise than by the knife, one cut off a foot, another a hand, and almost at the same time a third severed the head from the shoulders, throwing it into the crowd.[10]

Not every captive met the same fate. The fortunate ones were treated with lavish affection and adopted into the tribe. The women had a major say in the prisoner's fate, and the fittest had the best chance of being adopted; it was not uncommon for a widow to replace her lost husband in this way. However, once taken into the tribe, a captive was by no means secure for life; one Iroquois chief adopted forty prisoners but then later had them burned. Even those chosen by widows to replace their lost husbands were liable to be tortured to death if they proved unsatisfactory bedfellows.

Though many reports of North American Indian customs originate from clerics, they differ greatly from accounts by Sahagún and other Spaniards of Ancient Mexico. Whereas Sahagún inquired into every aspect of native religion, Jesuits and others who describe the North American tribes tell much of the treatment of victims but very little of the religious beliefs that prompted such treatment. Eyewitness accounts are so numerous that their general veracity is hardly in doubt. Yet they often imply that Indian cruelty arose from sheer joy in human suffering or from mere lust for human flesh. Nonetheless countless details included in these reports betray that fact that, however barbarous, the acts were essentially religious in nature. Le Jeune, for instance, insists that the Hurons began by treating their victim with a show of gentleness; he had to perform endless dances during the return journey after capture and was required to sing in each village on the way. Even the flesh-eating was highly ritualized and the heart, torn out just before death, was often given to the young men of the tribe. Among the Iroquois, women were sacrificed to the war god, and they even made a feast of bear meat to this deity as an atonement, if no human victims were available. Father Le Jeune also notes that before an Iroquois captive was sacrificed, the people were told by the chief that the sun god and the war god were present and would be watching the performance. Dreams played an important part in Iroquois religion: the seventeenth-century missionaries recorded many dreams relating to torture; in one case a man who dreamed that he was tortured by an enemy, insisted that his friends should tie him up and burn part of his flesh the next day in the belief that this would make the gods save him from real capture and torment.

The treatment of the scalp was highly ritualized, particularly in the southern United States, where the victim was ceremonially scalped before other agonies were inflicted. The Hasirai, living on the River Missouri, first hung scalps on trees and sang to them, after which they laid them in the ashes of the perpetual fire maintained in the temple and placed food offerings before them. The Pawnees used scalps as ceremonial offerings to the gods. Among the Natchez, old women carried the scalps in dances, praising the sun for victory. In general, in the South-east scalps were looked upon as sacrificial offerings, and, as in Mexico, skulls were collected and displayed in front of temples. Whether in the impaling of victims' heads or the burning of their bodies, the people of the Mississippi region took advantage of imported techniques, both Spanish and Aztec.

At the opposite extremity of the North American continent the tribes of the north-west coast of Canada practised forms of ritual cannibalism so exotic that they are far from being a mere repetition of Old World customs, though, like those of West Africa, they were based on secret societies. Of these north-western tribes, the Kwakiutls are the best documented. Their supreme god bore the formidable name of Baxbakualanuxsiwae (the Cannibal of the Northern Extremity of the World) and was a rabidly cannibal form of dying god, whose monstrous body was covered all over with gaping, blood-stained mouths. According to a strange legend, this giant man-eater had been roasted alive in a pit dug by his four brothers in his own house. As he came into his home, his brothers lay in wait for him and watched as he prowled round the room, bellowing his cannibal cry "Hap! Hap! Hap!" in a voice of mounting excitement. At last his feet came close to the pit which they had dug in the floor, the eldest suddenly snatched away the boards that lay over the opening, and Baxbakualanuxsiwae, still dancing frantically, plunged to the bottom and landed among the red-hot stones that glowed there. Quick as lightning, the brothers filled in the hole with more stones. The god's flesh hissed on the red-hot stones and he soon died.[11]

This cannibal hero was the supreme patron of a sect called the Hamatsas, who formed a kind of élite of licensed man-eaters. A youth who wished to join this élite had to live in solitary retreat for at least three months in the forest, where he sought to absorb the spirit of the god. Before he returned to the village as a fully-fledged member of the sect, he had to prepare a special meal of human flesh for the veteran Hamatsas. For this purpose he took advantage of the strange custom of tree burial. In order to provide the special fare, he would locate a suitable corpse hung in a tree. The body would first be smoked, according to strictly prescribed ritual, and then eaten in company with the other Hamatsas. After dancing in frenzied fashion round the corpse, each chose his portion in strict order of tribal seniority. The novice had to swallow every mouthful of his portion whole, without chewing, and wash it down with a draught of salt water. This inevitably led to a fit of vomiting, and it was vital that every single mouthful, which had been meticulously counted, was brought up. If the number of pieces failed to tally with those swallowed, his excrement had to be carefully examined, to make sure that none remained in his body.

Strictly speaking, this initial feast of the Hamatsa novice was not a true sacrifice, for, notwithstanding the bizarre ritual, the flesh was not taken from a victim specially killed for the purpose, but from someone who had already died. However, from initiation onwards he became dedicated to the god, and to the eating of human flesh, which was normally taken not from "natural" corpses but from living victims. Consumed in the prescribed manner, the meal can hardly have been enjoyable; instead, it was the outward sign that he was no longer an ordinary mortal, but had identified himself with the god. To satisfy the continuing need to eat other men, both slaves and captives were killed. If none were available, Hamatsas would even snatch mouthfuls of flesh from the living bodies of their own tribes-men, gnawing at anyone they chose. A former Hamatsa, still alive at the end of the nineteenth century, said that it was a common prac-tice to swallow hot water after a mouthful of flesh, taken from a liv-ing body, as it was believed that this would inflame the wound made by his teeth.[12]

In considering South America, Peru deserves pride of place as the cradle of the only higher civilization of that continent. Human sac-rifice has a long history in Peru in pre-Inca times, and the Incas themselves at the time of the Spanish conquest had many forms of offering, particularly involving children. Such killings are often ig-nored, since they are so much less spectacular than those of the Aztecs.

Ancient Peruvians had no system of writing and left no codices to bear witness to their beliefs and rituals. The Spanish chroniclers left voluminous records of what they saw but, as in Mexico, these were related more to the outward forms of religion than to its inner sub-stance; moreover, since the Spaniards were out to destroy the old gods, such forms soon ceased to exist and their accounts only de-scribe the situation in 1532, the year in which the Inca Empire sur-rendered to a hundred and fifty conquistadors. Nonetheless, ample evidence does survive from pre-Inca times. The Ancient Peruvians enjoyed a long tradition as superb weavers and potters. Sometimes this pre-Inca art depicts an actual sacrifice; in addition, several heads and limbs proliferate, and their meaning is unmistakable.

Some of the earliest data come from the vicinity of Casma, lying on the coast about two hundred miles north-west of Lima. The Tem-ple of Serro Sechin, which dates back to nearly 2000 B.C., has a num-ber of stone stelae. Certain of these depict human figures that are evidently dead, since their eyes are closed; but many slabs have also been found that display severed heads; other reliefs show limbs sepa-rated from the rest of the body; and certain full-length figures seem to represent people who were not only dead, but had been dismem-bered.

At Paracas, situated on the coast south-east of Lima, a great civili-zation flourished from about 700 to 200 B.C. Here a large number of ceremonial burials have been found, that suggest early origins for a custom so often mentioned by the sixteenth-century chroniclers—the interring of the living with the dead. Some of the Paracas tombs, formed by deep shafts with bottle-shaped stone chambers, contained thirty or forty individuals, mostly women and infants. According to Julio Tello, the Peruvian archaeologist who first excavated Paracas, the remains belonged to people of different social classes; some had rich mantles while others, presumably attendants, were wrapped in rough cotton sheets. Bodies of children were also found in ceramic urns.

In another part of Paracas, known as the Necropolis, quantities of mummy bundles were found, consisting mostly of elderly men, wrapped in layer after layer of some of the most fabulous textiles ever produced by man. Because of the very dry climate—it rains in this desert only once every twenty-five years—they were in almost perfect condition. These wrappings, some of which can be seen in the Archaeological Museum in Lima, combined a vast number of intricate designs. In almost every bundle a strange motif recurred, to which scholars have given the prosaic title of "Conventional Flying Oculate Being"; its presence is so universal as to amount to a kind of mortuary status symbol. In the larger bundles, up to one third of the total number of decorated textiles depict this Oculate Being, a figure both weird and sanguinary. It has a wide, leering mouth, holds a trophy head in one hand and a knife in the other, while streamers or appendages flow from its body. The motif occurs on pottery designs as well as on textiles. The Oculate Being is not the only figure to hold severed heads; even mythical condor birds and feathered killer whales bear similar trophies. The Paracas artists often show a corpse or a head held close to the mouth of one of these monsters, as if it were being eaten. As American archaeologists Edward and Jane Powell Dwyer point out, the flesh-eating connotation of such symbols is not in doubt, and the Oculate Being himself, so cherished by the élite, was clearly addicted to human sacrifice.[13]

The Moche civilization, which flourished on the northern coast of Peru during the first seven centuries of the Christian era, is renowned for the great skill of its potters. These Moche vessels, of which enormous numbers survive, are so lifelike as to constitute a kind of literature in clay, rich in descriptive detail of the people's temples, houses, animals, boats, dress and even their infirmities. They also tell us much about the gods, and depict human sacrifice with a freedom rare among Old World potters (see the illustration). For instance, one jar in the Ethnological Museum in West Berlin portrays a man about to be hurled from a rock, while another shows an opossum god in the act of beheading a victim with a knife.

An article by Dr Elizabeth Benson provides vivid drawings of Moche sacrifice.[14] On a painted pot from the Art Institute of Chicago, the central figure is surrounded by amputated arms and legs with cords attached; he is being dragged off by two women and his fate is clearly sealed. A vessel in the Anthropological Museum in Munich shows two bound and nude figures that are about to be decapitated. Elizabeth Benson suggests that many of the scenes on Moche pots, often endearingly described as "mother and child", really depict a female priest bearing off her victim (the latter is universally depicted as smaller than its sacrificer). The "children" in question often have their hair cut in the manner of victims or war prisoners. Another elaborate Moche pot shows a whole series of offerings at different levels, each with its trophy head and with a figure at the top being decapitated by monsters.

The people of Moche devised an ordeal, probably also inflicted on prisoners, for which it is hard to find any parallel elsewhere. Moche pots abound in skeletal figures and heads that were generally supposed to represent departed ancestors. However, Dr Alan Sawyer of the University of British Columbia read a paper to the Forty-third Congress of Americanists in August 1979 in which he pointed out that the cheeks of the so-called death-heads are flesh-covered, though the eyes, nose and mouth resemble those of skulls; they invariably have a zig-zag line running from ear to mouth. He most convincingly demonstrated that these were not dead people at all but victims, whose faces had been flayed, eyes reduced to sockets and noses cut down to the bone; enough skin had been left on the lower part of the jaw—as shown by the zig-zag line—for them to be able to eat (and perhaps scream during the ceremony). Doctors consulted by Sawyer confirmed that under such conditions a person could at least survive but would suffer drastic loss of weight, because of difficulties in eating and problems of saliva. If deprived of lips, a kind of pseudo lip would grow and the person could live on for a number of years but would present an emaciated and even skeletal appearance. These flayed figures, some of whom are female, are often attended by vultures, occasionally portrayed as attacking their eyes or genitals. They even appear in erotic scenes; one such skeletal being bears a child, conceivably his own that he has brought as an offering to the god.

Sawyer proposes that these "living dead" were sacred beings, who represented the afterlife amidst the living. They had, in a sense, been to the other world and returned; as such, like the blind drummers of later times in Peru, they belonged to the realm of the supernatural.

When we turn from these earlier civilizations to their heirs, the all-conquering Incas, we are presented with eye-witness accounts of sacrificial scenes. Both textual evidence and archaeology stress the primordial role of burial rites and ancestor worship throughout the history of ancient Peru. This cult is very apparent among the Incas, who carried it to such a pitch of intensity that the mortuary bundles of deceased rulers (the Emperor himself was known as "The Inca") kept their own households, owned property and even received tribute.

Since sacrifice among the Incas was very much a royal prerogative, the largest number of victims was claimed by the accession and death of the king; many of these were children from four to ten years old. In the absence of any writing system, the chroniclers had to rely on verbal accounts by natives; these refer mainly to events within living memory and their estimates of victims vary widely. A seemingly conservative figure comes from Fray Joseph de Acosta, who states that when the Inca Huayna Capac died, only a very few years before the Conquest, a thousand human offerings followed him to the next world. Acosta writes that when an Inca ruler died, they killed his favourites and concubines, together with servants and court officials; children were also slain. Garcilaso de la Vega, himself a scion of the Inca royal line, who wrote his history a century after the Conquest, at times seeks to absolve his forbears from the stain of sacrifice. Nonetheless he also admits that favourite servants and women were buried alive with a dead Inca, but insists, in mitigation, that this was a voluntary act. Several other chroniclers go much further and maintain that four thousand people lost their lives in the obsequies of Huayna Capac. Pedro Cieza de Leon gives this number but when, in another context, he insists that stories of two thousand children being killed for a single feast day were Spanish inventions, he inevitably casts doubt on his own figure for the Emperor's funeral.

People were also slain when some exalted person, other than the king, died or was threatened with death. In one such case, when an important nobleman was told by a soothsayer that his days were numbered, he promptly sacrificed his son to the sun as a surrogate for his own person. Sickness ranked high among the many pretexts for sacrifice; it was thought to be the outcome of sin, and when nobles fell ill, an offering was called for as a ransom to the gods. To quote the chronicler Antonio De Herrera: "When any person of note was sick, and the priest said he must die, they sacrificed his son, desiring the idol to be satisfied with him and not to take away his father's life. The ceremonies used at these offerings were strange, for they behaved themselves like mad men. They believed that all calamities were occasioned by sin, and that sacrifices were the remedy."

In Ecuador, a key province of the Inca Empire, the Jivaros, secluded in a world of their own beyond the towering Andes, showed great enthusiasm for human sacrifice and for headshrinking in particular. The Jivaros were unusual not only in their treatment of the human head, but in the beliefs that prompted the practice. The taking of heads for shrinking was not the automatic right of any warrior, but the jealous privilege of a coterie of killers, each of whom was known as "Kakaram", meaning "powerful one". To graduate as a Kakaram, a man had to kill several persons; as his reputation grew, he gained the right to wear special feather headdresses and ornaments. When he had become really famous, even his enemies would seek his help in getting a head for shrinking. Such requests had to be complied with, since a refusal would be looked upon as a sign of weakness.

Michael Harner, whose more controversial views on the Aztecs have already been cited, made a detailed study of the Jivaros and their religion, in which he stressed the key role played by hallucinogenic drugs. Their use stemmed from the belief that man was subject to invisible forces which could only be seen and then invoked with the aid of such narcotics. Within a few days of birth, a baby was given a drug to help it to enter the "real" world, and older children had to take stronger hallucinogens if they misbehaved. Many of these were prepared from datura and related plants, large doses of which were taken to produce a state of excitement, leading to delirium and hallucination. To obtain these effects, the Jivaros would also ingest the raw juice of datura stems.

Drugs helped not only to invoke spirits but also in the quest for Arutam, a particular kind of soul that was connected with killing and headshrinking. A person was not born with an Arutam soul; it had to be acquired in a variety of ways. Boys might begin their search at the age of six, when they would be taken by their father to fast at a sacred well in the remote forest. Once the long task was completed, the possessor of an Arutam soul would be seized with a desperate urge to kill; he would then, until recently, have joined a headhunting expedition, accompanied by his father if he were still a young boy. One of the stranger features of this odd cult was that a warrior, in the process of killing, lost his Arutam soul and had to acquire another one in the coming months.

The more direct motive for headshrinking, however, came not from the Arutam but from a second form of soul called the Muisak, which could only be acquired by someone who already possessed an Arutam. The sole purpose of a person's Muisak was to avenge its owner's death. It was only called a Muisak whilst it was still inside the corpse, from which it was able to spring forth and take the form of an avenging demon. But according to traditional beliefs, if the head of the corpse were duly shrunk (a shrunken head was called a Tsantsa), the Muisak was forced to enter the head trophy, from which it was powerless to escape. Hence the Tsantsa was prepared by the headhunting expedition as quickly as possible, even before it reached home. In addition, charcoal was rubbed into the skin so that the Muisak could not "see out". The hair was deemed a vital part of the Tsantsas. Some of them are preserved, together with their flowing locks, in museums throughout the world. White men's heads were normally of little interest, since the Jivaros suspected that whites had no Muisak or Arutam souls at all. The tree-sloth was the only non-human creature thought to possess one, because he moved so slowly; he, therefore, had to be very aged and must inevitably have acquired an Arutam during such a long life. Hence sloth heads were also shrunk.

The Jivaros' expeditions resembled those of other peoples. Long ceremonies preceded their launching, and the Wea, or master of ceremonies, had to be given a special new hut, which took several months to build. Usually such war parties did not capture a whole village, but confined their assault to a single house; the heads of all inside were taken, regardless of age or sex. While it is customary to talk of headshrinking, what was actually shrunk was the skin, cut away from the skull and its contents, which were merely thrown into the river. After all flesh had been scraped away, the skin was sown up and boiled in plain water, a process that reduced the size by half. It was then further shrunk by being filled with heated stones that were rolled round the inside; when it was too small to hold pebbles, hot sand was used to reduce the size even further.

Three great feasts celebrated the preparation of a Tsantsa. Five days in length, they were held at monthly intervals and all neighbouring villagers were invited. In the ritual dance the man who had first taken the head would bear it aloft, while two female relatives held onto him. In this way the power of the Muisak was thought to pass into their bodies. The Muisak itself was believed to remain in the shrunken head until the end of the third feast, when the celebrants expelled it and sent it back to its own people with the words: "Now, now, go back to your house where you lived. Your wife is there calling you from your house. You have come here to make us happy. Finally we have finished. So return." In recent decades the head was then commonly sold by the head-taker to one of the mestizo communities on the western edge of the tribal lands, though this was illegal under Ecuadorian law.

Harner writes of how he revisited Jivaro territory in 1969. By then the hunting and shrinking of heads had been greatly reduced but was not yet entirely at an end. The region has since been opened up by an airstrip used by missionaries, and has an air-supplied military base. Moreover, it lies in an area of oil exploration, and this has also helped to put an end to time-honoured customs. Jivaro headshrinking, which survived for so long, falls squarely within our definition of human sacrifice, both for its spiritual motivation and for its ritual. That the victim was killed beforehand hardly affects the issue; Dyak heads were taken on the battlefield and even the Tahitians killed their offering before the ceremonies began. However, as with many modern survivals of human sacrifice, when the outside world began to encroach the killings became more furtive, before finally ceasing. At times the Kakarams even resorted to securing a victim for headshrinking with a shotgun or with poison. Nowadays they merely shrink monkeys' heads for sale to tourists.

In Colombia, which lay beyond the northern border of the Inca Empire, the Spanish found customs similar to those of the Incas. Pedro Cieza de Leon was not a friar, like most of the chroniclers, but a soldier, who took part in the Spanish suppression of the great Inca uprising eighteen years after the Conquest. Before this, he had lived in Panama and Colombia and travelled to Peru from Panama in order to join the forces pitted against the rebels. He chronicled his journey through Colombia and Ecuador and, in place after place that he visited, he found the custom of live burial of widows with their husbands to have reached almost obsessive proportions. On the first part of the journey, he visited Cartagena, a port on the Caribbean coast of Colombia. A chief called Alaya, ruler of a large kingdom, had died only two years before Cieza arrived; the people told him of the ceremony that they had attended at which the majority of the ruler's women and servants were thrown alive into his tomb. Not only did Cieza find the same customs further on, in the vicinity of the present-day cities of Medellin and Cali, but also at Guayaquil, on the coast of Ecuador. He reveals that it was also rife in Peru itself, both on the southern coast and inland in Cajamarca, the place where the conqueror Pizarro first met and later killed the last Emperor, Atahualpa.

The Caucas, who lived in the fertile valley of the river still known as the Cauca, outrivalled all other tribes of Colombia in terms of sheer numbers sacrificed and eaten. The eminent German anthropologist, Herman Trimborn, quotes from a variety of written sources in describing their religion. Yet Cauca customs recall those of other lands in so many respects that the details serve only as a reminder that such rites were worldwide. Not only are exactly the same categories of people sacrificed in Colombia as elsewhere—slaves and captives, but the same methods are used, including the cutting out of the heart, though the victims were more often clubbed. The Caucas and their neighbours had a passion for severed heads and were certainly greedy cannibals, even if one discounts Cieza's figure of fifty thousand Indians devoured by their fellow humans in the province of Popayan, in southern Colombia, in the calendar year 1538. Perhaps the same writer is on stronger ground when he says that the Paucaras, a tribe of the Cauca Valley, sacrificed two humans every week on a platform outside their main temple. As an added refinement, the Caucas kept as trophies not only the heads but the stuffed bodies of their foes, a custom that finds parallels among the Incas, who made drums out of their enemies' skins.

For Cieza and other sixteenth-century writers, the ritual nature of human sacrifice and cannibalism in the Cauca Valley was not in doubt. The Armas offered victims' hearts to their gods, while tribes in the Medellin region did not eat their slaves, but burnt them in front of the statue of their creator god, Dobeiba. In Panama to the north, the Chibchas practised a variant on another familiar theme. When a chief died, his body was dried on a fire and suspended in a hammock beside the tomb. Gaspar de Espinosa, as quoted by Trimborn, attended the burial of a chief who was mummified in this way, festooned with jewels and duly placed in a hammock. His wives and servants had to follow him to the next world; some took poison of their own accord, while others were forced to do so, before they were thrown into the grave.[15]

The Tupinambas occupied a vast stretch of the coast of Brazil, extending from the present-day Rio de Janeiro northwards as far as the Amazon estuary. Forming part of an even larger language group, known simply as Tupi, the Tupinambas were remarkable for their strange forms of sacrifice of which ample records survive. Unlike the more recent reports on, say, the Iroquois or Kwakiutls, such records relate mainly to the sixteenth century, during which Portugal strove to subdue the never-ending coastline of Brazil (the sanguinary tale is well told by John Hemming in *Red Gold*).

The first landing was made in 1500 A.D. and certain Tupinambas had already been contacted by the Portuguese in 1511; others were still fighting them in northern Brazil in 1618. These would-be conquistadors, unlike the Spaniards in Mexico and Peru, could achieve no blitzkrieg. Brazil had no universal monarch, whose capture, like the king on the chessboard, was decisive. Instead, the defeat of one tribe merely led to a head-on clash with the next in line. Hence, over a long period, new contacts were continually being made with American Indian groups that had not yet been wrenched out of their ancient ways. Their customs were faithfully reported, both by the Portuguese and by a series of visitors from other countries; a few of these gained a rare inside view of Tupinamba rites, having been first captured and then cast in the long drawn-out role of prospective victims.

Outstanding among the latter was the German gunner, Hans Staden, seized by the Indians near the port of Santos in 1552. He first underwent the strange ritual decreed for future human offerings, and only escaped from the jaws of death by feigning a toothache, which prevented him eating and made him too thin to be worth killing and cooking. After this, he produced some daring prophesies and won for himself the status of a tribal oracle, too precious to be slain. Other reports of this kind come from two Englishmen. Anthony Knivet also became a Tupinamba slave and made several last-minute escapes from ritual execution; after this he became their military adviser, devising new and wily tactics for ensnaring enemies. Another English captive, Peter Carder, curried favour by revamping their arsenal of weapons.

The fullest accounts, however, come from French clerics who were active in Brazil from an early date. The Franciscan, André Thevet, in particular, made a serious study of Indian religion, whilst Capuchins such as Yves d'Evreux and Claude d'Abeville also wrote at length about the Brazilian Indians. Such evangelization was not without its risks: in 1556 the ship of the first Bishop of Brazil, Pero Fernandes Sardinha, was wrecked off the coast; the bishop, two canons and two ladies of rank, together with over a hundred whites in all, were stripped, sacrificed and eaten.

Notwithstanding such lapses, the Brazilian native acquired a special aura as the prototype of the noble savage, long before the Tahitians were ever heard of. The monolithic Aztec and Inca empires both impressed and repelled their conquerors. But the more fragmented and easy-going tribes of Brazil inspired a totally different image, summed up in the lines of the poet Pierre de Ronsard:

> Vivez, heureux gent, sans peine et sans souci.
> Vivez joyeusement; je voudrais vivre ainsi.

Montaigne interviewed three Tupinambas whom he met in France in 1562. In his essay *Des Cannibales* he used Tupinamba virtues as a means to criticise French society. The cult of the Tupinambas and their neighbours thus became a fashion, particularly in France; a tableau was even staged in 1550 near Rouen in honour of the visit of King Henry II and Queen Catherine de Medici, in which a meadow near the River Seine was exotically decked out to resemble the Brazilian jungle, complete with monkeys and parrots. Three hundred men took part, stripped naked, tanned and shaggy. Fifty of these were genuine Brazilian Indians brought in for the purpose, while the remainder were French sailors.[16]

Ever since Renaissance man began to learn about the tropics, he has been beset by the urge to exchange his careworn existence for a more happy-go-lucky life on a palm-fringed beach, shared by friendly and ingenuous natives. The illusion still persists. And yet, if this no-tion of a guileless people, innocent of greed, is never much more than an adolescent's dream, at the outset it may have contained a kernel of truth. The contrast between rapacious Europeans and re-laxed natives was real, whether in Brazil, or later, say, in Tahiti and Bali. Another French cleric, Jean de Léry, illustrates the point with the story of an elderly Tupinamba who asked what became of the wealth of a well-known French trader when he died. De Léry said that it was passed on to his children. The Indians replied: "I now see that you Frenchmen are great madmen. You cross the sea and suffer great inconvenience, as you say when you arrive here, and work so hard to accumulate riches for your children or for those who survive you. Is the land that nourished you not sufficient to feed you? We have fathers, mothers and children whom we love. But we are certain that after our death the land that nourished us will also feed them. We therefore rest without further care."

Alas, in all this theorizing about the noble savage loomed the in-escapable snag, already sensed by Montaigne. In his famous essay he relates how he had spoken to a Tupinamba prince and asked him what advantages he gained from his rank. The Prince replied, "to march first into battle". He was at no pains to conceal that the fa-vourite pursuit of the guileless savage was war, fought with the spe-cific aim of taking live captives, who were later to be sacrificed and eaten. In the end, this obvious stain so tarnished the native image, that a sharp reaction set in. The Brazilian Indian was then hauled off his pedestal and branded as the most debased of men. The Portuguese seized upon native vices as a pretext for their policy of slavery, lead-ing to extermination. They took every advantage of the Indian lust for sacrifice. For instance, at times they would entice a chief on to one of their ships and, having extracted from him all his wealth, hand him over to a rival group for ritual execution and eating. As a result, the enmity between the chief's tribe and his slayers reached a new pitch of intensity, resulting in further wars and a fresh flow of captives. This was precisely what the Portuguese wanted, because they claimed the right to seize such captives as slaves, desperately needed for their sugar plantations. The procedure was politely known as "ransoming", since the law allowed the colonists to "ransom", or in other words impound, prisoners about to be eaten by another tribe. It was even not unknown for Christians to kill ceremonially in the Indian manner and to adopt the name of their victim. They thereby set an example to the natives, abetted them in their tribal wars and increased their own haul of slaves.

The copious European accounts are in a different category to the Aztec and Inca data, based more on what the Spaniards learned from informants than on what they witnessed themselves. Unlike the sophisticated Aztecs, the Tupinambas were a tribal people with simple institutions, though they cultivated the soil, growing mainly manioc as their staple food. And yet, even whilst coming from opposite ends of the Americas, odd parallels arise between their forms of sacrifice. Tupinambas and Aztecs in war sought not to kill but to capture the enemy; both had a precise ritual for the taking of a prisoner; both cosseted future victims with a show of outward affection; both practised a form of gladiatorial sacrifice in which a pretence was made of giving the victim, tethered by a cord, a chance to fight back with mock weapons and missiles. Tupinamba prisoners, like those of the Aztecs, were conditioned to serve their captor and to die willingly, and instances can be cited of tribesmen who, once captured, preferred ritual death to release to the Portuguese.

When a Tupinamba warrior took a prisoner, he first clamped his hand upon his shoulder, saying, "I make you my slave", and from that day forth, the captive would faithfully serve his new master. The moral impact of this ritual of capture was profound; when Father Yves d'Evreux asked a Tupinamba why he seemed reluctant to serve him, the Indian replied that it was because he had not taken him in war, placing his hand on his shoulder in the prescribed way.[17] Hans Staden's account of his own capture shows that things did not always work out so smoothly. Sometimes disputes took place as to who was the true captor. "They began to quarrel around me. One said that he was the first to lay hands on me, while another said that it was he who had caught me. They came from different villages, and were unhappy at the prospect of returning home without a prisoner. This was why they quarrelled with those who held me. . . . Finally the chief who wished to become my owner spoke and said that they should bring me alive to their home, in order that the women could see me alive and rejoice at my expense, since they were going to kill me in the manner that they called cavivim pipig, that is to say they would prepare intoxicating drink, would gather for a festival and would eat me all together. The others agreed and they tied four ropes round my neck." [18]

After this initial ordeal, the captors would make a triumphant entry into any village that lay on their path, to display their new slaves. Staden tells how he was taken, along with other prisoners, to a village that lay on the way home and made to dance and brandish rattles. Before entering the home territory, the slaves' eyebrows and the front part of their heads had to be shaven; their whole body was then smeared with resin or honey, to which were stuck feathers or down. The next step was very significant: a captive would be taken by his master to his relatives' tomb, where he would take part in a ceremony of renewal, or re-dedication, just as if he were to be slain there and then to honour these ancestors. But in fact the future victim was kept alive for several years after his capture. During this period he was at times treated with love, at others heaped with scorn.

Staden remains the ideal witness of the earlier part of a victim's career, though he was lucky enough to avoid the rest of the proceedings and to live to tell the tale. At the home village he was welcomed with precisely those dances and songs that would be used on the still distant day of his sacrifice. But a love-hate relationship was apparent from the start when people attacked him with sticks saying, "With this blow, I avenge my friend who was killed by your people". After this he was allowed to rest in a hammock, before being dragged before the chief, as part of the initial ceremonies, to the accompaniment of yet more dancing.

The captor had a sacred obligation to take care of his slave; rather than let him go hungry, he would even have reduced his own fare. As an adopted tribesman, the captive was married a few days after his arrival, often to a daughter of his captor or to one of his secondary wives; other prisoners, as among the Iroquois, were betrothed to women who had lost their husbands in battle. He was also allowed to have relations with unmarried girls of the village. The wife's task was to coddle the future victim to whom she had been married, and to make him feel thoroughly at home; he was granted almost complete freedom of movement and even allowed to cultivate a plot of his own and to hunt and fish. Yet he never altogether lost his alternative status as an enemy. Any children born to his new wife were killed at birth, or when they were a few years old. Thevet saw two children killed who were six or seven years old; occasionally they were kept and sacrificed on the same day as their father.

Cherished at times, at others the adopted victim was heaped with indignities. He was never allowed to forget his dual status and had to attend feasts plumed and feathered as befitted a prisoner. As he walked through the village, bedecked with feathers in this way, people threw parrot plumes at him as a reminder that he was fated to die. Sometimes he was further humiliated by being brought bound to a ceremony. The length of this peculiar form of captivity varied greatly. Old men were soon slain, while the younger ones were allowed to live for several years at least, and in certain cases for twelve or fifteen. Yves d'Evreux writes of how one youth was captured as a child and grew to manhood among his captors, who had already eaten his mother; the knowledge of his fate did nothing to temper the genuine love that he felt for his adopted relations.

Once the date of the final rite was fixed by the elders, feverish preparations began and messengers were sent out with invitations to nearby villages. A very special task, reserved for seasoned warriors, was the making of the cord, thirty yards long, with which the victim was to be bound for the sacrifice. A new club was also fashioned, to crack the man's skull; the day before he was to die, it was decorated with strings and balls of cotton. The ceremonies were so long and elaborate as to recall those of the Aztecs. On the first day, according to Thevet's eye-witness account, the front part of the prisoner's head was again shaven and his body painted black and once more stuck with feathers. After these formalities he went to rest in a special hut, but got little sleep as old women, also painted black, slung their hammocks at his side and intoned ritual chants all night long. Two more days of singing and dancing followed, but the strangest rites were reserved for the fourth day. First the victim was cleansed in a nearby river; then, on his way back, a mock combat took place. Either he was forced to run along a track, as if trying to escape, and was "recaptured" by a warrior, or he was simply waylaid by a single adversary, while others stood ready to bind him with the ceremonial cord when he succumbed. If the first assailant failed to master the victim, another came and took his place.

On the fifth day, the captive was led to the place of execution. Here the cord was released from his neck and tied round his waist, leaving his arms and legs free. In front of him were placed hard-skinned fruits about the size of an apple, together with some pebbles. These he hurled at the spectators, as a kind of symbolic vengeance. In the course of this "vengeance", he would work himself into such a frenzy that he ended by throwing handfuls of earth at people, once his stock of ammunition was exhausted. Meanwhile, a group of old women would light the fire in which the body was to be cooked. The executioner, arrayed in gorgeous plumes, took the club from the hands of these hags and advanced upon the victim, addressing him as follows: "Are you not of the nation, who are our enemies? Have not you yourself killed and eaten our relatives and friends?" The prisoner would reply: "Yes, I am very strong, and I have killed and eaten several; I have been bold in assailing your people, whom I have eaten so many times." The slayer tried to fell his victim with a single blow, which the latter did his best to fend off; on occasion, he was allowed to defend himself with his own club. Once he was finally dispatched, children were encouraged to anoint themselves in his blood; sometimes they were even invited to plunge their hands into a hole made in his stomach and drag out the entrails. The body was then roasted and distributed to all present; tongue and brains were given to the young men, while the veterans took the skin of the skull and other parts of the body. The sexual organs, as fertility symbols, went to the women. For the benefit of those for whom no flesh could be spared, a kind of soup was made of the bones, hands and feet, and put in a pot from which all could take their share.

René Girard, in *La Violence et le Sacré*, cites Tupinamba rites in support of one of his basic themes—the element of contradiction in human sacrifice. Close bonds unite the sacrificer to his victim, who becomes both friend and foe, and has to be both good and bad.[19] Among the Tupinambas the notion survived that if the victim were to be ritually slain and eaten, he must first be made one of the group —he always had to come from an enemy tribe. The adoption is simply a preparation for his death as the universal scapegoat, a concept basic to tribal thought. First he has to be loaded with insults and then become a relative by marriage, cherished with a love which he fully reciprocates, before being ritually slain.

The alternative pampering and brutality that was the fate of the victim whether of the Iroquois or of the Tupinambas is a trait more often to be found in the New World, but it also conforms in reverse to Girard's pattern of the African ruler who is both good and evil, revered as king at one moment, at another forced to sin and, by flouting convention, to become an outsider, and then to fight a mock battle with his subjects. Among the Tupinambas, hatred engendered love, while in the African instance, love turned temporarily to hatred.

The plight of the captive leads Girard back to another major tenet: sacrifice restores the unanimity of the community, centred upon the person of the scapegoat who plays the part of the mythical hero, who died at the beginning of time. The Tupinambas, like so many peoples, traced their ancestry back to a legendary hero who laid down, for all time the rituals that they were to preserve. The fact that he had been burned, not eaten, is of lesser importance; offerings burned before the altar, as for instance in the Old Testament, were symbolically "consumed" by the god. Girard stresses that the Tupinamba victim had to be both cursed and esteemed; the cannibalistic finale merely reflected the primordial event, as handed down by immemorial tradition. He is supported by Mircea Eliade who reminds us in *The Sacred and the Profane* that sacrifice came first and that man-eating was mainly an additional, secondary rite. It was not a case of killing the man in order to eat him but of eating him because he had been sacrificed.

If Tupinamba practices are a thing of the past, the notion of ritual sacrifice has not altogether died out in Brazil, as evidenced by the following incident reported in the 5 May 1977 issue of the Mexican newspaper *Excelsior*.

On Ipitanga Beach, near the city of San Salvador de Bahía, Jose Mauricio Carvalho, pastor of a sect known as "The Universal Assembly of Saints", was arrested and charged with the drowning of eight children, aged from seven months to eight years old, by throwing them off a rock into the sea during the course of a ceremony. The "prophet" of the sect, Jose Maurino, explained that this sacrifice was made "for the glory of God". One woman who had lost three children also said when interviewed that this was "the will of God". The children were cast one by one into the sea, in the presence of the fanatical votaries. None of the group repented of what they had done, since they insisted that they had obeyed God's order.

II

The Urge to Kill

At the turn of the century human sacrifice was often treated as a sinister but passing vice with which men were cursed at a given stage in their history but which they later cast off in the name of progress. In 1904 it was still possible for Edward Westermarck to write: "We find that various peoples who at a certain period have been addicted to the practice of human sacrifice, have afterwards at a more advanced stage of civilization voluntarily given it up. . . . With the growth of enlightenment men would lose faith in this childish method of substitution, and consequently find it not only useless but objectionable; and any sentimental disinclination to the practice would by itself, in the course of time, lead to the belief that the deity no longer cares for it, or is averse to it." [1] The fallacy of this line of thought is exposed by Westermarck himself: to prove his point he cites the case of India, where Brahmans and Buddhists in the last millennium B.C. abolished human sacrifice, but he fails to add that it revived when Hinduism replaced Buddhism and then flourished as never before in the early days of the British Raj.

Another theory, current at the time, reduced sacrifice, whether human or animal, to the status of a bribe to the gods. This view of the human victim as a mere commodity, immolated in exchange for tangible benefits, takes little account of the complex links that bound him both to the priest who took his life and to the community for which he died. More recent attempts at over-simplification treat sacrifice as a handy weapon for waging class warfare—a scourge with which the ruling class could terrorize the masses. In societies such as Aztec Mexico, the same stick also served as a carrot, since the common people were supposedly goaded into fighting their masters' wars with the bait of a hunk of human flesh—a notion that I have shown to be false.

In the present study of human sacrifice, the custom is more often seen to be neither a bribe to the gods nor a bait to their worshippers but rather an act of abnegation, tinged with devotion. By this act a single victim, raised to the status of the deity, served to bridge the gap between the gods and man. Through the medium of the victim's death, man momentarily became God, and God became man. The word Pontiff, as applied to Christ's successors on the throne of St Peter, derives from the Latin *pons*, meaning "bridge". The word "sacrifice" itself means "to make sacred". By being made sacred—or sacrificed—the victim, at the supreme moment of his agony, creates an instant of oneness between man and his god. His death is then no longer a bribe but a rite of deep intensity, that reunites the community and restores its equilibrium. The act would have no meaning unless all present lived in the knowledge that it was both necessary and right. The ritual would also serve no purpose if it were painless. The price of salvation, momentary or eternal, has to be high, for in man's striving to rise above himself, only the blood of the sufferer can forge the link that binds him to God—the god he has created in his own image. The transformation of man into God through the medium of another man has been sought by all peoples at all times, by means of their many religions.

Sacrifice brings not only unity but purification and renewal. This renewal is often symbolized by ritual bathing or baptism, for resurrection finds its roots in the unclean; it is born of sin, which must be washed away. For a people who felt no guilt and knew no sin, the ceremony would also be meaningless. In its higher forms sacrifice is, therefore, a way of release from sin by ablution and "rebirth". Whether in the initiation rites of the Australian aboriginal or in the Greek Eleusinian mysteries, people were "reborn" as new infants. Christian baptism is only one form of this cleansing and rebirth. In India the suttee widow was ritually washed; in Africa the king had first to err symbolically before being made pure. In Tahiti, by sacrifice to Oro, people sought atonement from sin; the Greek Pharmakos took upon himself the city's load of guilt; the Japanese Samurai committed seppuku to make amends for wrongs that dishonoured the community.

Hence the victim, as a bridge between God and fallen man, must possess the qualities of both, must be both pure and impure. Redemption stems from blood and shame and the scapegoat, in one form or another, has to combine the role of deliverer and wrongdoer, when he takes upon himself the load of human sin. The victim had to be loved, but also in a sense hated. As we have seen, this paradox is foremost among Tupinambas of Brazil, who could not offer up a captive until he had first been insulted as a foe and then cossetted as a foster child. In order to be sacrificed, he had to be both loved and hated—just as the Dyaks of Borneo could only slay the pliant slave after he had first been made odious and cursed. Among the Iroquois, some captives were tortured without further ado, while others were cherished to the end of their days.

As we have also seen, many forms of ritual killing—however time honoured—were modified over the centuries. The best documented changes are those reported after the first contact with Europeans. Under this baleful influence chiefs acquired deadlier weapons and wider ambitions, and the pace of sacrifice even quickened. If missionaries were not themselves offered as victims, their arrival was often hailed as a portent, to which only a sacrificial feast could do justice. American Indians seem to have copied the Inquisition burnings, and Africans, out of deference to their new masters, took to tree crucifixion; in the South Seas, the demand for heads soared, no longer for religious uses, but as collector's pieces; campaigns for taking them were stepped up accordingly. However, these very Europeans, for all their cruelties, in the end put a stop to ritual killing among their native subjects, though this was done more by force than by persuasion. In the final analysis, the most radical change in sacrifice was its banning after European conquest.

At the very basis of human offering lies the cult of the human head that has existed since time immemorial. Primitive man sensed that, if he differed from the apes, his genius sprang not from his heart or liver but from the skull that encased his enlarged brain. He worshipped himself in the person of a man-made god and the skull throughout history was made the symbol of the durable and the divine. The cult of the head up to, say, ten thousand years ago, probably claimed only occasional ritual victims, whose remains have been found in Monte Circeo and elsewhere. But once chiefdoms, under a single ruler, took the place of classless nomad bands, tribal warfare followed, which in turn served to produce more human heads, so that the cult of the skull gained a new impetus, fuelled by these headhunting raids. Possibly the very origins of tribal warfare lies not in the need to punish or pillage but in the demand for captives to sacrifice.

While the cult of the head has survived to the present day, new forms of sacrifice followed the invention of agriculture and the rise of the first civilizations. People who had formerly belonged to tiny bands of hunters or served local chiefs were now subject to great kings. These were often seen as the living god, descended from the creator who had dwelt on earth as a legendary hero and who fathered the tribe. The story of such creator-heroes often ended in a primaeval act of violence, that in turn gave rise to the practice—widespread but not universal—of killing the king himself; after a fixed term he had to die, as a descendant of the god who had once been sacrificed. Hence these new forms were a re-enactment of an original sacrifice. Their rites, culminating in rebirth or resurrection, also often involved the eating of the god in the person of his victim and representative. The myth of the dying god thus became basic to human sacrifice, although the idea that the king, regarded as divine, should himself meet a violent end was in most places abandoned; rulers were only too ready to delegate to others the privilege of dying for the common good. But whether the king died or one of his subjects, the notion of re-enactment is vital. Religious man is mesmerized by the idea of the eternal return. What happened once has to be continually repeated in order to preserve the living and provide for the dead. In Egypt only people whose funerary rites exactly reproduced those of the legendary Osiris could aspire to an afterlife.

For Sir James Frazer, the death of the god-king or his representative was a fertility rite; if the king's strength ebbed he had to die, because his people knew that otherwise the crops would not ripen nor the cattle fatten. But once the king himself ceased to be the victim, this interpretation loses force. For further changes occurred, as these early cultures devised forms of sacrifice not based on fertility. The purpose of the burial in the Royal Cemetery of Ur of scores of retainers with a king who had died a natural death was to honour his person and provide for his wellbeing in the hereafter. Frequent also in many places was the slaying of men, women and children to keep a ruler in good health and to prevent him from dying if he became sick. Equally, the universal burial of people, often alive, to dedicate temples, palaces and even bridges, gave added protection to such structures. All these rites had no direct bearing on harvests, though others still served this end, such as the burying of victims' flesh in the fields or drowning them in rivers (to ensure water supplies), as well as seasonal offerings at the time of sowing and reaping.

If sacrifice no longer required the death of the king, it was often, though not always, still centred upon his person. In India and Mexico, some killings were directly inspired by the ruler and in the greater part of Africa, as well as in the islands of the Pacific, sacrifice was the king's prerogative, designed to secure his and his family's wellbeing and hence that of the community. In those places where kings and emperors took the place of tribal chiefs, war captives continued to be the main victims. As the scale of warfare mounted, so the supply of prisoners increased; these were always sacrificed by the Aztecs, whereas in Ancient Egypt and Mesopotamia this was less often the case.

Warfare on an imperial scale paved the way for a new and sinister development: the cult of mass sacrifice. One victim was no longer enough to placate the gods and many had to die at once. Mass offering took several forms. It was unthinkable that a great ruler should enter the next world without a huge retinue, which included both war captives and members of his own household, slain in his honour. In the tombs of Ur, excavated by Woolley, numerous personal retainers were buried; to the deceased kings of Dahomey mostly prisoners were offered, as witnessed by many European visitors. In Ancient Mexico, the death of the ruler was only one of many pretexts for multiple killing; hundreds if not thousands also died when a king was crowned or a temple completed. Mass sacrifice, which was not, in any case, universally practised, is surely a debasement of the nobler and more basic rite whereby the one died to save and reunite the many. By a shocking kind of inflation, an end formerly brought about by the death of one man now required the slaughter of hundreds.

On the other hand, cannibalism, though it may shock our susceptibilities, appears less a debasement than a variant on the sacrificial theme, practised since the remotest times. Anthropophagy—the eating of the human body—is the logical, though not inevitable, development from theophagy, the eating of the god. Where the victim is eaten, the practice has to be repeated again and again, as a periodical renewal of what the God himself had suffered. As I have continually stressed, to treat cannibalism as mere gluttony is to ignore the whole basis of religious sacrifice and custom. Man-eating was always accompanied by ceremonial in commemoration of an original act performed at the beginning of time. Whether among the Kwakiutls of northwest Canada, the Papuas of New Guinea or the Tupinambas of Brazil, the myth of a cannibal creator underlies the ceremonial.

In writing of human sacrifice throughout the world, one is ever conscious of a sameness in the rites—in the ends to be sought and in the choice of victim. Inevitably, however, differences also emerge, though simple explanations of why they occur are hard to find. Anthropologists are divided in their views as to man's development. One important school rejects the chance factor and sees all change as the product of set rules, arising out of material circumstances. But the incidence of sacrifice in human society tends to be rather haphazard and defies analysis on a cause and effect basis. Among the Jews, for instance, human offering died out, while it thrived unabated among the civilised nations of South-East Asia. At a lower level of culture, the Melanesians avidly sacrificed men to their gods and ate them, while the Eskimos did not, though they killed infants. The spread of cannibalism in Africa is erratic and follows no logical pattern. In Polynesia customs varied from one island to the next; certain non-cannibals lived almost within hailing distance of man-eaters and would sell their prisoners to the latter, though they themselves were repelled by human flesh.

At times the white man's presence influenced events, even to the point of raising the tempo of sacrifice. But wide disparities between one place and another were not solely due to European occupation; for example, the British impact on Indian religion was at first minimal and suttee thrived until public opinion in Britain forced the hand of the Calcutta government. Nor can suttee be treated merely as an instrument in the hands of heirs eager to seize the property of the dead, even if they had to burn their own mothers in the process. Sons have always been, and still are, keen to enter into their inheritance but this constant factor throws little light on why in some parts of the world widows were burned or strangled while in others they were cherished. It is not easy, for instance, to find a logical explanation for the widespread custom among the Incas of burying widows with their husbands and its apparent absence among those sacrificial zealots, the Aztecs.

If sacrifice varied in form and method from one place to the next, it also differed in intensity. In general, it thrived among religious fanatics, such as the peoples of India and Mexico, to a much greater extent than among the more pragmatic nations such as the Chinese. Moreover, only a tentative explanation can be offered for its disappearance in some places long ago and its prospering in others until modern times. The need to shed blood upon the altar abated whenever people embraced an ethic which treated human behaviour as more important than bizarre rites to honour a pitiless pantheon. Such a moral code gave a nobler status to the individual, who was no longer treated as a mere chattel, arbitrarily expendible if the god needed to be placated and the conscience of his worshippers to be eased. The Ancient Greeks may be taken as an example; following the sacrificial death of Socrates, the first of the great philosophers, the élite sought solace in what is commonly called the Greek ethic rather than in the ancient gods, whose legends were filled with gory tales. This Greek ethic, however, as we have seen, reduced the will to sacrifice but did not end it, since the old gods would still claim an occasional human victim. Among the Hebrews of the Old Testament, sacrifice first increased as the worship of the tribal Yahweh came under Canaanite influence, but a strong reaction set in. Inspired by its great prophets, Israel embraced a monotheism that was almost as much ethic as religion, more concerned with conduct here on earth than with the hereafter. These religious leaders demanded that people should "walk in the way of the Lord", marked not by material offering but by moral rectitude. As a result, human and even animal sacrifice waned and finally disappeared.

Human offering was also reduced when a single saviour, the essence of goodness, took the place of impassive deities who were sometimes good and sometimes bad. Among Christians, the death of the Saviour was seen as a once-and-for-all event that, at least in theory, absolved man from the need to kill. But however benign its early impact, a saviour religion nurtures within it the germ of new cruelties. Once the religion has won full recognition, dissenters—even those who cavil at a single syllable in its litany—become the saviour's enemies and, like tribal foes in Africa and Oceania, must be hunted to their death; and leniency ranks as a betrayal of the redeemer or prophet. Muslims killed infidels and Christians killed Jews and heretics, in ceremonies that often recalled pagan rituals. So if a human ethic or a divine teacher may have a restraining influence, this may abate and the urge to kill reassert itself. Of this Christianity is not the only example; in India the rise of Buddhism, the kindliest and the least sanguinary of religions, marked the virtual end of sacrifice but once Buddhism had been expelled from its homeland, sacrifice was promptly revived. Hence, even the most generalized principle is only partly valid and the patchy distribution of sacrifice gives little support to writers who would reduce history to a set of rules.

Human sacrifice is an essential factor to be taken into account when trying to understand how ancient societies worked, but it also sheds light on a pressing theme in the modern world: the problem of violence. Anthropologists and sociologists are also deeply divided over this. One school of thought maintains that man, ever since the time when the primitive Australopithecus made the first weapons in Africa, has been an inveterate killer; unlike the other animals, he has preyed upon his own species. Such theories command a wide following, perhaps because many people are eager for some explanation of man's "beastliness" with which to justify their own and others' behaviour.

This view of man the killer was first put forward in the early 1950s by Raymond Dart, the South African professor of anatomy, and has since been popularized by a number of authors, among whom the best known are Konrad Lorenz, Desmond Morris and Robert Ardrey. Other writers, such as Ashley Montague, are equally adamant that violence is not our inescapable heritage and that some but not all people are conditioned to be brutal in the course of their upbringing. The two opposing views, that human aggression is innate and that it is largely acquired, go to the very root of modern man's predicament, his inability to live at peace with his neighbour.

Desmond Morris in *The Human Zoo* likens our conduct to that of mice and other rodents that eat their own kind only when kept in close confinement. Man, so the argument runs, owing to the cramped environment of big cities and to his captive state, as prisoner to his own wants, behaves like these caged mice rather than like wild animals, who only prey on other species. Yet according to this same thesis, modern man merely displays the more infamous qualities of his distant and primitive forbears, an idea based on Freud's notion that we are still driven by the same instincts as our primaeval ancestors. But primitive man, whose aggressiveness we supposedly inherit, did not live in cities and his wants were simple. This is true not only of early hunters but of their tribal successors. The Maoris of New Zealand were inveterate warriors and cannibals but their conditions were anything but cramped, nor were those of the Australian aboriginals, who also at times ate each other.

Our study of human sacrifice has consistently shown that man does not "prey" on man in the sense that a lion hunts an antelope, simply to obtain food. As a rule, tribes did not make war to satisfy their lust for killing or their hunger for their enemies' flesh. Where prisoners were eaten—a practice less universal than Morris and others suggest—almost invariably this was done more to honour the gods than to increase the supply of animal protein. Paradoxically, then, the violence of homo sapiens may be said to have arisen through the very thing that differentiates him from beasts—his faith. Religion offered him both a release from death in the hereafter and in this life a mechanism to meet those needs created by his genius but absent in the animal kingdom—to make the crops ripen, to preserve buildings and to honour the person of the chief. To achieve these ends wars had to be waged and captives sacrificed.

Unlike the animals, man developed both the arms with which to kill his fellow beings and the convictions, however mistaken, that promoted such violence. The practice of human sacrifice, so widespread, does indeed lend support to the view held by Dart and others that man is at least a potential killer. But it denies the reasoning behind the viewpoint, for it indicates that the urge to kill derives not from an innate curse or from an unnatural and over-rapid development of the brain but rather from a striving to escape from evil through the medium of a religious faith. Reaching out for something higher than himself, man was driven to kill so as to placate his idols with the greatest prize of all, a human life.

Robert Ardrey in his *Territorial Imperative* no longer describes man as worse than the beasts but grudgingly places him on the same level. He is presented as very similar to mammals, birds and even fish, all aggressively obsessed with gaining and keeping a given territory. Erich Fromm, in writing of aggression, refutes this thesis and Ashley Montague offers a formidable list of animals without the slightest leanings towards this territorial imperative; among them are the other members of the superfamily to which we belong, the chimpanzee, the orang and the gorilla.[2]

But whatever the truth of Ardrey's theory for the animal kingdom, in the case of tribal man it would be more just to speak of an obsession with religion than with territory. I have already shown that the main motive for his endless warfare was not conquest. This can still be seen from the tribal wars that rage among the Yanomamis and Waraos of the Venezuelan jungle and in the remoter parts of New Guinea; Cambridge anthropologist Paul Sillitoe in his computerized study of the reasons for warfare today in the highlands of New Guinea states that the aspirations of a chief constitute the main reason, whilst secondary causes include "redress, revenge, economic gain and religious necessity".[3] It is only the rise of states and empires that made of territory the prime cause for war and slaughter.

A variant on the Ardrey theme is the Harner-Harris proposal that, because of his pressing need for animal protein, man resorts to war in search of captives that he can eat. But Harris himself cuts the ground from under his feet by using his argument to explain the incessant wars of the Yanomamis, who are not cannibals and have been shown by anthropologist Paul Shagnon, of Pennsylvania State University, to be quite well supplied with protein. Writers on protein deficiency tend to limit their discussion to the American continent but their ideas are better refuted by what happened in the West African kingdom of Dahomey. For centuries its rulers were deeply involved in the slave trade. With arms provided by the slave traders, they conquered the port of Wydah on the coast, which then became one of the most prosperous of all the slave entrepots. Dahomans were prized as docile slaves in the West Indies; many Haitians, for example, trace their origins to the Dahomey region, whence the voodoo cult stemmed.

The King of Dahomey, as we have seen, sacrificed each year hundreds of people to honour his predecessor on the throne. But these solemn, if inhumane, rites to honour the king's gods and ancestors deprived him of part of his yearly revenue in the form of the human merchandise that supported a booming trade, vital to his wellbeing and prosperity. If this trade did not produce protein or other food, it provided the king with ample supplies of firearms and rum, in which he was far more interested. Since the kings, not their humbler subjects, decided every issue to their own advantage, it would be more accurate to speak not of a protein deficiency but of a royal thirst for liquor as the cause of violence. This was the European product most in demand and one which, whether in West Africa or in Hawaii, the rulers consumed in prodigious quantities.

Whatever the roots of man's propensity to kill his fellows, the urge has not abated in our century. Not only is the toll of victims greater than ever before; in addition, modern despots, say in Cambodia or Uganda, are yet more infamous and massacre not external foes as in former times but hundreds of thousands, if not millions, of their own people. Nevertheless human sacrifice has inevitably waned as a semblance of Western culture has been imposed on every corner of the globe. Desert strips and tropical reefs have assumed the trappings of statehood and their chiefs become prime ministers or presidents. As members of the United Nations, they sign declarations on human rights; if they continue to kill people, the methods are more discreet and the pretexts more political than ritual. The caprices of the local gods yield to those of international bankers—deities who have little sympathy with the local needs when these include regalia for headhunters or cutlery for cannibals.

Thus most forms of ritual sacrifice have abated as the last uncharted regions have submitted to the modern state with its apparatus of police, army, teachers and health officers. Yet certain forms have clung on tenaciously into the modern day. Headhunting continued among the hill tribes of India until the 1940s and among the Jivaros of Ecuador until the 1960s; people were slain in 1959 to make magic medicine in Basutoland; the Asmats of New Guinea were still seeking fresh skulls to initiate their youth in 1954 and other practices survived into the late 1960s. Indeed, our "civilized" twentieth century has had its share of sacrificial fervour. The psychologist Erich Fromm in *The Anatomy of Human Destructiveness* compares the slaughter of the aristocratic youth of England and Germany at the outset of World War I to a child sacrifice to the god of national honour. It would have made little difference, according to Fromm, if fathers had killed their offspring themselves, instead of sending them off gladly to their deaths. No-one would pretend, however, that the hideous slaughter that ensued was a human sacrifice in the sense that we have been studying here, even if the endless series of offensives on the Western front had the character of a futile and bloody ritual, performed for the god of nationalism.

This sacrificial fervour of 1914 was entirely lacking from World War II, with perhaps one exception—the Japanese Kamikaze pilots.

In Chapter VI I referred to ritual suicide in Japan in earlier times, arising out of the Shinto religion and the Samurai ethic, based on two principles: an absolute devotion to the Emperor and a rigid code of honour. This code, known as Bushido (the Way of the Warrior), demanded of the young soldier that he sacrifice his own life after killing as many enemies as possible. The Meiji revolution of 1867 launched Japan on an all-out course of westernization. But far from dying out, Shintoism took on a new lease of life when in 1868 it was raised by the Emperor to the status of the official religion of Japan. Accordingly, the Samurai ethic survived almost intact in the modern armed forces which were then created. Religion and militarism remained inseparable in the new and westernized Japan, in which the soldier was still taught to view death with a profound indifference. His fanatical courage sprang from the conviction that if he died for his Emperor, he would attain a kind of Nirvana, or Paradise, for heroes, where he would rejoin his illustrious forbears of the ancient and feudal Japan. The Samurai code was not merely preserved but extended; formerly confined to the aristocracy, it was now adopted by the middle classes, who formed the backbone of the officer corps of the new army, and thus served as a basis for the future expansion of the Empire of the Rising Sun.

This rigorous Samurai ethic rested on a long tradition not only of individual but also of mass suicide as the only alternative to dishonour. For example, when in 1582 the Shogun Nobunega faced defeat at the hand of rebels, he slit his wife's throat and then committed seppuku, or ritual suicide; the fifty men of his bodyguard also killed themselves. The most notable instance of its kind is the death of the Forty-Seven Ronin. This band of Samurai committed collective seppuku after they had avenged the honour of their master, a scene often re-enacted today in a classic Kabuki play (see the illustration).

Following this tradition, instances of mass suicide occurred in World War II. For example, when on 8th July 1944 the U.S. marines were about to storm the last Japanese redoubt of Marpi Point in the Marianas Archipelago, they were horrified to witness the self-slaughter of hundreds of Japanese, both military and civil. Some shot themselves while others jumped over a cliff; a few soldiers were even decapitated by their own officers. But by far the most spectacular suicides were those of the corps of pilots known as Kamikaze. Their history dates from October 1944, when two unplanned suicide assaults were made against U.S. warships: one was by Rear-Admiral Arimi in person, when he unsuccessfully tried to attack a carrier during the Battle of Formosa. The first Kamikaze unit, formed soon after this by Vice-Admiral Onishi, the naval commander-in-chief on the Island of Mindanao, was the 201st Fighter Squadron, based on Clark Field. After orthodox tactics had failed and he was left with only thirty operative fighters, Oshiri resorted to this extreme, although not all his officers shared his enthusiasm.

Kamikaze means "Divine Wind" and the Special Attack Corps, as the Kamikaze were officially called, was divided into four groups, Shikishima (Beautiful Island), Yamato (the Japanese People), Asahi (Rising Sun) and Yamazakura (Wild Cherry Blossom). The names were taken from a traditional poem:

> *If you ask me what is the soul of the Japanese,*
> *The people of the Beautiful Island,*
> *I will tell you that it is the Wild Cherry Blossom*
> *That scatters its perfume in the light of the Rising Sun.*

The wild cherry, which, having scattered its perfume, falls without regrets, symbolized the readiness of these pilots to die for their country without wavering.[4]

Notwithstanding such evocative titles, the task of effectively committing suicide for one's country and its emperor demanded much skill and training. The best results were obtained not by diving onto the deck of a warship but by skimming the ocean and releasing the bomb in such a manner that it bounced off the sea and struck the flight deck of a carrier. After much perilous practice, it was found that the bomb had to be dropped at an altitude of 30 feet and a distance of 325 yards from the target. The fighter normally then crashed into the ship 2.4 seconds later, and chances of escape were negligible. For such a spectacular sacrifice the results were often meagre, because one bomb could not destroy carriers and other large ships. On 6th April 1945 six Kamikaze hits badly damaged USS *Newcomb* but did not sink her. In all, eighteen battleships and eleven carriers received hits from Kamikazes but none were lost. To achieve this end, 1700 pilots laid down their lives, mostly between 6th April and 22nd June 1945.

Such acts of self-slaughter were directly inspired by the Samurai code of Bushido, based on Shintoism. Their spirit of abnegation is expressed in the letter of Isao Matsuo to his parents on the eve of his Kamikaze sortie:

Dear Parents,

Please congratulate me. I have been given a splendid opportunity to die. This is my last day. The destiny of our homeland hinges on the decisive battle in the seas to the south where I shall fall like a blossom from a radiant cherry tree.

I shall be a shield for His Majesty and die cleanly along with my squadron leader and other friends. I wish that I could be born seven times, each time to smite the enemy.

How I appreciate a chance to die like a man! I am grateful from the depths of my heart to the parents who have reared me with their constant prayers and tender love. And I am grateful as well to my squadron leader and superior officers who have looked after me as if I were their own son and given me such careful training.

Thank you, my parents, for the twenty-three years during which you have cared for me and inspired me. I hope that my present deed will in some small way repay what you have done for me. Think well of me and know that your Isao died for our country. This is my last wish and there is nothing else that I desire.

I shall return in spirit and look forward to your visit at the Yasukuni shrine. Please take good care of yourselves. . . .

We are sixteen manning the bombers. May our deaths be as sudden and clean as the shattering of crystal.

Written at Manila on the eve of our sortie,

Isao

P.S. Soaring into the sky of the southern seas, it is our glorious mission to die as the shields of His Majesty. Cherry blossoms glisten as they open and fall.

Wherever the modern world has encroached and as time has passed, the motivation of all forms of "ritual" violence has become ever more political and less religious. Moreover the distinction between politics and religion tends to be more clearcut now than before. As long as the ruler was divine or semi-divine, it was impossible to make this distinction, a situation that did not change in Japan until 1945. But since most modern states have now gone out of their way to divorce religion from politics—with many of them writing this principle into their constitutions—a political act has ceased to be a religious one, and if a life is lost in the process, this is no longer a human sacrifice as we have defined it. The famous suicides of the Reverend Jim Jones and nine hundred of his followers of the People's Temple in Guyana in November 1978 are a case in point. Ritual was absent and the religious motives nebulous—although Jones' interminable sermons at Jonestown focussed on himself as God—so that the mass suicide was scarcely in the tradition of the Forty-Seven Ronin or of the Indian mass suicides known as Jauhar. However, this modern act of self-slaughter may help us to understand man's past acquiescence in his role as victim. Eye-witness survivors of the Jonesville holocaust are vague as to how far people were *forced* to die. All refer to the presence of armed guards but since they themselves found a pretext to escape the vigilance of these very guards, they may tend to magnify their role. When one woman, Christine Miller, challenged Jones' suggestion that they all had to kill themselves, the crowd shouted her down. If anyone wanted to disobey, the very worst that the guards could do was to kill such dissenters, and death by a bullet was surely preferable to taking strychnine. The impression remains that the vast majority died voluntarily, however circumscribed their "free will" may have been.

Jones has much in common with another fanatical "leader", Charles Manson. Admittedly he differed from Manson in that he ordered his followers to kill themselves, rather than to kill others, but both believed in a holocaust from which only their own group would be spared by taking refuge in jungle or desert, and both were obsessed with racial problems, though they took opposite sides: Manson was a racist who believed that the blacks would destroy the whites, while Jones was a rabid anti-racist. Manson, to his "family" of followers, was himself Jesus; when first arrested, he was booked as "Manson, Charles M., also known as Jesus Christ, God". Several witnesses at his trial declared that they were sure that he was Jesus. Both Manson and Jones had a diabolical hold over their flock, and at times used sex as a weapon to maintain this hold. Under Manson's hypnotic spell Sandy Good was able to declare, "I have finally reached the point where I can kill my parents". Equally Jones mesmerized his people to the degree that they were ready to kill themselves and their children.

Therefore, even in the world of today, where to keep alive the incurably sick has become almost a cult in itself, people can still be mentally programmed to kill themselves en masse. This surely makes it easier to appreciate an indifference towards ritual death in older societies that at first sight seems to go against human nature —whether the detached air of the Dahoman victims seen by Burton or the impassive mien of the suttee widow as she mounted her husband's pyre. For them death was a mere staging-post on the road to a renewal of life. In this century the Kamikaze pilots and even the disciples of Jim Jones were promised an afterlife as a sequel to self-slaughter, so that if today a single demonic will can drive hundreds to self-slaughter, it becomes less surprising that in ancient times people were ready if not eager to be slain on the god's altar, when the whole fabric of society and the whole weight of religious tradition demanded this of them.

Present-day attitudes towards death are ambivalent. On the one hand, our doctors struggle to prolong the ordeal of the chronically sick, even for a matter of days. But at the same time we accept with a mere shrug of resignation reports of mass murders, provided that they happen far enough away from our own doorstep. This indifference may be in part the result of our daily exposure to new and myriad forms of violence. The principle may be the same for the mother taking her children to see a mass sacrifice in the Aztec capital as for the modern parent setting them in front of the television to watch an endless series of gun battles. Only the scale and frequency differ; for it has been calculated that in the United States a child, before he grows up, witnesses an average of 36,000 mock deaths on television. The vicarious thrill of watching others being killed is catered for today as never before; and for the child the distinction may be hazy between simulated and actual death, between tomato ketchup and real blood.

Faced with the mass brutality of our century, real as well as simulated, one may ask whether, in its place, man might not do better to revert to the ritualized killings of the past. If the need for scapegoats persists, could this not be met with less bloodshed through the medium of a solemn ceremony, in which one stoic victim meets his end on the god's altar, dying with dignity for the common good? If violence is endemic, sacrificial violence is at least a more restrained form. Even at its worst, when it involved mass offerings, the cumbersome ritual hampered the rate of slaughter. Yet the value of these stately ceremonies sprang from the knowledge, shared alike by victim and slayer, that they would produce specific results. If no longer based on that assurance, ritual death ceases to have a purpose. At the root of human sacrifice lay a belief in a hereafter that was not unlike life on earth. Even where victims were not slain with the precise end of serving their master in the next world, they never doubted the future blessings in store for them.

In almost all cultures but our own the living and the dead belonged to one single community, and death did not signify separation from a man's loved ones. Only in the world of today has death been demythologized. It has become a separate state, divorced from life, and we strive obsessively to save the dying from crossing this great divide. Once people share the belief that this life is the be-all and end-all of their existence, ritual sacrifice must abate, regardless of what other forms of killing take its place. In this respect, the modern ideologies differ absolutely from the old religions. However elusive their new promise of paradise, its gates are to be sought in this world, not the next. If modern dogmas also claim their victims, they die without hope and their end is not sacrificial.

Traditional society catered for both material and spiritual needs; sacrifice and religious rituals ("religion" comes from the Latin *religere*, meaning to bind together) were a vital uniting force in the community. Human sacrifice thus played its part in man's striving to live in harmony with the cosmos. Whilst rituals may vanish and beliefs change, the need seems no less urgent in our modern fragmented society for man to recover that lost sense of cohesion.

Sources

Chapter I

1 Evans Pritchard, pp. 202–3
2 Robertson Smith, p. 361
3 Gusdorf, pp. 76–7
4 Westermarck, p. 464
5 Ibid, p. 464
6 Ibid, p. 462
7 Ibid, p. 466
8 Lévi-Strauss, pp. 296–7
9 Gusdorf, pp. 75–81
10 Ibid, p. 69
11 Girard, p. 23
12 Eliade, *The Sacred and The Profane*, p. 100

Chapter II

1 Woolley, pp. 70–71
2 Ibid, p. 69
3 James, *The Ancient Gods*, p. 56
4 Budge, p. 199
5 Ibid, p. 204
6 Ibid, p. 208
7 Ibid, p. 216
8 Pfeiffer, p. 215
9 Budge, p. 175
10 Kramer, p. 118
11 Groot, vol. 2, p. 722

12 Ibid, p. 725
13 Ibid, p. 731

CHAPTER III

1 Branston, p. 115
2 Strackerjan, p. 127
3 MacCulloch, p. 147
4 Piggott, p. 117
5 *Encyclopedia of Religion and Ethics*, vol. 2, p. 11
6 Ibid, p. 12
7 Branston, p. 149
8 Westermarck, p. 435
9 *Encyclopedia of Religion and Ethics*, vol. 6, p. 861
10 Westermarck, p. 439
11 *National Geographic* magazine, vol. 153, no. 2
12 *Encyclopedia of Religion and Ethics*, vol. 6, p. 848

CHAPTER IV

1 Joshua 6:26
2 James, *The Origins of Sacrifice*, p. 258
3 Genesis 22:17
4 Isaiah 30:33
5 Toynbee, p. 38
6 Jeremiah 6:31
7 James, *The Origins of Sacrifice*, p. 266
8 Frankfurt, p. 33
9 Hick, p. 113
10 Ibid, pp. 100–101
11 Eliade, *Rites and Symbols of Initiation*, p. 11
12 Kramer, p. 132
13 Girard, pp. 150–55
14 Toynbee, p. 294

CHAPTER V

1 Westermarck, p. 464
2 Ibid, p. 437

3   *Encyclopedia of Religion and Ethics*, vol. 6, p. 850
4   Ibid, p. 850
5   Westermarck, p. 458
6   Panigrahi, p. 15
7   Frazer, pp. 503–7
8   Ibid, p. 505
9   Hodson, p. 136
10 Fuerer-Haimendorf, p. 23
11 Mitra Chandra, *Note on Another Instance* . . .
12 Zimmer, p. 212
13 Woodruff, vol. 1, p. 262
14 Wightman, pp. 20–21
15 Bruce, pp. 51–4
16 Ibid, p. 108
17 Kincaird, p. 41
18 Toynbee, p. 24
19 Schweizer, p. 189
20 Zimmer, p. 172
21 Hick, p. 183

CHAPTER VI

1   Thakur, *The History of Suicide* . . . , p. 80
2   Thakur, *Self-Immolation in India*, p. 128
3   Ibid, p. 120
4   Ibid, p. 139
5   Ibid, p. 140
6   Thakur, *The History of Suicide* . . . , p. 95
7   Mukhopadhyay, p. 99
8   Mair, pp. 72–3
9   Ellis, A. B., pp. 124–7
10 Groot, vol. 2, p. 726
11 Ibid, p. 736
12 Ibid, pp. 748–9
13 Thakur, *Self-Immolation in India*, p. 127
14 Mukhopadhyay, p. 102
15 Zakiuddin, p. 154
16 Ibid, p. 159
17 Mukhopadhyay, p. 102
18 Ibid, pp. 105–7
19 Woodruff, vol. 1, p. 256

20 *Encyclopedia of Religion and Ethics*, vol. 6, p. 843
21 Satow, pp. 345–6
22 Alvarez, p. 53
23 Ibid, p. 65

Chapter VII

1 Her Majesty's Stationery Office, *Report to the Secretary* . . . , pp. 11–12
2 Tannahil, pp. 72–3
3 Beatty, passim
4 Ibid, p. 11
5 Ibid, p. 26
6 Ibid, pp. 45–55
7 Parrinder, *African Traditional Religion*, pp. 88–9
8 Frobenius, pp. 134–9
9 Ellis, A. B., p. 123
10 Ibid, p. 126
11 Burton, p. 237
12 Ibid, p. 223
13 Frazer, vol. 3, pp. 138–40
14 Herskovitz, p. 53
15 Meek, pp. 54–5
16 Bentley, vol. 2, pp. 210–14
17 Ibid
18 Spiel, p. 56
19 Schweinfurt, vol. 2, pp. 93–4
20 Tannahil, pp. 149–9
21 Hecquard
22 Parrinder, *African Traditional Religion*, p. 63
23 Budge, p. 177

Chapter VIII

1 Brooke, pp. 203–7
2 Ling-Roth, pp. 142–3
3 Bock, p. 218
4 Schaerer, *Die Bedeutung* . . . , p. 3
5 Ling-Roth, p. 164
6 Schaerer, *Das Menschenopfer* . . . , p. 558

7 Schaerer, *Die Bedeutung* . . . , p. 12
8 Zegwaard, pp. 1032–3
9 Seligman, p. 550
10 Schoch, p. 37
11 Ibid, pp. 45–6
12 Parkinson, pp. 31–45
13 Oliver, vol. 1, p. 117
14 Oliver, vol. 2, pp. 909–11
15 Schoch, p. 20
16 Ellis, W., p. 297
17 Oliver, vol. 2, p. 953
18 Tregear, p. 337
19 Vayda, pp. 96–7
20 Murray, p. 232

CHAPTER IX

1 Moser
2 Díaz del Castillo, p. 369
3 Lines
4 Piña Chan
5 Joralemon
6 Sahagún, *Florentine Codex*, Bk. 2, pp. 42–4
7 Sahagún, *Historia General* . . . , vol. 1, p. 188
8 Durán, vol. 1, p. 248
9 Torquemada, vol. 2, p. 73
10 Durán, vol. 2, p. 394
11 Tezozómoc, p. 112
12 Sahagún, *Florentine Codex*, Bk. 9, Ch. 13
13 Harner, *The Ecological Basis* . . .

CHAPTER X

1 O'Brien, p. 69
2 Ibid, pp. 43–4
3 Ibid, p. 105
4 Ibid, p. 44
5 Kamen, pp. 190–92
6 Davies, Ch. 2
7 Knowles, p. 167

8 Ibid, p. 171
9 Ibid, pp. 181–4
10 Driver, p. 377
11 Hogg, p. 58
12 Goddard, passim
13 Dwyer, passim
14 Benson, passim
15 Trimborn, *Die Religionen des Alten Amerika*
16 Hemming, p. 16
17 Métraux, p. 45
18 Ibid, p. 45
19 Girard, pp. 380–5

CHAPTER XI

1 Westermarck, p. 468
2 Sillitoe, p. 253
3 Montagu, p. 237
4 Nagatsuka, p. 144

Bibliography

Alvarez, A., *The Savage God: A Study of Suicide* (London: Weidenfeld & Nicolson, 1971).

Anderson, Rufus, *The Hawaiian Islands* (Boston: Gould & Linden, 1865).

Anesaki, Paul, *Masaharu: The History of Japanese Religion* (London: Kegan Paul, 1930).

Ardrey, Robert, *The Territorial Imperative: A Personal Enquiry into the Animal Origins of Property and Nations* (New York: Atheneum, 1966).

Arens, William, *The Man-eating Myth: Anthropology and Anthropophagy* (New York: Oxford University Press, 1979).

Balandier, Georges, *The Kingdom of the Congo from the Sixteenth to the Eighteenth Century* (London: Allen & Unwin, 1968).

Ballantyne, R. M., *The Cannibal Islands, or Captain Cook's Adventures in the South Seas* (London: James Nisbet & Co., 1888).

Barth, Fredrik, *Ritual and Knowledge among the Baktaman of New Guinea* (New Haven, Conn.: Yale University Press, 1975).

Basutoland, *see* H.M. Stationery Office.

Baudrillard, Jean, *L'Échange Symbolique et la Mort* (Paris: Editions Gallimard, 1976).

Beatty, K. J., *Human Leopards* (London: Hugh Rees, 1915).

Benson, Elizabeth, "Death-Associated Figures on Mochica Pottery," in *Death and the After-life in Pre-Columbian America* (Washington, D.C.: Dumbarton Oaks Research Library, 1975).

Bentley, W. Holman, *Pioneering on the Congo*, 2 vols. (London: The Religious Tract Society, 1900).

Bergman, Sten, "My Father is a Cannibal," in *The Explorer's Journal*, vol. XLI, no. 2 (New York, 1963).

Boas, Franz, "The Social Organization and Secret Societies of the Kwakiutl," in *Report of the U.S. National Museum* (Washington, D.C., 1895).

Bock, Carl, *The Headhunters of Borneo* (London: Sampson Low, 1882).

Brain, Robert, *The Last Primitive People* (New York: Crown, 1976).

Brandon, S. G. E., *Religion in Ancient History* (London: Allen & Unwin, 1969).

────── (ed.), *The Saviour God* (Manchester: Manchester University Press, 1963).

Branston, Brian, *Gods of the North* (London: Thames & Hudson, 1955).

Brinkley, F., *Japan: Its History, Arts and Literature* (London: T. C. Jack, 1903).

Brooke, Rajah Sir James, *Narrative of Events in Borneo and Celibu*, journal ed. Rodney Mundy (London: John Murray, 1848).

Brown, G., *Melanesians and Polynesians* (London: Macmillan, 1910).

Browne, Courtney, *The Last Banzai* (New York: Holt, Rinehart & Winston, 1967).

Bruce, George, *The Stranglers. The Cult of Thuggee and Its Overthrow in British India* (London: Longman, 1968).

Budge, Sir Wallis, *Osiris and the Egyptian Resurrection* (London: The Medici Society, 1911).

Buijtenhuijs, Robert, *Le Mouvement "Mau Mau"* (Paris and The Hague: Mouton, 1971).

Burton, Sir Richard, *A Mission to Gelele, King of Dahome* (London: Routledge & Kegan Paul, 1966).

Chakravarti, Chintaharan, "Kali Worship in Bengal," in *Adyar Library Bulletin*, vol. XII, pp. 296–303, (Madras, 1957).

──────, "The Hindu Rituals", in *Bulletin of the Ramakrishna Mission*, vol. VIII, pp. 212–17, (Singapore, 1957).

Charlevoix, Pierre Francois de, *Journal of a Voyage to North America* (Chicago: The Custom Club, 1923).

Clark, Grahame, *World Prehistory* (London: Cambridge University Press, 1969).

Cohn, Norman, *Europe's Inner Demons* (London: Heinemann, 1975).

Coles, J. M. and Higgs, E. S., *The Archaeology of Early Man* (London: Faber & Faber, 1969).

Conquest, Robert, *The Great Terror* (New York: Macmillan, 1968).

Cook, Captain James, *Captain Cook's Journal during his First Voyage Round the World, made in H.M. Bark Endeavour 1768-71*, ed. W. J. L. Wharton (London: E. Stock, 1893).

———, *The Journals of Captain James Cook on his Voyages of Discovery*, ed. J. C. Beaglehole, 4 vols. (London: Cambridge University Press, 1955-7).

Cook, Sherburne, "Human Sacrifice and Warfare as Factors in the Demography of Pre-Colonial Mexico", in *Human Biology*, vol. XVIII (Baltimore, 1946).

Crawford, J., "Cannibalism in Relation to Ethnology", in *Transactions of the Ethnological Society of London*, vol. IV (1866).

Dalzel, Archibald, *The History of Dahomey* (London: T. Spilsbury & Son, 1793).

Davies, Nigel, *Voyagers to the New World, Fact and Fantasy* (London: Macmillan, 1978; New York: Morrow, 1979).

Detzner, M., *Moeurs et Coutumes des Papous* (Paris: Payot, 1935).

Devore, Irvine, *see* Lee, Richard.

Días del Castillo, Bernal, *The Bernal Díaz Chronicles*, trans. and ed. Albert Idell (New York: Doubleday, 1956).

Douglas, Mary, *Witchcraft Confessions and Accusations* (London: Tavistock Publications, 1970).

Driver, Harold E., *The Indians of North America* (Chicago: University of Chicago Press, 1971).

Durán, Fray Diego, *Historia de Las Indias de Nueva España e Islas de la Tierra Firme*, 2 vols. (Mexico City: Porrua, 1967).

Dussaud, René, *Les Sacrifices Humains chez les Cananéens* (Paris: Leroux, 1910).

Dwyer, Jane Powell and Edward B., "The Paracas Cemeteries: Mortuary Patterns in Pre-Columbian America", in *Death and the Afterlife in Pre-Columbian America* (Washington, D.C.: Dumbarton Oaks Research Library, 1975).

Eichhorn, Werner von, *Die Religionen Chinas* (Stuttgart: Verlag W. Kohlhammer, 1973).

Eliade, Mircea, *Rites and Symbols of Initiation. The Mysteries of Birth and Rebirth* (New York: Harper Torchbooks, 1958).

———, *The Sacred and the Profane. The Nature of Religion* (New York: Harper & Row, 1959).

Ellis, A. B., *The Ewe-speaking Peoples of the Slave Coast of West Africa* (London: Chapman & Hall, 1890).

Ellis, William, *Narrative of a Tour through Hawaii* (London: Fisher, Son & Jackson, 1826).

———, *Polynesian Researches* (London: Fisher, Son & Jackson, 1829).

Encyclopedia of Religion and Ethics, ed. James Hastings, 13 vols. (New York: Scribners, 1951).

Evans Pritchard, E., *Nuer Religion* (Oxford Clarendon Press, 1956).

Firth, Raymond "Offering and Sacrifice. Problems of Organization", in *Journal of the Royal Anthropological Institute*, vol. XCIII (London, 1963).

Florentine Codex, *see* Sahagún.

Flornoy, Bertrand, *Haut-Amazone* (Paris: Plon, 1939).

Fornander, Abraham, *An Account of the Polynesian Race. Its Origins and Migrations*, 3 vols. (London: Kegan Paul, Trench and Trübner, 1890).

Frankfurt, Henry, *Kingship and the Gods* (Chicago: University of Chicago Press, 1948).

Frazer, Sir James G., *The Golden Bough*, abridged edition (London: Macmillan, 1922).

Frobenius, Leo, *Erithräa. Länder und Zeiten des Heiligen Königsmördes* (Berlin: Atlantisverlag, 1930).

Fuchs, Stephen, *The Aboriginal Tribes of India* (Delhi: Macmillan India, 1973).

Fuerer-Haimendorf, Professor C. von, "Beliefs Concerning Human Sacrifice among the Hill Reddis", in *Man in India*, vol. XXIV, pp. 14–41 (Ranchi).

Gait, E. A. "Human Sacrifices in Ancient Assam", in *Journal of the Asiatic Society of Bengal*, vol. LXVII, part 3 (Calcutta, 1898).

Garcilasco de la Vega, Inca, *Historia General del Peru*, 3 vols. (Lima: Editorial Universo, 1970).

Girard, René, *La Violence et le Sacré* (Paris: Grasset, 1972).

Glasse, Robert, "Cannibalism in the Kuru Region of New Guinea", in *Transactions of the New York Academy of Science, Series 2*, vol. XXIX, no. 6, pp. 748–54 (1967).

Goddard, Pliny E., *Indians of the Northwest Coast* (New York: American Museum of Natural History, 1924).

Gray, George Buchanan, *Sacrifice in the Old Testament* (Oxford: Clarendon Press, 1925).

Grierson, Sir George Abraham, *Bihar Peasant Life* (London: Trübner & Co., 1885).

Groot, J. J. J. M. de, *The Religious System of Ancient China* (Leyden: E. B. Brill, 1894).

Guiart, Jean, *Histoire de l'Inquisition au Moyen Age* (Paris: Auguste Picard, 1935).

———, *Les Religion de l'Océanie* (Paris: Presses Universitaires de France, 1962).

Gusdorf, Georges, *L'Expérience Humaine de Sacrifice* (Paris: Presses Universitaires de France, 1948).

Harner, Michael J., "The Ecological Basis for Aztec Sacrifice", in *American Ethnologist*, vol. IV, no. 1 (Washington, D.C., 1977).

——— *The Jivaro: People of the Sacred Waterfalls* (New York: Doubleday, 1972).

Harner, Michael J., and Meyer, Alfred, *Cannibal* (New York: Morrow, 1979).

Harris, Marvin, *Cannibals and Kings; The Origins of Cultures* (New York: Random House, 1977).

Hecquard, H., *Reise an die Küste und in das Innere von Westafrika* (Leipzig, 1890).

Helfrich, Klaus, *Menschenopfer und Tötungsrituale im Kult der Maya* (Berlin: Gebr. Mann Verlag, 1973).

Hemming, John, *Red Gold: The Conquest of the Brazilian Indians* (London: Macmillan, 1978).

Herbert, Jean, *Shinto. At the Foundation-head of Japan* (London: Allen & Unwin, 1961).

Hérissée, le A., *L'Ancien Royaume de Dahomey* (Paris: Emile Larose, 1911).

Her Majesty's Stationery Office, *A Report on the Recent Outbreak of Diretlo Murders in Basutoland* (London, 1951).

————, *Report to the Secretary of State for the Colonies by the Parliamentary Delegation to Kenya* (London, 1954).

Herrera, Antonio de, *Historia General de los Hechos de los Castellanos*, 10 vols. (Asunción, Paraguay: Editorial Guariana, 1944).

Herskovits, Melville J., *Dahomey: An Ancient West African Kingdom*, 2 vols. (New York: J. J. Augustin, 1938).

Hick, John (ed.), *The Myth of God Incarnate* (London: S. C. M. Press Ltd., 1977).

Higgs, E. S., *see* Coles.

Hillebrandt, Alfred, *Die Freiwillige Feuertod in Indien und die Soma Weihe* (Munich: Die Königliche Bayerische Akademie der Wissenschaft, 1917).

Hirschberg, W., *Religionsethnologie und Ethnohistorische Religionsforschung: eine Gegenüberstellung* (Vienna: Institut für Völkerunde, 1972).

Hodson, T. C., "Headhunting among the Hill Tribes of Assam", in *Folklore*, vol. 20, pp. 132–143 (London, 1909).

Hogg, Gary, *Cannibalism and Human Sacrifice* (New York: The Citadel Press, 1966).

Hubert, H. and Mauss, M., *Mélanges d'Histoire des Religions* (Paris: Felix Allan, 1909).

Hunt, George T., *The Wars of the Iroquois* (Madison: University of Wisconsin Press, 1940).

Hutton, J. H., "Divided and Decorated Heads as Trophies", in *Man*, vol. 22, no. 67 (London, 1922).

————, "Headhunters of the North-East Fronier", in *Journal of the Royal Society of Arts*, vol. 85 (London, 1936).

————, "Sacrifice by Hurling from the Roof", in *Man*, vol. 23, no. 110 (London, 1923).

————, "The Significance of Headhunting in Assam", in *The Journal of the Royal Anthropological Institute*, vol. 58, pp. 399–408 (London, 1928).

James, E. O., *The Ancient Gods* (London: Weidenfeld and Nicolson, 1960).

————, *The Origins of Sacrifice* (London: John Murray, 1933).

Joralemon, David, "Ritual Blood Sacrifice among the Ancient Maya", in *First Round Table Conference on Palenque, Pt. 2*, pp. 59–76, ed. Merle Greene Robertson (Robert Louis Stevenson School, Round Pebble Beach, Cal., 1974).

Kamakau, Samuel Manaiakalani, *Ka Poe Kahika: The People of Old* (Honolulu: Bishop Museum Press, 1964).

Kamen, Henry, *The Spanish Inquisition* (New York: New American Library, 1965; London: Weidenfeld & Nicolson, 1965).

Kendrick, T. D., *The Druids. A Study in Celtic Prehistory* (London: Methuen, 1927).

Kincaird, Dennis, *British Social Life in India, 1608–1937* (London: Routledge and Kegan Paul, 1973).

Knowles, Nathaniel, "The Torture of Captives by the Indians of North America" in *Proceedings of the American Philosophical Society*, vol. 82, pp. 151–225 (Philadelphia, 1940).

Kramer, S. N., *The Sacred Marriage Rite* (Bloomington: Indiana University Press, 1969).

Lawson, John Cuthbert, *Modern Greek Folklore and Ancient Greek Religion* (London: Cambridge University Press, 1910).

Leakey, L. S. B., *Defeating Mau Mau* (London: Methuen, 1954).

Lee, Richard B. and Devore, Irvine, (eds.), *Man the Hunter* (Chicago: Aldine Publishing, 1968).

Lévi, Sylvan, *La Doctrine du Sacrifice dans les Brahmanas* (Paris: Presses Universitaires de France, 1966).

Lévi-Strauss, Claude, *La Pensée Sauvage* (Paris: Plon, 1962).

Lines, Jorge A., "Estatuaria Huetar del Sacrificio Humano", in *Revista Mexicana es Estudios Antropológicos*, vol. 6, pp. 36–50 (Mexico City, 1942).

Ling-Roth, Henry, *The Natives of Sarawak and British North Borneo*, 2 vols. (London: Truslove and Hanson, 1896).

Linton, Ralph, "The Origin of the Skidi Pawnee Sacrifice to the Morning Star", in *American Anthropologist*, vol. 28, no. 3 (Washington, D.C., 1926).

Lizot, Jacques, "Aspects Économiques et Sociaux du Changement Cultural chez les Yanomamis", in *L' Homme*, vol. II, pp. 2–51 (Paris, 1971).

———, "Population, Resources and Warfare among the Yanomami", in *Man*, vol. 12, no. 3–4, pp. 497–517 (London, 1977).

Lorentz, Konrad, *On Aggression* (New York: Harcourt, Brace and World, 1966).

Luschan, Felix von, *Die Altertümer von Benin* (Berlin and Leipzig: Vereinigung Wissenshaftlicher Verleger, 1919).

MacCulloch, J. A., *The Celtic and Scandinavian Religions* (London: Hutchinson, 1911).

Mair, Lucy, *Witchcraft* (London: World University Library, 1969).

Maringer, Johannes, *Menschenopfer und Bestattungsbrauch Alteuropas* (Freiburg, Switzerland: Paulusdrückerei).

Marks, Alfred, *Tyburn Tree. Its History and Annals* (London: Brown, Langham & Co., 1908).

Martin, R., *Uber Skeletkult und Verwandte Vorstellungen* (Zürich: Mitteilungen der Geographisch-Ethnographischen Gesellschaft, 1923).

Mauss, M., *see* Hubert.

Meek, C. K., *The Northern Tribes of Nigeria* (London: Oxford University Press, 1925).

Meinicke, Karl, "Die Neukaledonier", in *Globus*, vol. 15 (Braunschweig, 1869).

Métraux, Alfred, *Religions et Magies Indiennes d'Amérique du Sud* (Paris: Gallimard, 1967).

Meyer, Alfred, *see* Harner.

Michelsen, Oscar, *Cannibals Won for Christ* (London: Morgan & Scott, 1893).

Midelfort, H. C. E., *Witch Hunting in Southwestern Germany* (Stanford, Cal.: Stanford University Press, 1972).

Millot, Bernard, *L'Epopée Kamikaze* (Paris: Robert Laffont, 1970).

Mills, J. P., "A Note on Headhunting among the Mishmis of the Lohit Valley, Assam", in *Man in India*, vol. 27, pp. 74–5 (Ranchi, 1947).

———, "The Naga Headhunters of Assam", in *Journal of the Royal Central Asian Society*, vol. 6, pp. 65–7 (London, 1938).

Mitra Chandra, Sarat, "Further Note on the Custom of Offering Human

Sacrifice to Water Spirits", in *Quarterly Journal of the Mythic Society*, no. 2, pp. 589–94 (1923).

———, "Note on Another Instance of the Khasi Custom of Offering Human Sacrifice to the Snake Deity Thlen", in *Man in India*, vol. 12, pp. 184–7 (Ranchi, 1932).

———, "Notes on Magic and Human Sacrifice in Mediaeval Northern Bengal", in *Journal of the Anthropological Society of Bombay*, vol. 15, pp. 548–55 (1932).

———, "On a Recent Instance of Offering Human Sacrifice to the Snake Deity", in *Journal of the Anthropological Society of Bombay*, vol. 13, pp. 192–8, (1924–1928).

Mock, E., "Das Menschenopfer bei den Germanen", in *Abhandlungen der Universität Leipzig*, vol. 27 (1909).

Mommert, C., *Menschenopfer bei den Alten Hebräern* (Leipzig, 1905).

Montagu, Ashley, *The Nature of Human Aggression* (New York: Oxford University Press, 1976).

Morris, Desmond, *The Human Zoo* (New York: McGraw Hill, 1969).

Moser, C., "Human Decapitation in Ancient Mexico", in *Studies in Pre-Columbian Art and Archaeology, no. 11* (Washington, D.C.: Dumbarton Oaks Research Library, 1973).

Mukhodpadhyay, Amitabha, "Sati as a Social Institution in Bengal", in *Bengal Past and Present*, vol. 76, pp. 99–115 (Calcutta Historical Society, 1957).

Munz, Peter, *When the Golden Bough Breaks* (London: Routledge and Kegan Paul, 1973).

Murray, J. H. P., *Papua or British New Guinea* (London: T. Fisher Unwin, 1912).

Nagatsuka, Ryuji, *I Was a Kamikaze. The Knights of the Divine Wind* (London: Abelard Shuman, 1973).

Nathan, John, *Mishima, a Biography* (Boston and Toronto: Little Brown, 1974).

Nevermann, Hans, *Götter der Südsee: die Religion der Polynesier* (Stuttgart: W. Spemann Verlag, 1947).

Nock, A. D., *Essays on Religion in the Ancient World*, 2 vols. (Oxford: Clarendon Press, 1972).

Nordmann, Paul I., "Contribution à l'étude de l'infanticide à Tahiti", in *Bulletin de la Societé des Études Océaniennes*, vol. 6, no. 9 (Paris, 1943).

Noury, C., "Chants Marquisiens pendant les Sacrifices Humains", in *Bulletin de la Societé des Études Océaniennes*, vol. 3, no. 3 (Paris, 1928).

O'Brien, John A., *The Inquisition* (New York: Macmillan, 1973).

Oliver, Douglas L., *Ancient Tahitian Society*, 3 vols. (Honolulu: University Press of Hawaii, 1974).

Panigrahi, Lalita, *British Social Policy and Female Infanticide in India* (New Delhi: Munshiram, 1976).

Parkinson, Sydney, *A Journal of a Voyage to the South Seas on His Majesty's Ship the Endeavour* (London: C. Dilley, 1784).

Parrinder, E. G., "An African Saviour God", in *The Saviour God*, ed. S. G. E. Brandon (Manchester: Manchester University Press, 1963).

————, *African Traditional Religion* (London: Hutchinson, 1954).

Parry, Leonard Arthur, *The History of Torture in England* (London: Patterson Smith, 1975).

Peekel, Gerhard, *Religion und Zauberei auf dem Mittleren Neu-Mecklenburg Bismarck-Archipel, Südsee* (Munster: Anthropos-Bibliothek, 1909).

Pfeiffer, Karlheinz, "Menschenopfer in den Hochkulturen der Welt," in *Die Wage*, vol. 10 (1971).

Piggott, Stuart, *The Druids* (London: Thames and Hudson, 1968).

Piña Chan, Ramón, "Exploración del Cenote de Chichén Itzá", in *Boletín del Instituto Nacional de Antropología e Historia*, no. 31 (Mexico City, 1968).

Pouillon, Jean (ed.), *Destins du Cannibalisme* (Paris: Gallimard, 1972).

Preuss, Theodor, *Der Dämonische Ursprung des Griekischen Dramas* (Leipzig: B. G. Tenoner Verlag, 1906).

Rice, Arthur P., "Cannibalism in Polynesia", in *American Antiquarian*, vol. 32, pp. 77–84.

Rinde, Peter, *Harakiri. Unterordnung und Auflenung in Japan* (Wollzeilenverlag, 1965).

Robertson Smith, W., *The Religion of the Semites* (London: A. and C. Black, 1927).

Rosaldo, Michelle Zimbalist, "Skulls and Causality", a letter in *Man*, vol. 12, no. 1, pp. 168–9 (London, 1977).

Rouse, W. H. D., *Greek Votive Offerings* (London: Cambridge University Press, 1902).

Ryder, Alan, *Benin and the Europeans, 1485–1897* (London: Longman, 1969).

Sabine, Sir Edward, *Narrative of an Expedition to the Polar Sea in the Years 1820, 1821, 1822 and 1823* (London: James Madden, 1840).

Sabourin, Léopold, *Rédemption Sacrificielle* (Brussels: Desclée de Brouwer, 1961).

Sahagún, Fray Bernardino de, *Florentine Codex*, trans. from the Nahuatl by J. O. Anderson and Charles E. Dibble, 12 vols. (Santa Fe, N.M.: School of American Research, 1950).

———, *Historia General de las Cosas de Nueva España*, 6 vols. (Mexico City: Porrua, 1956).

St. Johnston, Alfred, *Camping among Cannibals* (London: Macmillan, 1883).

Satow, Sir Edward, *A Diplomat in Japan* (London: Seely Service, 1921).

Schaerer, H., "Das Menschenopfer bei den Katinganern", in *Tijdschrift voor Indische Taalland en Volkenkunde* (Batavia, 1938).

———, "Die Bedeutung des Menschenopfer im Dajakischen Totenkult", in *Mitteilungsblatt der Gesellschaft für Völkerkunde* (Leipzig, 1940).

Schoch, Alfred, *Rituelle Menschentötungen in Polynesien* (Ulm: A. Leufke, 1954).

Schweinfurt, Georg, *The Heart of Africa*, 2 vols. (London: Sampson Low, 1873).

Schweizer, Albert, *Indian Thought and Its Development* (London: A. and C. Black, 1951).

Schwenn, Friedrich, *Die Menschenopfer bei den Griechen und Römern* (Berlin: Töpelmann, 1966).

Seeman, Berthold, *Viti. An Account of a Government Mission to the Vitian or Fijian Islands in the Years 1860–1861* (London: Macmillan, 1862).

Seligman, C. G., *The Melanesians of British New Guinea* (London: Cambridge University Press, 1910).

Sillitoe, Paul, "Big men and war in New Guinea", in *Man*, vol. 13, no. 2 (London, 1978).

Siméon, Delmas P., *La Religion ou le Paganisme des Marquisiens* (Paris: Gabriel Beauchesne, 1927).

Speck, Frank G., "The Iroquois. A Study in Cultural Evolution", in *Cranbrook Institute of Science Bulletin*, no. 23 (Bloomfield Hills, 1945).

Spiel, Christian, *Menschen essen Menschen* (Frankfurt: Fischer, 1974).

Stietepcron, Heinrich von, "Suicide as a Religious Institution", in *Bharatiya Vidya*, vol. 27, pp. 7–24 (Bombay, 1967).

Strack, Hermann, *Das Blut im Glauben und Aberglauben der Menschheit* (Berlin: Institutum Judaicum, 1900).

Strackerjan, L., *Aberglaube und Sagen aus dem Herzogthum Oldenburg* (Oldenburg, 1967).

Talbot, P. Amaury, *Life in Southern Nigeria*, 2 vols. (London: Macmillan, 1923).

Tannahil, Reay, *Flesh and Blood* (London: Abacus, 1976).

Tezozómoc, Alvarado, *Cronica Mexicana* (Mexico City: Leyenda, 1948).

Thakur, Upendra, *The History of Suicide in India: an Introduction* (New Delhi: Munshi Ram Manohar Lal, 1963).

———, "Self-Immolation in India (1201–1765 A.D.)", in *Journal of the Bihar Research Society*, vol. 52, pp. 117–42 (1966).

Torquemada, Fray Juan de, *Monarquía Indiana*, 3 vols. (Mexico City: Editorial Chávez Hayhoe, 1943–4).

Toynbee, Arnold, *A Historian's Approach to Religion* (London: Oxford University Press, 1956).

Tregear, Edward, *The Maori Race* (London: A. D. Willis, 1910).

Trimborn, Hermann, *Das alte Amerika* (Stuttgart: Kilpper, 1959).

———, *Die Religionen des alten Amerika* (Stuttgart: W. Kohlhammerverlag, 1961).

———, *Quellen zur Kulturgeschichte des Präkolumbischen Amerika* (Stuttgart: Strecker, 1936).

———, *Señorío y Barbarie en el Valle del Cauca* (Madrid: Instituto Gonzalo Fernández de Oviedo, 1947).

Vayda, A. P., *Maori Warfare* (Wellington, N.Z.: The Polynesian Society, 1960).

Volhard, Ewald, *Kannibalismus* (Stuttgart: Stricker und Schröder, 1951).

Ward, Herbert, *Five Years with the Congo Cannibals* (London: Chatto and Windus, 1891).

———, *A Voice from the Congo* (London: Heinemann, 1910).

Wavrin, Marquis de, *Chez les Indiens de Colombie* (Paris: Plon, 1953).

Westermarck, Edward, *The Origin and Development of the Moral Ideas* (London: Macmillan, 1906).

Westervelt, W. D., "Chief Man-Eater", in *Paradise of the Pacific*, vol. 17, no. 7 (Honolulu, 1904).

Wightman, A. J., *No Friend for Travellers* (London: Robert Hale, 1959).

Wilbert, Johannes, "Eschatology in a Participatory Universe. Destinies of the Soul among the Warao Indians in Venezuela", in *Death and the Afterlife in Pre-Columbian America*, ed. Elizabeth Benson (Washington, D.C.: Dumbarton Oaks Research Library, 1975).

Williams, F. E., *The Natives of the Purari Delta* (Port Moresby, 1924).

Wirz, Paul, "Der Ersatz für die Kopfjägerei und die Trophäenimitation", in *Beiträge zur Gesellungs—and Völkerwissenschaft* (Berlin: Gebr. Mann Verlag, 1950).

Wisse, Jacob, *Selbstmord und Todesfurcht bei den Naturvölker* (Zutphen: W. J. Thieme, 1933).

Wolff, Hans Walter, *Anthropologie des Alten Testaments* (Munich: C. Kaiser, 1973).

Woodruff, Philip, *The Men who Ruled India*, 2 vols., Vol. 1: *The Founders* (London: Jonathan Cape, 1953–4).

Woolley, Sir Leonard, *Excavations at Ur* (London: Ernest Benn, 1954).

Zakiuddin, Ahmed, "Sati in Eighteenth-century Bengal", in *Journal of the Asiatic Society of Pakistan*, vol. 13, pp. 147–64 (Dacca, 1968).

Zegwaard, Gerard A., "Headhunting Practices of the Asmat of Netherlands New Guinea", in *American Anthropologist*, vol. 61, pp. 1021–41 (Washington, D.C.: 1959).

Zimmer, Heinrich, *Myths and Symbols in Indian Art and Civilization* (New York: Pantheon Books, 1946).

Index

Aaron, 62
A-bar-gi, King, 29, 31
Abeville, Claude d', 267
Abolition Act (1833), 145
Abraham, 18, 56, 62–63, 65
Achilles, 52, 53, 54
Acosta, Fray Joseph de, 261
Adonis, 52, 67
  cult of, 57
  ritual death followed by rebirth, 67–68
Africa, 19, 24
  ancestor-worship in, 141, 142
  animal sacrifice in, 20
  cannibalism in, 15, 16, 153–165
  foundation sacrifice in, 22
  headhunting in, 239
  ritual sacrifice in, 143–144
  widow sacrifice in, 104
  See also names of countries; names of
    tribes
Agamemnon, 52, 55–56, 195
Aguilar, Jerónimo de, 220
Ahmadnagar, Rajah of, 126
Ahuitzotl, 216, 217
Albigensians, *see* Catharists
Alexander the Great, 102, 107
Algonkian Indians, 253
Amenhotep II, King, 36, 37, 103
American Ethnologist, 235
Anatomy of Human Destructiveness, The
  (Fromm), 284
Ancient Tahitian Society (Oliver), 189
Anderson, Dr. Arthur, 206
Andromeda, 41
Angola, cannibalism in, 161
Ani, Papyrus of, 35
Anthropological Museum (Munich), 260
Anthropology and Anthropophagy
  (Arens), 153–154

Anthropophagy, 278
Aphrodite, 57
Apollo, 52, 57
Archaeological Museum (India), 259
Ardrey, Robert, 281, 282–283
Arens, William, 15, 153–154
Arguelles, Edgar, 182
Ariadne, 56
Arimi, Rear-Admiral, 286
Arioi tribe, child sacrifice of, 193
Art Institute of Chicago, 260
Artemis, 52, 55–56, 59
Ashanti tribe, 161, 162
Asiatic Society, 78
Asmat tribe, 175, 179, 284
Assassins, the, 92
Atahualpa, Emperor, 265
Atonement, Day of, 65
Atreus, King, 54
Attis, 57–58
  ritual death followed by rebirth, 67–68
Augustine, St., 130–131
Augustus, Emperor, 47, 50
Australia, 22, 23, 182
  cannibalism in, 163
  infanticide in, 192
  ritual death followed by rebirth among
    the tribes of, 69
Australopithecus, 281
Austronesian languages, 166
Auun, King, 44
Aztec Stone of the Sun, 216
Aztecs, 14, 16, 73, 198–241, 274–275
  cannibalism in rites, 154
  the coronation of Moctezuma II, 216
  dance of the severed heads, 209
  divine self-immolation, 99
  elaborate preparations for festivals,
    211–212